C-630   CAREER EXAMINATION SERIES

This is your
PASSBOOK for...

Public Health Educator

Test Preparation Study Guide
Questions & Answers

COPYRIGHT NOTICE

This book is SOLELY intended for, is sold ONLY to, and its use is RESTRICTED to individual, bona fide applicants or candidates who qualify by virtue of having seriously filed applications for appropriate license, certificate, professional and/or promotional advancement, higher school matriculation, scholarship, or other legitimate requirements of education and/or governmental authorities.

This book is NOT intended for use, class instruction, tutoring, training, duplication, copying, reprinting, excerption, or adaptation, etc., by:

1) Other publishers
2) Proprietors and/or Instructors of "Coaching" and/or Preparatory Courses
3) Personnel and/or Training Divisions of commercial, industrial, and governmental organizations
4) Schools, colleges, or universities and/or their departments and staffs, including teachers and other personnel
5) Testing Agencies or Bureaus
6) Study groups which seek by the purchase of a single volume to copy and/or duplicate and/or adapt this material for use by the group as a whole without having purchased individual volumes for each of the members of the group
7) Et al.

Such persons would be in violation of appropriate Federal and State statutes.

PROVISION OF LICENSING AGREEMENTS – Recognized educational, commercial, industrial, and governmental institutions and organizations, and others legitimately engaged in educational pursuits, including training, testing, and measurement activities, may address request for a licensing agreement to the copyright owners, who will determine whether, and under what conditions, including fees and charges, the materials in this book may be used them. In other words, a licensing facility exists for the legitimate use of the material in this book on other than an individual basis. However, it is asseverated and affirmed here that the material in this book CANNOT be used without the receipt of the express permission of such a licensing agreement from the Publishers. Inquiries re licensing should be addressed to the company, attention rights and permissions department.

All rights reserved, including the right of reproduction in whole or in part, in any form or by any means, electronic or mechanical, including photocopying, recording, or by any information storage and retrieval system, without permission in writing from the Publisher.

Copyright © 2024 by
National Learning Corporation

212 Michael Drive, Syosset, NY 11791
(516) 921-8888 • www.passbooks.com
E-mail: info@passbooks.com

PUBLISHED IN THE UNITED STATES OF AMERICA

PASSBOOK® SERIES

THE *PASSBOOK® SERIES* has been created to prepare applicants and candidates for the ultimate academic battlefield – the examination room.

At some time in our lives, each and every one of us may be required to take an examination – for validation, matriculation, admission, qualification, registration, certification, or licensure.

Based on the assumption that every applicant or candidate has met the basic formal educational standards, has taken the required number of courses, and read the necessary texts, the *PASSBOOK® SERIES* furnishes the one special preparation which may assure passing with confidence, instead of failing with insecurity. Examination questions – together with answers – are furnished as the basic vehicle for study so that the mysteries of the examination and its compounding difficulties may be eliminated or diminished by a sure method.

This book is meant to help you pass your examination provided that you qualify and are serious in your objective.

The entire field is reviewed through the huge store of content information which is succinctly presented through a provocative and challenging approach – the question-and-answer method.

A climate of success is established by furnishing the correct answers at the end of each test.

You soon learn to recognize types of questions, forms of questions, and patterns of questioning. You may even begin to anticipate expected outcomes.

You perceive that many questions are repeated or adapted so that you can gain acute insights, which may enable you to score many sure points.

You learn how to confront new questions, or types of questions, and to attack them confidently and work out the correct answers.

You note objectives and emphases, and recognize pitfalls and dangers, so that you may make positive educational adjustments.

Moreover, you are kept fully informed in relation to new concepts, methods, practices, and directions in the field.

You discover that you are actually taking the examination all the time: you are preparing for the examination by "taking" an examination, not by reading extraneous and/or supererogatory textbooks.

In short, this PASSBOOK®, used directedly, should be an important factor in helping you to pass your test.

PUBLIC HEALTH EDUCATOR

DUTIES:
An employee in this class engages in community public relations and marketing activities designed to increase public awareness regarding the resources and services available through the Department of Health, and other health services available in the community. The employee has responsibility for organizing and implementing the dissemination of information pertaining to health problems, issues and solutions. The work is performed under the general supervision of the Public Health Director with leeway allowed for the exercise of independent judgment and initiative in carrying out the duties of the position. Supervision may be exercised over the work of others. Does related work as required.

EXAMPLES OF WORK:
- Conducts presentations among community populations at risk, aimed at improving the level of health information, motivating positive health habits and eliminating high risk injury and illness factors;
- Organizes and directs education efforts to influence public attitudes and behaviors with regard to given health needs;
- Designs, implements, and evaluates health promotion and prevention programs to improve wellness through increased awareness of health risk behavior and targeted risk factor reduction programs;
- Prepares and distributes health education materials including curricula, pamphlets, posters, exhibits, and audiovisual presentations;
- Initiates and evaluates surveys of public health education needs in the community and evaluates the materials and methods used to determine the effectiveness of the programs;
- Collaborates with other health specialists and civic groups to ascertain health needs, develop desirable health goals, and determine availability of health services;
- Collaborates with and conducts public health staff presentations, workshops, and forums to discuss common public health needs;
- Prepares and maintains health education components for nursing staff for use with home care and Prevent patients;
- Serves on community committees for health promotions;
- Coordinates, monitors and evaluates grant programs through state and internal statistics and reports;
- Prepares budget requests for health education operations.

SUBJECT OF EXAMINATION:
The written test will cover knowledge, skills, and/or abilities in such areas as:
1. Behavioral science concepts related to public health education;
2. Disease control and prevention;
3. Educating and interacting with the public;
4. Planning, implementing, and evaluating health education programs;
5. Preparing written material; and
6. Principles of educating and training.

HOW TO TAKE A TEST

I. YOU MUST PASS AN EXAMINATION

A. WHAT EVERY CANDIDATE SHOULD KNOW

Examination applicants often ask us for help in preparing for the written test. What can I study in advance? What kinds of questions will be asked? How will the test be given? How will the papers be graded?

As an applicant for a civil service examination, you may be wondering about some of these things. Our purpose here is to suggest effective methods of advance study and to describe civil service examinations.

Your chances for success on this examination can be increased if you know how to prepare. Those "pre-examination jitters" can be reduced if you know what to expect. You can even experience an adventure in good citizenship if you know why civil service exams are given.

B. WHY ARE CIVIL SERVICE EXAMINATIONS GIVEN?

Civil service examinations are important to you in two ways. As a citizen, you want public jobs filled by employees who know how to do their work. As a job seeker, you want a fair chance to compete for that job on an equal footing with other candidates. The best-known means of accomplishing this two-fold goal is the competitive examination.

Exams are widely publicized throughout the nation. They may be administered for jobs in federal, state, city, municipal, town or village governments or agencies.

Any citizen may apply, with some limitations, such as the age or residence of applicants. Your experience and education may be reviewed to see whether you meet the requirements for the particular examination. When these requirements exist, they are reasonable and applied consistently to all applicants. Thus, a competitive examination may cause you some uneasiness now, but it is your privilege and safeguard.

C. HOW ARE CIVIL SERVICE EXAMS DEVELOPED?

Examinations are carefully written by trained technicians who are specialists in the field known as "psychological measurement," in consultation with recognized authorities in the field of work that the test will cover. These experts recommend the subject matter areas or skills to be tested; only those knowledges or skills important to your success on the job are included. The most reliable books and source materials available are used as references. Together, the experts and technicians judge the difficulty level of the questions.

Test technicians know how to phrase questions so that the problem is clearly stated. Their ethics do not permit "trick" or "catch" questions. Questions may have been tried out on sample groups, or subjected to statistical analysis, to determine their usefulness.

Written tests are often used in combination with performance tests, ratings of training and experience, and oral interviews. All of these measures combine to form the best-known means of finding the right person for the right job.

II. HOW TO PASS THE WRITTEN TEST

A. NATURE OF THE EXAMINATION

To prepare intelligently for civil service examinations, you should know how they differ from school examinations you have taken. In school you were assigned certain definite pages to read or subjects to cover. The examination questions were quite detailed and usually emphasized memory. Civil service exams, on the other hand, try to discover your present ability to perform the duties of a position, plus your potentiality to learn these duties. In other words, a civil service exam attempts to predict how successful you will be. Questions cover such a broad area that they cannot be as minute and detailed as school exam questions.

In the public service similar kinds of work, or positions, are grouped together in one "class." This process is known as *position-classification*. All the positions in a class are paid according to the salary range for that class. One class title covers all of these positions, and they are all tested by the same examination.

B. FOUR BASIC STEPS

1) Study the announcement

How, then, can you know what subjects to study? Our best answer is: "Learn as much as possible about the class of positions for which you've applied." The exam will test the knowledge, skills and abilities needed to do the work.

Your most valuable source of information about the position you want is the official exam announcement. This announcement lists the training and experience qualifications. Check these standards and apply only if you come reasonably close to meeting them.

The brief description of the position in the examination announcement offers some clues to the subjects which will be tested. Think about the job itself. Review the duties in your mind. Can you perform them, or are there some in which you are rusty? Fill in the blank spots in your preparation.

Many jurisdictions preview the written test in the exam announcement by including a section called "Knowledge and Abilities Required," "Scope of the Examination," or some similar heading. Here you will find out specifically what fields will be tested.

2) Review your own background

Once you learn in general what the position is all about, and what you need to know to do the work, ask yourself which subjects you already know fairly well and which need improvement. You may wonder whether to concentrate on improving your strong areas or on building some background in your fields of weakness. When the announcement has specified "some knowledge" or "considerable knowledge," or has used adjectives like "beginning principles of..." or "advanced ... methods," you can get a clue as to the number and difficulty of questions to be asked in any given field. More questions, and hence broader coverage, would be included for those subjects which are more important in the work. Now weigh your strengths and weaknesses against the job requirements and prepare accordingly.

3) Determine the level of the position

Another way to tell how intensively you should prepare is to understand the level of the job for which you are applying. Is it the entering level? In other words, is this the position in which beginners in a field of work are hired? Or is it an intermediate or advanced level? Sometimes this is indicated by such words as "Junior" or "Senior" in the class title. Other jurisdictions use Roman numerals to designate the level – Clerk I, Clerk II, for example. The word "Supervisor" sometimes appears in the title. If the level is not indicated by the title, check the description of duties. Will you be working under very close supervision, or will you have responsibility for independent decisions in this work?

4) Choose appropriate study materials

Now that you know the subjects to be examined and the relative amount of each subject to be covered, you can choose suitable study materials. For beginning level jobs, or even advanced ones, if you have a pronounced weakness in some aspect of your training, read a modern, standard textbook in that field. Be sure it is up to date and has general coverage. Such books are normally available at your library, and the librarian will be glad to help you locate one. For entry-level positions, questions of appropriate difficulty are chosen — neither highly advanced questions, nor those too simple. Such questions require careful thought but not advanced training.

If the position for which you are applying is technical or advanced, you will read more advanced, specialized material. If you are already familiar with the basic principles of your field, elementary textbooks would waste your time. Concentrate on advanced textbooks and technical periodicals. Think through the concepts and review difficult problems in your field.

These are all general sources. You can get more ideas on your own initiative, following these leads. For example, training manuals and publications of the government agency which employs workers in your field can be useful, particularly for technical and professional positions. A letter or visit to the government department involved may result in more specific study suggestions, and certainly will provide you with a more definite idea of the exact nature of the position you are seeking.

III. KINDS OF TESTS

Tests are used for purposes other than measuring knowledge and ability to perform specified duties. For some positions, it is equally important to test ability to make adjustments to new situations or to profit from training. In others, basic mental abilities not dependent on information are essential. Questions which test these things may not appear as pertinent to the duties of the position as those which test for knowledge and information. Yet they are often highly important parts of a fair examination. For very general questions, it is almost impossible to help you direct your study efforts. What we can do is to point out some of the more common of these general abilities needed in public service positions and describe some typical questions.

1) General information

Broad, general information has been found useful for predicting job success in some kinds of work. This is tested in a variety of ways, from vocabulary lists to questions about current events. Basic background in some field of work, such as sociology or economics, may be sampled in a group of questions. Often these are principles which have become familiar to most persons through exposure rather than through formal training. It is difficult to advise you how to study for these questions; being alert to the world around you is our best suggestion.

2) Verbal ability

An example of an ability needed in many positions is verbal or language ability. Verbal ability is, in brief, the ability to use and understand words. Vocabulary and grammar tests are typical measures of this ability. Reading comprehension or paragraph interpretation questions are common in many kinds of civil service tests. You are given a paragraph of written material and asked to find its central meaning.

3) Numerical ability

Number skills can be tested by the familiar arithmetic problem, by checking paired lists of numbers to see which are alike and which are different, or by interpreting charts and graphs. In the latter test, a graph may be printed in the test booklet which you are asked to use as the basis for answering questions.

4) Observation

A popular test for law-enforcement positions is the observation test. A picture is shown to you for several minutes, then taken away. Questions about the picture test your ability to observe both details and larger elements.

5) Following directions

In many positions in the public service, the employee must be able to carry out written instructions dependably and accurately. You may be given a chart with several columns, each column listing a variety of information. The questions require you to carry out directions involving the information given in the chart.

6) Skills and aptitudes

Performance tests effectively measure some manual skills and aptitudes. When the skill is one in which you are trained, such as typing or shorthand, you can practice. These tests are often very much like those given in business school or high school courses. For many of the other skills and aptitudes, however, no short-time preparation can be made. Skills and abilities natural to you or that you have developed throughout your lifetime are being tested.

Many of the general questions just described provide all the data needed to answer the questions and ask you to use your reasoning ability to find the answers. Your best preparation for these tests, as well as for tests of facts and ideas, is to be at your physical and mental best. You, no doubt, have your own methods of getting into an exam-taking mood and keeping "in shape." The next section lists some ideas on this subject.

IV. KINDS OF QUESTIONS

Only rarely is the "essay" question, which you answer in narrative form, used in civil service tests. Civil service tests are usually of the short-answer type. Full instructions for answering these questions will be given to you at the examination. But in case this is your first experience with short-answer questions and separate answer sheets, here is what you need to know:

1) Multiple-choice Questions

Most popular of the short-answer questions is the "multiple choice" or "best answer" question. It can be used, for example, to test for factual knowledge, ability to solve problems or judgment in meeting situations found at work.

A multiple-choice question is normally one of three types—
- It can begin with an incomplete statement followed by several possible endings. You are to find the one ending which *best* completes the statement, although some of the others may not be entirely wrong.
- It can also be a complete statement in the form of a question which is answered by choosing one of the statements listed.

- It can be in the form of a problem – again you select the best answer.

Here is an example of a multiple-choice question with a discussion which should give you some clues as to the method for choosing the right answer:

When an employee has a complaint about his assignment, the action which will *best* help him overcome his difficulty is to
- A. discuss his difficulty with his coworkers
- B. take the problem to the head of the organization
- C. take the problem to the person who gave him the assignment
- D. say nothing to anyone about his complaint

In answering this question, you should study each of the choices to find which is best. Consider choice "A" – Certainly an employee may discuss his complaint with fellow employees, but no change or improvement can result, and the complaint remains unresolved. Choice "B" is a poor choice since the head of the organization probably does not know what assignment you have been given, and taking your problem to him is known as "going over the head" of the supervisor. The supervisor, or person who made the assignment, is the person who can clarify it or correct any injustice. Choice "C" is, therefore, correct. To say nothing, as in choice "D," is unwise. Supervisors have and interest in knowing the problems employees are facing, and the employee is seeking a solution to his problem.

2) True/False Questions

The "true/false" or "right/wrong" form of question is sometimes used. Here a complete statement is given. Your job is to decide whether the statement is right or wrong.

SAMPLE: A roaming cell-phone call to a nearby city costs less than a non-roaming call to a distant city.

This statement is wrong, or false, since roaming calls are more expensive.

This is not a complete list of all possible question forms, although most of the others are variations of these common types. You will always get complete directions for answering questions. Be sure you understand *how* to mark your answers – ask questions until you do.

V. RECORDING YOUR ANSWERS

Computer terminals are used more and more today for many different kinds of exams.

For an examination with very few applicants, you may be told to record your answers in the test booklet itself. Separate answer sheets are much more common. If this separate answer sheet is to be scored by machine – and this is often the case – it is highly important that you mark your answers correctly in order to get credit.

An electronic scoring machine is often used in civil service offices because of the speed with which papers can be scored. Machine-scored answer sheets must be marked with a pencil, which will be given to you. This pencil has a high graphite content which responds to the electronic scoring machine. As a matter of fact, stray dots may register as answers, so do not let your pencil rest on the answer sheet while you are pondering the correct answer. Also, if your pencil lead breaks or is otherwise defective, ask for another.

Since the answer sheet will be dropped in a slot in the scoring machine, be careful not to bend the corners or get the paper crumpled.

The answer sheet normally has five vertical columns of numbers, with 30 numbers to a column. These numbers correspond to the question numbers in your test booklet. After each number, going across the page are four or five pairs of dotted lines. These short dotted lines have small letters or numbers above them. The first two pairs may also have a "T" or "F" above the letters. This indicates that the first two pairs only are to be used if the questions are of the true-false type. If the questions are multiple choice, disregard the "T" and "F" and pay attention only to the small letters or numbers.

Answer your questions in the manner of the sample that follows:

32. The largest city in the United States is
    A. Washington, D.C.
    B. New York City
    C. Chicago
    D. Detroit
    E. San Francisco

1) Choose the answer you think is best. (New York City is the largest, so "B" is correct.)
2) Find the row of dotted lines numbered the same as the question you are answering. (Find row number 32)
3) Find the pair of dotted lines corresponding to the answer. (Find the pair of lines under the mark "B.")
4) Make a solid black mark between the dotted lines.

VI. BEFORE THE TEST

Common sense will help you find procedures to follow to get ready for an examination. Too many of us, however, overlook these sensible measures. Indeed, nervousness and fatigue have been found to be the most serious reasons why applicants fail to do their best on civil service tests. Here is a list of reminders:

- Begin your preparation early – Don't wait until the last minute to go scurrying around for books and materials or to find out what the position is all about.
- Prepare continuously – An hour a night for a week is better than an all-night cram session. This has been definitely established. What is more, a night a week for a month will return better dividends than crowding your study into a shorter period of time.
- Locate the place of the exam – You have been sent a notice telling you when and where to report for the examination. If the location is in a different town or otherwise unfamiliar to you, it would be well to inquire the best route and learn something about the building.
- Relax the night before the test – Allow your mind to rest. Do not study at all that night. Plan some mild recreation or diversion; then go to bed early and get a good night's sleep.
- Get up early enough to make a leisurely trip to the place for the test – This way unforeseen events, traffic snarls, unfamiliar buildings, etc. will not upset you.
- Dress comfortably – A written test is not a fashion show. You will be known by number and not by name, so wear something comfortable.

- Leave excess paraphernalia at home – Shopping bags and odd bundles will get in your way. You need bring only the items mentioned in the official notice you received; usually everything you need is provided. Do not bring reference books to the exam. They will only confuse those last minutes and be taken away from you when in the test room.
- Arrive somewhat ahead of time – If because of transportation schedules you must get there very early, bring a newspaper or magazine to take your mind off yourself while waiting.
- Locate the examination room – When you have found the proper room, you will be directed to the seat or part of the room where you will sit. Sometimes you are given a sheet of instructions to read while you are waiting. Do not fill out any forms until you are told to do so; just read them and be prepared.
- Relax and prepare to listen to the instructions
- If you have any physical problem that may keep you from doing your best, be sure to tell the test administrator. If you are sick or in poor health, you really cannot do your best on the exam. You can come back and take the test some other time.

VII. AT THE TEST

The day of the test is here and you have the test booklet in your hand. The temptation to get going is very strong. Caution! There is more to success than knowing the right answers. You must know how to identify your papers and understand variations in the type of short-answer question used in this particular examination. Follow these suggestions for maximum results from your efforts:

1) Cooperate with the monitor

The test administrator has a duty to create a situation in which you can be as much at ease as possible. He will give instructions, tell you when to begin, check to see that you are marking your answer sheet correctly, and so on. He is not there to guard you, although he will see that your competitors do not take unfair advantage. He wants to help you do your best.

2) Listen to all instructions

Don't jump the gun! Wait until you understand all directions. In most civil service tests you get more time than you need to answer the questions. So don't be in a hurry. Read each word of instructions until you clearly understand the meaning. Study the examples, listen to all announcements and follow directions. Ask questions if you do not understand what to do.

3) Identify your papers

Civil service exams are usually identified by number only. You will be assigned a number; you must not put your name on your test papers. Be sure to copy your number correctly. Since more than one exam may be given, copy your exact examination title.

4) Plan your time

Unless you are told that a test is a "speed" or "rate of work" test, speed itself is usually not important. Time enough to answer all the questions will be provided, but this does not mean that you have all day. An overall time limit has been set. Divide the total time (in minutes) by the number of questions to determine the approximate time you have for each question.

5) Do not linger over difficult questions

If you come across a difficult question, mark it with a paper clip (useful to have along) and come back to it when you have been through the booklet. One caution if you do this – be sure to skip a number on your answer sheet as well. Check often to be sure that you have not lost your place and that you are marking in the row numbered the same as the question you are answering.

6) Read the questions

Be sure you know what the question asks! Many capable people are unsuccessful because they failed to *read* the questions correctly.

7) Answer all questions

Unless you have been instructed that a penalty will be deducted for incorrect answers, it is better to guess than to omit a question.

8) Speed tests

It is often better NOT to guess on speed tests. It has been found that on timed tests people are tempted to spend the last few seconds before time is called in marking answers at random – without even reading them – in the hope of picking up a few extra points. To discourage this practice, the instructions may warn you that your score will be "corrected" for guessing. That is, a penalty will be applied. The incorrect answers will be deducted from the correct ones, or some other penalty formula will be used.

9) Review your answers

If you finish before time is called, go back to the questions you guessed or omitted to give them further thought. Review other answers if you have time.

10) Return your test materials

If you are ready to leave before others have finished or time is called, take ALL your materials to the monitor and leave quietly. Never take any test material with you. The monitor can discover whose papers are not complete, and taking a test booklet may be grounds for disqualification.

VIII. EXAMINATION TECHNIQUES

1) Read the general instructions carefully. These are usually printed on the first page of the exam booklet. As a rule, these instructions refer to the timing of the examination; the fact that you should not start work until the signal and must stop work at a signal, etc. If there are any *special* instructions, such as a choice of questions to be answered, make sure that you note this instruction carefully.

2) When you are ready to start work on the examination, that is as soon as the signal has been given, read the instructions to each question booklet, underline any key words or phrases, such as *least, best, outline, describe* and the like. In this way you will tend to answer as requested rather than discover on reviewing your paper that you *listed without describing*, that you selected the *worst* choice rather than the *best* choice, etc.

3) If the examination is of the objective or multiple-choice type – that is, each question will also give a series of possible answers: A, B, C or D, and you are called upon to select the best answer and write the letter next to that answer on your answer paper – it is advisable to start answering each question in turn. There may be anywhere from 50 to 100 such questions in the three or four hours allotted and you can see how much time would be taken if you read through all the questions before beginning to answer any. Furthermore, if you come across a question or group of questions which you know would be difficult to answer, it would undoubtedly affect your handling of all the other questions.

4) If the examination is of the essay type and contains but a few questions, it is a moot point as to whether you should read all the questions before starting to answer any one. Of course, if you are given a choice – say five out of seven and the like – then it is essential to read all the questions so you can eliminate the two that are most difficult. If, however, you are asked to answer all the questions, there may be danger in trying to answer the easiest one first because you may find that you will spend too much time on it. The best technique is to answer the first question, then proceed to the second, etc.

5) Time your answers. Before the exam begins, write down the time it started, then add the time allowed for the examination and write down the time it must be completed, then divide the time available somewhat as follows:
   - If 3-1/2 hours are allowed, that would be 210 minutes. If you have 80 objective-type questions, that would be an average of 2-1/2 minutes per question. Allow yourself no more than 2 minutes per question, or a total of 160 minutes, which will permit about 50 minutes to review.
   - If for the time allotment of 210 minutes there are 7 essay questions to answer, that would average about 30 minutes a question. Give yourself only 25 minutes per question so that you have about 35 minutes to review.

6) The most important instruction is to *read each question* and make sure you know what is wanted. The second most important instruction is to *time yourself properly* so that you answer every question. The third most important instruction is to *answer every question*. Guess if you have to but include something for each question. Remember that you will receive no credit for a blank and will probably receive some credit if you write something in answer to an essay question. If you guess a letter – say "B" for a multiple-choice question – you may have guessed right. If you leave a blank as an answer to a multiple-choice question, the examiners may respect your feelings but it will not add a point to your score. Some exams may penalize you for wrong answers, so in such cases *only*, you may not want to guess unless you have some basis for your answer.

7) Suggestions
   a. Objective-type questions
      1. Examine the question booklet for proper sequence of pages and questions
      2. Read all instructions carefully
      3. Skip any question which seems too difficult; return to it after all other questions have been answered
      4. Apportion your time properly; do not spend too much time on any single question or group of questions

5. Note and underline key words – *all, most, fewest, least, best, worst, same, opposite*, etc.
6. Pay particular attention to negatives
7. Note unusual option, e.g., unduly long, short, complex, different or similar in content to the body of the question
8. Observe the use of "hedging" words – *probably, may, most likely*, etc.
9. Make sure that your answer is put next to the same number as the question
10. Do not second-guess unless you have good reason to believe the second answer is definitely more correct
11. Cross out original answer if you decide another answer is more accurate; do not erase until you are ready to hand your paper in
12. Answer all questions; guess unless instructed otherwise
13. Leave time for review

  b. Essay questions
1. Read each question carefully
2. Determine exactly what is wanted. Underline key words or phrases.
3. Decide on outline or paragraph answer
4. Include many different points and elements unless asked to develop any one or two points or elements
5. Show impartiality by giving pros and cons unless directed to select one side only
6. Make and write down any assumptions you find necessary to answer the questions
7. Watch your English, grammar, punctuation and choice of words
8. Time your answers; don't crowd material

8) Answering the essay question

Most essay questions can be answered by framing the specific response around several key words or ideas. Here are a few such key words or ideas:

M's: manpower, materials, methods, money, management
P's: purpose, program, policy, plan, procedure, practice, problems, pitfalls, personnel, public relations

  a. Six basic steps in handling problems:
1. Preliminary plan and background development
2. Collect information, data and facts
3. Analyze and interpret information, data and facts
4. Analyze and develop solutions as well as make recommendations
5. Prepare report and sell recommendations
6. Install recommendations and follow up effectiveness

  b. Pitfalls to avoid
1. *Taking things for granted* – A statement of the situation does not necessarily imply that each of the elements is necessarily true; for example, a complaint may be invalid and biased so that all that can be taken for granted is that a complaint has been registered

2. *Considering only one side of a situation* – Wherever possible, indicate several alternatives and then point out the reasons you selected the best one
3. *Failing to indicate follow up* – Whenever your answer indicates action on your part, make certain that you will take proper follow-up action to see how successful your recommendations, procedures or actions turn out to be
4. *Taking too long in answering any single question* – Remember to time your answers properly

IX. AFTER THE TEST

Scoring procedures differ in detail among civil service jurisdictions although the general principles are the same. Whether the papers are hand-scored or graded by machine we have described, they are nearly always graded by number. That is, the person who marks the paper knows only the number – never the name – of the applicant. Not until all the papers have been graded will they be matched with names. If other tests, such as training and experience or oral interview ratings have been given, scores will be combined. Different parts of the examination usually have different weights. For example, the written test might count 60 percent of the final grade, and a rating of training and experience 40 percent. In many jurisdictions, veterans will have a certain number of points added to their grades.

After the final grade has been determined, the names are placed in grade order and an eligible list is established. There are various methods for resolving ties between those who get the same final grade – probably the most common is to place first the name of the person whose application was received first. Job offers are made from the eligible list in the order the names appear on it. You will be notified of your grade and your rank as soon as all these computations have been made. This will be done as rapidly as possible.

People who are found to meet the requirements in the announcement are called "eligibles." Their names are put on a list of eligible candidates. An eligible's chances of getting a job depend on how high he stands on this list and how fast agencies are filling jobs from the list.

When a job is to be filled from a list of eligibles, the agency asks for the names of people on the list of eligibles for that job. When the civil service commission receives this request, it sends to the agency the names of the three people highest on this list. Or, if the job to be filled has specialized requirements, the office sends the agency the names of the top three persons who meet these requirements from the general list.

The appointing officer makes a choice from among the three people whose names were sent to him. If the selected person accepts the appointment, the names of the others are put back on the list to be considered for future openings.

That is the rule in hiring from all kinds of eligible lists, whether they are for typist, carpenter, chemist, or something else. For every vacancy, the appointing officer has his choice of any one of the top three eligibles on the list. This explains why the person whose name is on top of the list sometimes does not get an appointment when some of the persons lower on the list do. If the appointing officer chooses the second or third eligible, the No. 1 eligible does not get a job at once, but stays on the list until he is appointed or the list is terminated.

X. HOW TO PASS THE INTERVIEW TEST

The examination for which you applied requires an oral interview test. You have already taken the written test and you are now being called for the interview test – the final part of the formal examination.

You may think that it is not possible to prepare for an interview test and that there are no procedures to follow during an interview. Our purpose is to point out some things you can do in advance that will help you and some good rules to follow and pitfalls to avoid while you are being interviewed.

What is an interview supposed to test?

The written examination is designed to test the technical knowledge and competence of the candidate; the oral is designed to evaluate intangible qualities, not readily measured otherwise, and to establish a list showing the relative fitness of each candidate – as measured against his competitors – for the position sought. Scoring is not on the basis of "right" and "wrong," but on a sliding scale of values ranging from "not passable" to "outstanding." As a matter of fact, it is possible to achieve a relatively low score without a single "incorrect" answer because of evident weakness in the qualities being measured.

Occasionally, an examination may consist entirely of an oral test – either an individual or a group oral. In such cases, information is sought concerning the technical knowledges and abilities of the candidate, since there has been no written examination for this purpose. More commonly, however, an oral test is used to supplement a written examination.

Who conducts interviews?

The composition of oral boards varies among different jurisdictions. In nearly all, a representative of the personnel department serves as chairman. One of the members of the board may be a representative of the department in which the candidate would work. In some cases, "outside experts" are used, and, frequently, a businessman or some other representative of the general public is asked to serve. Labor and management or other special groups may be represented. The aim is to secure the services of experts in the appropriate field.

However the board is composed, it is a good idea (and not at all improper or unethical) to ascertain in advance of the interview who the members are and what groups they represent. When you are introduced to them, you will have some idea of their backgrounds and interests, and at least you will not stutter and stammer over their names.

What should be done before the interview?

While knowledge about the board members is useful and takes some of the surprise element out of the interview, there is other preparation which is more substantive. It *is* possible to prepare for an oral interview – in several ways:

1) Keep a copy of your application and review it carefully before the interview

This may be the only document before the oral board, and the starting point of the interview. Know what education and experience you have listed there, and the sequence and dates of all of it. Sometimes the board will ask you to review the highlights of your experience for them; you should not have to hem and haw doing it.

2) Study the class specification and the examination announcement

Usually, the oral board has one or both of these to guide them. The qualities, characteristics or knowledges required by the position sought are stated in these documents. They offer valuable clues as to the nature of the oral interview. For example, if the job involves supervisory responsibilities, the announcement will usually indicate that knowledge of modern supervisory methods and the qualifications of the candidate as a supervisor will be tested. If so, you can expect such questions, frequently in the form of a hypothetical situation which you are expected to solve. NEVER go into an oral without knowledge of the duties and responsibilities of the job you seek.

3) Think through each qualification required
Try to visualize the kind of questions you would ask if you were a board member. How well could you answer them? Try especially to appraise your own knowledge and background in each area, *measured against the job sought*, and identify any areas in which you are weak. Be critical and realistic – do not flatter yourself.

4) Do some general reading in areas in which you feel you may be weak
For example, if the job involves supervision and your past experience has NOT, some general reading in supervisory methods and practices, particularly in the field of human relations, might be useful. Do NOT study agency procedures or detailed manuals. The oral board will be testing your understanding and capacity, not your memory.

5) Get a good night's sleep and watch your general health and mental attitude
You will want a clear head at the interview. Take care of a cold or any other minor ailment, and of course, no hangovers.

What should be done on the day of the interview?
Now comes the day of the interview itself. Give yourself plenty of time to get there. Plan to arrive somewhat ahead of the scheduled time, particularly if your appointment is in the fore part of the day. If a previous candidate fails to appear, the board might be ready for you a bit early. By early afternoon an oral board is almost invariably behind schedule if there are many candidates, and you may have to wait. Take along a book or magazine to read, or your application to review, but leave any extraneous material in the waiting room when you go in for your interview. In any event, relax and compose yourself.

The matter of dress is important. The board is forming impressions about you – from your experience, your manners, your attitude, and your appearance. Give your personal appearance careful attention. Dress your best, but not your flashiest. Choose conservative, appropriate clothing, and be sure it is immaculate. This is a business interview, and your appearance should indicate that you regard it as such. Besides, being well groomed and properly dressed will help boost your confidence.

Sooner or later, someone will call your name and escort you into the interview room. *This is it.* From here on you are on your own. It is too late for any more preparation. But remember, you asked for this opportunity to prove your fitness, and you are here because your request was granted.

What happens when you go in?
The usual sequence of events will be as follows: The clerk (who is often the board stenographer) will introduce you to the chairman of the oral board, who will introduce you to the other members of the board. Acknowledge the introductions before you sit down. Do not be surprised if you find a microphone facing you or a stenotypist sitting by. Oral interviews are usually recorded in the event of an appeal or other review.

Usually the chairman of the board will open the interview by reviewing the highlights of your education and work experience from your application – primarily for the benefit of the other members of the board, as well as to get the material into the record. Do not interrupt or comment unless there is an error or significant misinterpretation; if that is the case, do not hesitate. But do not quibble about insignificant matters. Also, he will usually ask you some question about your education, experience or your present job – partly to get you to start talking and to establish the interviewing "rapport." He may start the actual questioning, or turn it over to one of the other members. Frequently, each member undertakes the questioning on a particular area, one in which he is perhaps most competent, so you can expect each member to participate in the examination. Because time is limited, you may also expect some rather abrupt switches in the direction the questioning takes, so do not be upset by it. Normally, a board member will not pursue a single line of questioning unless he discovers a particular strength or weakness.

After each member has participated, the chairman will usually ask whether any member has any further questions, then will ask you if you have anything you wish to add. Unless you are expecting this question, it may floor you. Worse, it may start you off on an extended, extemporaneous speech. The board is not usually seeking more information. The question is principally to offer you a last opportunity to present further qualifications or to indicate that you have nothing to add. So, if you feel that a significant qualification or characteristic has been overlooked, it is proper to point it out in a sentence or so. Do not compliment the board on the thoroughness of their examination – they have been sketchy, and you know it. If you wish, merely say, "No thank you, I have nothing further to add." This is a point where you can "talk yourself out" of a good impression or fail to present an important bit of information. Remember, *you close the interview yourself.*

The chairman will then say, "That is all, Mr. _____, thank you." Do not be startled; the interview is over, and quicker than you think. Thank him, gather your belongings and take your leave. Save your sigh of relief for the other side of the door.

How to put your best foot forward
Throughout this entire process, you may feel that the board individually and collectively is trying to pierce your defenses, seek out your hidden weaknesses and embarrass and confuse you. Actually, this is not true. They are obliged to make an appraisal of your qualifications for the job you are seeking, and they want to see you in your best light. Remember, they must interview all candidates and a non-cooperative candidate may become a failure in spite of their best efforts to bring out his qualifications. Here are 15 suggestions that will help you:

1) Be natural – Keep your attitude confident, not cocky
If you are not confident that you can do the job, do not expect the board to be. Do not apologize for your weaknesses, try to bring out your strong points. The board is interested in a positive, not negative, presentation. Cockiness will antagonize any board member and make him wonder if you are covering up a weakness by a false show of strength.

2) Get comfortable, but don't lounge or sprawl
Sit erectly but not stiffly. A careless posture may lead the board to conclude that you are careless in other things, or at least that you are not impressed by the importance of the occasion. Either conclusion is natural, even if incorrect. Do not fuss with your clothing, a pencil or an ashtray. Your hands may occasionally be useful to emphasize a point; do not let them become a point of distraction.

3) Do not wisecrack or make small talk
This is a serious situation, and your attitude should show that you consider it as such. Further, the time of the board is limited – they do not want to waste it, and neither should you.

4) Do not exaggerate your experience or abilities

In the first place, from information in the application or other interviews and sources, the board may know more about you than you think. Secondly, you probably will not get away with it. An experienced board is rather adept at spotting such a situation, so do not take the chance.

5) If you know a board member, do not make a point of it, yet do not hide it

Certainly you are not fooling him, and probably not the other members of the board. Do not try to take advantage of your acquaintanceship – it will probably do you little good.

6) Do not dominate the interview

Let the board do that. They will give you the clues – do not assume that you have to do all the talking. Realize that the board has a number of questions to ask you, and do not try to take up all the interview time by showing off your extensive knowledge of the answer to the first one.

7) Be attentive

You only have 20 minutes or so, and you should keep your attention at its sharpest throughout. When a member is addressing a problem or question to you, give him your undivided attention. Address your reply principally to him, but do not exclude the other board members.

8) Do not interrupt

A board member may be stating a problem for you to analyze. He will ask you a question when the time comes. Let him state the problem, and wait for the question.

9) Make sure you understand the question

Do not try to answer until you are sure what the question is. If it is not clear, restate it in your own words or ask the board member to clarify it for you. However, do not haggle about minor elements.

10) Reply promptly but not hastily

A common entry on oral board rating sheets is "candidate responded readily," or "candidate hesitated in replies." Respond as promptly and quickly as you can, but do not jump to a hasty, ill-considered answer.

11) Do not be peremptory in your answers

A brief answer is proper – but do not fire your answer back. That is a losing game from your point of view. The board member can probably ask questions much faster than you can answer them.

12) Do not try to create the answer you think the board member wants

He is interested in what kind of mind you have and how it works – not in playing games. Furthermore, he can usually spot this practice and will actually grade you down on it.

13) Do not switch sides in your reply merely to agree with a board member

Frequently, a member will take a contrary position merely to draw you out and to see if you are willing and able to defend your point of view. Do not start a debate, yet do not surrender a good position. If a position is worth taking, it is worth defending.

14) Do not be afraid to admit an error in judgment if you are shown to be wrong

The board knows that you are forced to reply without any opportunity for careful consideration. Your answer may be demonstrably wrong. If so, admit it and get on with the interview.

15) Do not dwell at length on your present job

The opening question may relate to your present assignment. Answer the question but do not go into an extended discussion. You are being examined for a *new* job, not your present one. As a matter of fact, try to phrase ALL your answers in terms of the job for which you are being examined.

Basis of Rating

Probably you will forget most of these "do's" and "don'ts" when you walk into the oral interview room. Even remembering them all will not ensure you a passing grade. Perhaps you did not have the qualifications in the first place. But remembering them will help you to put your best foot forward, without treading on the toes of the board members.

Rumor and popular opinion to the contrary notwithstanding, an oral board wants you to make the best appearance possible. They know you are under pressure – but they also want to see how you respond to it as a guide to what your reaction would be under the pressures of the job you seek. They will be influenced by the degree of poise you display, the personal traits you show and the manner in which you respond.

ABOUT THIS BOOK

This book contains tests divided into Examination Sections. Go through each test, answering every question in the margin. We have also attached a sample answer sheet at the back of the book that can be removed and used. At the end of each test look at the answer key and check your answers. On the ones you got wrong, look at the right answer choice and learn. Do not fill in the answers first. Do not memorize the questions and answers, but understand the answer and principles involved. On your test, the questions will likely be different from the samples. Questions are changed and new ones added. If you understand these past questions you should have success with any changes that arise. Tests may consist of several types of questions. We have additional books on each subject should more study be advisable or necessary for you. Finally, the more you study, the better prepared you will be. This book is intended to be the last thing you study before you walk into the examination room. Prior study of relevant texts is also recommended. NLC publishes some of these in our Fundamental Series. Knowledge and good sense are important factors in passing your exam. Good luck also helps. So now study this Passbook, absorb the material contained within and take that knowledge into the examination. Then do your best to pass that exam.

EXAMINATION SECTION

EXAMINATION SECTION
TEST 1

DIRECTIONS: Each question or incomplete statement is followed by several suggested answers or completions. Select the one the BEST answers the question or completes the statement. *PRINT THE LETTER OF THE CORRECT ANSWER IN THE SPACE AT THE RIGHT.*

1. Which of the following is an example of primary health education?　　1.____

    A. Helping clients with maturity-onset diabetes to reverse imbalances in blood sugar
    B. Teaching community members about the elements of an adequate and balanced diet
    C. Helping a diabetic who has lost a limb to amputation how to maximize his potential for healthy living
    D. Teaching overweight clients how to adjust their diet in order to lose weight

2. Which of the following is a disadvantage associated with the use of videotapes for instruction or promotion?　　2.____

    A. Not appropriate for group settings
    B. Expensive to produce
    C. Distribution is complicated
    D. Low probability of audience identification with subjects

3. The foundation of any community health promotion program is generally considered to be　　3.____

    A. remediation
    B. advocacy
    C. prevention
    D. maintenance

4. When writing materials for adults with limited reading skills, readability tests performed on the materials should indicate a level of about _____ grade.　　4.____

    A. 3rd
    B. 5th
    C. 7th
    D. 9th

5. To spread the word about a health promotion program, a health educator wants to make use of a local television station. Which of the following personnel would probably be LEAST useful as a contact?　　5.____

    A. Commentator
    B. Health/medical reporter
    C. News assignment editor
    D. Talk show producer/host

1

6. In a large urban area, members of a geographically concentrated Chinese immigrant community seem to suffer disproportionately from foodborne illnesses. In the past, adults from this community have proven reluctant to share personal opinions or feelings in front of others. A health educator, hoping to reduce the risk of these kinds of illnesses, launches a needs assessment program to determine whether a program should be designed for this group. Which of the following approaches to needs assessment is probably LEAST appropriate for this community?

    A. Focus group
    B. Written survey
    C. Literature review
    D. Observation

7. A county health department has observed that educational print materials about breast cancer, which the department received from the state health administration, are written at too high a reading level and are not culturally appropriate for the older, low-income Asian American women in the department's target community. For health educators at the department, the most appropriate next step would be to

    A. hire a professional graphic artist to create illustrations of older Asian American women to accompany the materials
    B. develop materials for other media, such as visuals or radio announcements
    C. conduct focus groups to identify appropriate communication channels, credible information sources, and the acceptability of breast cancer materials
    D. simplify the text of the materials

8. Prior to the full implementation of a marketing strategy for health education services, it will be necessary for program designers to conduct _____ research.

    A. experimental
    B. ethnographic
    C. longitudinal
    D. formative

9. As a funding source for health education programs, corporate grants

    A. usually require a more formal proposal preparation than a foundation grant
    B. may take the form of matching gifts
    C. are issued through an RFP or RFA process
    D. are typically easier to obtain than foundation grants

10. Among the cultural group of clients broadly classified as "Native American," a health educator should expect to find the most traditional of these to be characterized by

    A. patriarchal family systems
    B. independence and individualism
    C. acceptance of death as part of the natural life cycle
    D. a focus on the nuclear family

11. Which of the following is NOT a problems or barrier involved in performing an impact analysis of a health education program?

    A. Impact evaluations involve extended commitment from members of the agency.
    B. They are not as comprehensive or thorough as other forms of evaluation.

C. They frequently rely on other strategies in addition to communication.
D. Results often cannot be directly related to the effects of a program.

12. When collecting the morbidity data of a community, a health educator must keep in mind that

    A. reporting any listed diagnosis does not accurately represent the disease burden associated with a condition
    B. reporting only primary diagnosis data will often underrepresent the actual prevalence of a particular disease
    C. it is usually difficult to obtain hospital discharge data
    D. morbidity data should be collected independent of any opinion data collected among community members

13. The most successful worksite health education programs will typically include a(n)

    A. co-enrollment and participation by employees of other local companies
    B. advisory or coordinating committee composed of employees from various levels and departments
    C. built-in referral service
    D. steering committee composed of health education professionals from various levels and departments in the local community

14. To some degree, a health educator usually tries to include community members in the planning process of a health education program. When possible, a health educator should involve community members in
    I. adapting or developing materials
    II. choosing appropriate strategies to reach the intended audience
    III. evaluating the program
    IV. developing the health messages

    A. I and IV
    B. II only
    C. II, III and IV
    D. I, II, III and IV

15. As a general rule, the budget considerations for a health education program that is planned on an ongoing basis should reflect a_____ -year projection

    A. 1
    B. 3
    C. 5
    D. 10

16. Pre-testing health messages and materials is considered to be essential as a condition for acceptance in a program. However, it does have limitations. The most significant of these is that pre-testing

    A. is of little use when messages contain especially sensitive or controversial content
    B. can assess emotional responses, but does little to demonstrate the extent of client comprehension
    C. is essentially qualitative in nature, and does not involve statistical precision
    D. has no provision for determining the perceived personal relevance of messages

17. Of the following steps in establishing a community health education program, which should typically occur LAST?

    A. Promoting the organization
    B. Conducting a needs analysis
    C. Recruiting volunteers
    D. Developing job descriptions

18. Each of the following is a guideline to be used in adapting a health education program to a different culture, EXCEPT

    A. trying to personalize the delivery of the program, rather than use the mass-media approach
    B. asking community members to choose a name for the program
    C. organizing health education activities around recreational activities or community celebrations
    D. providing word-for-word translations of audio, video, or written program materials

19. A health educator is helping to plan a school health center for a large and culturally diverse urban high school. The most compelling reason to adopt a school-based, rather than school-linked, structure for this school health center is the

    A. avoidance of professional turf wars
    B. issue of legal liability
    C. greater school control over service delivery
    D. low health-seeking behavior of adolescents

20. Which of the following is NOT a risk factor associated with heart disease?

    A. High blood cholesterol
    B. Alcohol abuse
    C. Environmental factors
    D. Hypertension

21. The most significant criticism of the educational approach to health promotion is that programs and personnel

    A. focus too much on individuals and does little to alter their environment
    B. impose medical values on the client
    C. is likely to induce feelings of guilt if clients choose not to follow prescribed regimes
    D. assumes that clients believe that health "experts" know best

22. At a bare minimum, a comprehensive health promotion program at a major worksite should include each of the following activities, EXCEPT

    A. group smoking cessation programs
    B. support groups of various types
    C. blood pressure control programs
    D. health education classes on selected topics

23. Which of the following steps in developing a successful health education program would typically be performed FIRST?

    A. Writing a mission statement
    B. Writing goals and objectives
    C. Inventory of organizational resources
    D. Needs assessment

24. In dealing with largely ethnic communities, it is helpful for the health educator to recognize the differences between other cultures and the dominant Anglo-American culture. Which of the following is NOT typically identified as a generalized Anglo-American cultural trait?

    A. Formality
    B. Human equality
    C. Practicality and efficiency
    D. Individualism and privacy

25. A community's health education needs are assessed directly through the value judgements of the health educator and other professionals. This is an example of _____ need.

    A. expressed
    B. normative
    C. felt
    D. comparative

KEY (CORRECT ANSWERS)

1.	B	11.	B
2.	B	12.	B
3.	C	13.	B
4.	B	14.	D
5.	A	15.	B
6.	A	16.	C
7.	C	17.	C
8.	D	18.	D
9.	B	19.	D
10.	C	20.	C

21. A
22. B
23. A
24. A
25. B

TEST 2

DIRECTIONS: Each question or incomplete statement is followed by several suggested answers or completions. Select the one the BEST answers the question or completes the statement. *PRINT THE LETTER OF THE CORRECT ANSWER IN THE SPACE AT THE RIGHT.*

1. Which of the following types of information is LEAST likely to be produced by the outcome evaluation of a health education program?

    A. Long-term maintenance of desired behavior
    B. Policies initiated or other institutional changes made
    C. Expressed intentions of the target clientele
    D. Knowledge and attitude changes

    1.____

2. In dealing with ethnic communities, it is helpful for the health educator to recognize the differences between other cultures and the dominant Anglo-American culture. Which of the following is typically identified as a generalized Anglo-American cultural trait?

    A. Orientation toward being, rather than action or work
    B. Emphasis on duration of life, rather than overall quality
    C. Cooperation, rather than competition
    D. Tradition, rather than change

    2.____

3. Which of the following is NOT a risk factor typically associated with pneumonia or influenza?

    A. Tobacco use
    B. Health care access
    C. Workplace hazards
    D. Biological factors

    3.____

4. For the health educator, the most significant difference between grants and contracts as funding sources for programs is that grants

    A. allow more creativity and flexibility in a particular project
    B. are more likely to be awarded to unsolicited proposals
    C. provide 100 percent funding for initiatives
    D. usually go to for-profit organizations

    4.____

5. Which of the following is an advantage associated with the use of interactive media for instruction or promotion?

    A. Applicability to group settings
    B. Minimal computer literacy requirements of learners
    C. Minimal staff support requirements
    D. Requires little technical skill to develop

    5.____

6. In the context of health promotion, the purposes of health education include each of the following, EXCEPT providing

    A. awareness
    B. maintenance
    C. advocacy
    D. prevention

    6.____

7. A focus group has convened as part of a health educator's community assessment. Of the following, the LEAST useful or appropriate question for the educator to ask group members would be

    A. How do you feel about the general quality of life for people in this community?
    B. Do you agree that there are people in this community who would benefit from changing certain behaviors?
    C. How have people responded in the past to health education programs?
    D. What do you think about the idea of promoting an exercise class for seniors?

8. The first phase of the PRECEDE model of planning health education is the _____ diagnosis.

    A. epidemiological
    B. educational
    C. behavioral
    D. administrative

9. When working one-one-one or in small groups with clients from different cultures, a health educator should remember that in general, people from _____ communities will prefer the greatest distance between themselves and people with whom they are speaking.

    A. African-American
    B. Hispanic-American
    C. Anglo-American
    D. Asian-American

10. Which of the following would NOT be a guideline for presenting educational programs to groups of older adults?

    A. Encourage participation, such as answering questions, role-playing, and real-life scenarios
    B. Begin presentations with an introductory overview.
    C. Adjust the environment to accommodate sensory deficits that are common among older people.
    D. Plan to present information in 1 - to 2-hour blocks, and leave time for questioning.

11. A 60-year-old male with an enlarged prostate returns to his to a physician because he's had abdominal pain for two days. Four days ago, his physician prescribed Benadryl for his allergies. After he began to take Benadryl, the man's urine slowed down and then he developed abdominal pain. This case is an example of

    A. iatrogenesis
    B. blaming the victim
    C. secondary morbidity
    D. treating symptoms, rather than the cause

12. To pre-test a draft copy of a flier that will distributed during a cancer awareness workshop, a health educator mails the flier directly to a sampling of community members, along with a questionnaire about its content and format. The potential disadvantages of using the self-administered questionnaire include
    I. low response rates
    II. uncontrolled exposure to draft materials
    III. typically require follow-up
    IV. extended time lapse between production and responses

    A. I and II
    B. II and IV
    C. III only
    D. I, II, III and IV

13. In the coalition model of health education and promotion, which of the following organizations usually consists of citizens who are appointed by official bodies?

    A. Commissions
    B. Advisory committees
    C. Task forces
    D. Consortia/alliances

14. Guidelines for the composition of print materials as health instruction media include
    I. Abbreviations and acronyms should be used for the purpose of simplicity
    II. Text should be written in active, not passive, voice
    III. Graphics should be immediately identifiable
    IV. No type smaller than 10-point should be used

    A. I only
    B. II and IV
    C. II, III and IV
    D. I, II, III and IV

15. As part of a community assessment, a health educator wants to compile information on primary care services and community services. As a source of this information, the first and best choice would be

    A. the state department of human services
    B. the state department of health
    C. the state department of aging
    D. local information and referral service inventories

16. As a mass media channel for the communication of a health-related message or public service announcement, television

    A. is an inexpensive and relatively easy way to get a message out
    B. is most likely to reach low-income and other audiences who are unlikely to turn to health sources for help
    C. involves a relatively high degree of client attention and involvement
    D. allows for the communication of more complex health issues or behaviors

17. Which of the following methods for recruiting volunteers for a health education program is generally LEAST effective? 17.____

    A. Articles placed in business/community newsletters
    B. Person-to-person contact
    C. News releases/public service announcements
    D. Classified advertising

18. A health educator designs a number of goals for his substance abuse treatment program, beginning at the individual consciousness level and moving to social change. The educator will have accomplished a behavior change goal if, after completing the program, a client can say that he 18.____

    A. now drinks less than he used to
    B. understands that drinking too much is bad for him
    C. is aware that he is drinking too much
    D. finds that soft drinks are becoming more socially acceptable in bars and clubs

19. The first step in any community assessment performed prior to the design of a health education program is usually a(n) 19.____

    A. oral survey
    B. literature review
    C. focus group
    D. community observation

20. When developing and writing specific objectives, it is important to remember that each objective must include 20.____
    I. the performance or action being stated
    II. a measurable factor
    III. a time element
    IV. a standard of performance or condition

    A. I and II
    B. I, II and IV
    C. II and IV
    D. I, II, III and IV

21. Which of the following activities would MOST likely be associated with the social change model of health education? 21.____

    A. Limiting and challenging cigarette advertising and sports sponsorship
    B. Persuasive education to prevent non-smokers from starting
    C. Helping clients to learn how to stop smoking if they want to
    D. Screening clients for tobacco-related illnesses

22. Health promotion and health education programs should NOT be developed to 22.____

    A. include interventions that will focus on a single risk factor
    B. operate in ways that can be specifically measured and evaluated
    C. apply methods that are universally proven among different settings
    D. conform to the needs and preferences of the target group(s)

23. A modestly-funded local health agency wants to perform an outcome analysis of the publicity campaign for its vaccination program. Which of the following procedures would be most appropriate?

    A. Telephone survey of self-reported behavior
    B. Focus groups
    C. Calculation of the percentage of the target audience who participated
    D. Study of long-term disease trends

24. The leading cause of death and injury of children under 12 in the United States is

    A. violence outside the home
    B. home health hazards
    C. automobile accidents
    D. abuse and neglect

25. Which of the following is LEAST likely to be successful as a means of assessing employees' health needs in a worksite wellness outreach?

    A. Asking for health risk information including smoking, weight, exercise, etc.
    B. Surveying employees about their interest in wellness programs
    C. Take-home, self-administered health-risk appraisals
    D. Measuring blood pressure and cholesterol

KEY (CORRECT ANSWERS)

1. A		11. A	
2. B		12. D	
3. C		13. A	
4. A		14. C	
5. C		15. D	
6. C		16. B	
7. B		17. D	
8. A		18. A	
9. D		19. B	
10. D		20. D	

21. A
22. C
23. C
24. B
25. C

TEST 3

DIRECTIONS: Each question or incomplete statement is followed by several suggested answers or completions. Select the one the BEST answers the question or completes the statement. *PRINT THE LETTER OF THE CORRECT ANSWER IN THE SPACE AT THE RIGHT.*

1. As part of the needs assessment process, a health educator attempts to assemble a community profile. In this process, advantages of using geographic and political boundaries in defining a community include
    I. easier data collection
    II. greater likelihood of influencing the use of government resources and policies to address priority health problems
    III. greater likelihood of a shared identity among community members
    IV. increased probability of common demographic trends

    A. I only
    B. I and II
    C. II, III and IV
    D. I, II, III and IV

    1.____

2. Of the following, which element of a health education program is MOST likely to have the greatest impact on producing lasting changes?

    A. Preventing injury and disease
    B. Changing health behaviors
    C. Enhancing awareness of positive health habits
    D. Creating a supportive environment for good health practices

    2.____

3. According to the PATCH model of health education planning developed by the Centers for Disease Control and prevention, five elements are considered critical to the success of any community health education process. Which of the following is NOT one of these?

    A. Data are used to guide the development of programs
    B. The capacity of community members to promote health should be increased.
    C. Evaluation should emphasize feedback and improvement.
    D. Participants develop a solution-focused approach to solving specific health problems.

    3.____

4. Before deciding upon a means of instruction, a health educator should know that people tend to retain 90 percent of what they

    A. do and say
    B. see and hear
    C. read
    D. say

    4.____

5. When developing materials for clients with limited reading skills, it is important to remember that low-literacy clients typically

    A. depend on auditory cues to clarify and interpret words
    B. rely on a broad set of inferences outside their personal experience when reading

    5.____

C. have longer attention spans than expected
D. have difficulty understanding complex ideas, especially those with several elements

6. A health educator is participating in the writing of a grant proposal for a risk reduction program among an urban immigrant community. Typically, the cover letter that accompanies a proposal for a government or foundation grant should include a brief explanation of each of the following, EXCEPT the

A. total funding requirement
B. methods for evaluating program success
C. purpose of the project
D. project's relevance to the foundation's or agency's interest

7. Which of the following would be a useful resource for discovering a local wellness council?
   I. Local chamber of commerce
   II. Wellness Councils of America (WELCOA)
   III. Local recreation department
   IV. YMCA of USA

A. I and II
B. II and III
C. III only
D. I, II, III and IV

8. Advantages associated with the coalition model of health education and promotion include each of the following, EXCEPT

A. enhanced credibility
B. appropriateness for brief, task-based interventions
C. conservation of community resources
D. broader reach within a community

9. In a written objective for a health promotion program, which of the following verbs would be LEAST appropriate for describing a client outcome?

A. Classify
B. Interpret
C. Know
D. Define

10. A health educator wants to study the relationships between age, gender, ethnic background and two dependent variables: drug use and sexual behavior. The type of study to be conducted will be

A. ex post facto
B. multivariate
C. pre-test/post-test
D. longitudinal

11. Which of the following activities would MOST likely be associated with the educational model of health education?

    A. Lobbying for a no-smoking policy in public places.
    B. Encouraging people to seek early detection and treatment of smoking-related disorders.
    C. Helping clients to explore their own values and attitudes about smoking.
    D. Responding to clients' self-identified concern with smoking as a health issue with printed educational materials.

12. Which of the following needs assessment activities is MOST likely to yield only quantitative data?

    A. Written survey
    B. Observation
    C. Focus group
    D. In-depth interview

13. As a mass media channel for the communication of a health-related message or public service announcement, radio does NOT

    A. generally reach fewer people than television
    B. offer a greater potential for audience targeting than television
    C. involve relatively high production and distribution expenses
    D. offer the opportunity for direct audience involvement

14. When designing a program targeted to African-American clients, a health educator should know that African-American parenting styles generally result in each of the following, EXCEPT that children

    A. have less body contact (breast feeding, holding, etc.) with their parents than most other American children.
    B. are taught to comply with requests that do not have immediate tangible rewards
    C. are taught that there is a supreme being that is greater than themselves
    D. learn the responsibility of caring for other children

15. A health educator wants to test the readability of some written instructional materials he has designed for a stop-smoking seminar. The quickest and most efficient way to do this would be to

    A. have the materials screened by colleagues
    B. consult with a reading instructor from the community
    C. give the materials to volunteers who are representative of the target population, and follow up with comprehension questions
    D. use the Fry scale

16. Of the following risk factors, which plays a contributing role in ALL leading causes of death in America?

    A. Diet
    B. Stress
    C. Substance abuse
    D. Health care access

17. In order to secure volunteers to help implement a health education program, the best approach is usually to emphasize the

    A. rewards of participating in the program
    B. numbers of children and infants who will benefit from the program
    C. risk factors in the community that need to be changed
    D. moral imperative of improving community health

18. Which of the following is an example of tertiary health education?

    A. Campaigning for safer roads and stricter enforcement of traffic laws
    B. Conducting a smoking cessation workshop in a group format
    C. Teaching a client with juvenile-onset diabetes how to adjust eating habits
    D. Teaching basic skin care to clients with acne.

19. The basic purpose of a formative program evaluation is to

    A. document the short-term results of the program
    B. maximize the chance for program success before the communication activity starts
    C. help determine whether outcomes were in fact produced by elements of the program
    D. obtain descriptive data on a project

20. A health educator decides that in conducting a course for teenage alcoholics on the health risks associated with drinking, she will adopt an authoritarian communication style. The most likely positive outcome associated with this approach is that clients will

    A. appreciate others' own rights and opinions about how to solve problems
    B. be encouraged to explore their feelings more freely and to be creative about finding solutions
    C. be given clear guidance on how to resolve their problems
    D. feel protected from harm and able to cope with their problems

21. Which of the following is LEAST likely to be successful as a means of recruiting employees for a worksite wellness outreach?

    A. On-the-spot sign-ups during screenings
    B. Follow-up personal visits to workstations or job sites
    C. Individual telephone calls
    D. Persistent use of the media and individual mailings

22. In innovation-diffusion theory, an individual who influences the client's decision in a more desirable direction is known as a(n)

    A. innovator
    B. motivator
    C. change agent
    D. impeller

23. A health agency has composed draft materials for a nutrition awareness program, and wants to hear what members of the community think of the materials. The coordinator schedules individual interviews with a number of people who represent different sub-groups in the community. The advantages associated with the individual interview as a program pre-test include

    I. rapid response analysis
    II. small time requirements
    III. the ability to explore emotional or complex issues
    IV. the ability to communicate with hard-to-reach audiences

    A. I and II
    B. II, III and IV
    C. III and IV
    D. I, II, III and IV

23.____

24. According to the Society for Public Health Education's (SOPHE) code of ethics, each of the following is a responsibility of a health educator, EXCEPT to

    A. further health education through applied research
    B. share skills and experience with students and colleagues
    C. advocate for change and legislation, and speak out on issues harmful to public health
    D. guide communities in their choices through selective and judicious provision of information

24.____

25. The most significant advantage of the medical model of health education is that it

    A. takes into account the social factors that influence client behaviors
    B. encourages clients to seek and discover information about healthy lifestyle choices
    C. assumes that individual behavior is the primary cause of ill health
    D. draws on the knowledge of trained professionals to identify the most effective mode of intervention

25.____

KEY (CORRECT ANSWERS)

1. B	11. C
2. D	12. A
3. D	13. C
4. A	14. A
5. D	15. D
6. B	16. D
7. A	17. A
8. B	18. C
9. C	19. B
10. B	20. C

21. D
22. C
23. C
24. D
25. D

EXAMINATION SECTION
TEST 1

DIRECTIONS: Each question or incomplete statement is followed by several suggested answers or completions. Select the one the BEST answers the question or completes the statement. *PRINT THE LETTER OF THE CORRECT ANSWER IN THE SPACE AT THE RIGHT.*

1. A health educator helps collect data for an epidemiological study that will examine the relationship, during the months of December and January, between the incidence of influenza in a community and the behaviors of the community members. The type of study to be conducted will be

    A. longitudinal
    B. ex post facto
    C. cross-sectional
    D. pre-test/post-test

2. In a worksite wellness program, which of the following is LEAST likely to help employees change their health risks?

    A. The use of "engagement" strategies that are individually designed
    B. A solid and focused array of health improvement classes and seminars
    C. Repeated follow-up contacts after programs or classes have ended
    D. Persistent, personalized outreach to at-risk employees

3. The final phase of the PRECEDE model of planning health education is the _____ diagnosis.

    A. behavioral
    B. administrative
    C. educational
    D. social

4. Typically, a health promotion effort in a community should begin with a(n)

    A. enhancement of community awareness about the program
    B. behavioral change strategy
    C. screening and appraisal of health risks
    D. socioemotional intervention

5. Role-playing exercises are sometimes a useful means of instruction in health education. Generally, a disadvantage associated with this activity is that it

    A. focuses on a narrow band of skills
    B. tends to truncate discussions
    C. makes learning more abstract
    D. requires a well-trained facilitator

6. In researching a community profile, which of the following items of information would probably be LEAST useful to a health educator?

    A. Average educational level of residents
    B. Age distribution

C. Political affiliations
D. Average household income

7. A health educator decides that in conducting a course for young teenagers on the dangers of unprotected sex, he will adopt a paternalistic communication style. A potential disadvantage associated with this decision is that

   A. attention is often diverted from real problems
   B. clients may become reluctant to take independent action
   C. clients may become likely to rebel or reject the views of the health educator
   D. the health educator may be perceived as neither supportive nor caring

8. To help conduct effective meetings, health educators and other program members should

   A. begin only when all members of the group are present
   B. record minutes of each meeting and distribute them before the next
   C. take collective responsibility for tasks and deadlines
   D. let people raise issues that are important to them, even if they are not on the agenda

9. Though the cultural groups that make up the broad category known as "Asian American" are varied in their beliefs and customs, it should generally be expected that first-generation immigrants from Asia will share a set of traditional values and behavior. Which of the following would be LEAST likely to be included in these values and behaviors?

   A. Assertive help-seeking in time of need
   B. Blame of self for failure
   C. Control of strong feelings
   D. Respect for authority

10. As a general rule, sentences that appear in a health education brochure should each contain about _____ or fewer words.

    A. 8
    B. 12
    C. 17
    D. 25

11. A health educator is participating in the writing of a grant proposal for a hygiene awareness program for migrant workers. Typically, the body of a proposal should FIRST contain

    A. specific goals and objectives of the program
    B. a description of the target population
    C. an itemized budget for the program, including all expenses and a justification for each
    D. a one-page summary of the entire proposal

12. When defining and organizing a message for an adult audience with limited reading skills, a health educator should NOT

    A. put the most important information in the middle of the presentation
    B. present one idea on a single page, or two facing pages

C. frequently summarize or repeat concepts
D. start with the completed idea one wants understood, then provide a breakdown or explanation

13. Which of the following theories would be MOST helpful in designing a program for treating alcohol abuse?

    A. Consensus
    B. Innovation-diffusion
    C. Conflict
    D. Self-regulation

14. As a mass media channel for the communication of a health-related message or public service announcement, magazines

    A. are more approachable and involve easier placement of PSAs than audiovisual media
    B. do not enable agencies to more specifically target segments of the public
    C. can explain more complex health issues and behaviors
    D. generally involve passive consumption

15. Which of the following is a risk factor associated with stroke?

    A. Alcohol abuse
    B. Obesity
    C. Home hazards
    D. Infectious agents

16. Before deciding upon a means of instruction, a health educator should know that people generally retain only about 10 percent of content that they

    A. say
    B. read
    C. do
    D. hear

17. For participants in a breast and cervical cancer control program, a health educator adapted a low-literacy flier developed by another organization. The flier was pre-tested among community members, and found to be written at the appropriate level. Staff at the agency observed that women in the program, after receiving the fliers, folded them to fit them in their purses, and many women left the fliers behind in the clinic. The most appropriate next step would be to

    A. conduct a focus group to discover what kind of format women would prefer for written information
    B. modify the format but keep the original text, to produce a flier that will fit into a woman's purse
    C. discontinue production of the fliers, and instead rely on visual presentation of the material on-site
    D. monitor the women as they leave the clinic and encourage them to take the flier with them

18. As part of a community assessment, a health educator wants to conduct a focus group interview. The ideal number of members to participate in this sort of group is usually about

    A. 3 to 5
    B. 4 to 8
    C. 10 to 12
    D. 15 to 20

18.____

19. In the client-centered model of health education, interventions are best described as

    A. promotion of medical interventions to prevent or alleviate ill health
    B. instruction about the causes and effects of health-demoting factors
    C. changing clients' attitudes and behaviors to promote the adoption of a healthier lifestyle
    D. collaborations with clients to identify and act on health-related concerns

19.____

20. Each of the following is a guideline that should be used in acquiring information from clients who are of different cultural or language backgrounds, EXCEPT

    A. asking questions in the exact same way repeatedly, to ensure understanding
    B. adjusting the style of the interaction to reflect differences in age between oneself and the client
    C. establishing rapport and showing genuine warm concern for the client, to build trust
    D. using open-ended questions to increase the amount of information obtained

20.____

21. The local newspaper has just run a story about a homeless encampment near the downtown area of a small city. An educator with the local health agency wants to write a letter to the editor of the paper, in order to draw attention to the services it offers to homeless people in the community. Guidelines for writing letters to be printed on the editorial page include

    I. the most important point should be made at the end of the letter
    II. letters should be saved for the most important issues
    III. letters should be signed by an officer of the organization
    IV. they should be no longer than 50-100 words

    A. I and II
    B. II and III
    C. III and IV
    D. I, II, III and IV

21.____

22. The lead agency in a coalition for health education and promotion should usually expect extensive staff demands in each of the following areas, EXCEPT

    A. clerical
    B. service delivery
    C. fund-raising
    D. research and fact gathering

22.____

23. A health agency conducts a readability test on one of its brochures. This is a(n) _____ evaluation of a health education procedure. 23._____

    A. impact
    B. process
    C. outcome
    D. formative

24. Most nationwide initiatives focusing on public health, such as Healthy People 2000, place the highest priority on 24._____

    A. physical activity and fitness
    B. family planning
    C. occupational safety and health
    D. violent and abusive behavior

25. A health educator designs a number of goals for his exercise education program, beginning at the individual consciousness level and moving to social change. The educator will have accomplished a decision-making change goal if, after completing the program, a client can say that she 25._____

    A. feels unfit because she gets out of breath easily
    B. will take fitness classes
    C. states the belief that she would feel better if she exercised more
    D. now goes to the gym regularly and is generally more physically active

KEY (CORRECT ANSWERS)

1.	C	11.	D
2.	B	12.	A
3.	B	13.	D
4.	C	14.	C
5.	D	15.	A
6.	C	16.	B
7.	B	17.	B
8.	B	18.	C
9.	A	19.	D
10.	C	20.	A

21. B
22. B
23. D
24. A
25. B

TEST 2

DIRECTIONS: Each question or incomplete statement is followed by several suggested answers or completions. Select the one the BEST answers the question or completes the statement. *PRINT THE LETTER OF THE CORRECT ANSWER IN THE SPACE AT THE RIGHT.*

1. Which of the following is an example of secondary health education? 1._____

    A. Demonstrating the proper installation of a child car seat
    B. Explaining to a group of teens how to avoid contracting sexually transmitted diseases such as AIDS
    C. Showing clients how to give first aid after an accident
    D. Teaching a client with food allergies how to adjust eating habits to ensure minimum complications

2. A health educator wants to print a brochure on safe sex to be distributed among local teenagers. The educator should know that the greatest expense involved in printing materials is 2._____

    A. making the printing plates
    B. paper
    C. distribution costs
    D. original artwork or graphics

3. In the beginning phase of a health education program, a good needs assessment process can help the program designers to do each of the following, EXCEPT to 3._____

    A. identify which programs to implement first
    B. identify the types of programs needed
    C. establish a set of baseline data to demonstrate later improvements
    D. establish incentives for behavioral change

4. The most common mistake health educators make in designing a worksite wellness program is to 4._____

    A. depend solely on a schedule of classes for health improvement intervention
    B. focus only on at-risk employees
    C. use the "menu approach" to offering a variety of programs
    D. spend too much time tracking down employees to persuade them to take part in programs or classes

5. A health educator working in a Hispanic/Latino community should remember that the diverse Hispanic cultures in America tend to share some common values and behaviors. Which of the following is NOT one of these? 5._____

    A. Family as the primary source of emotional and psychological support.
    B. Matriarchal family structures.
    C. Consultation with several family members before seeking health care.
    D. Modesty and personal privacy.

6. Which of the following interventions does NOT conform to the medical model of health education?

    A. Persuading parents to bring their children in for vaccinations
    B. Teaching a course on how to care for teeth and gums
    C. Participating in a self-help group to discuss the issue of menopause
    D. Screening middle-aged men for high blood pressure

7. Of the following, which element should typically appear FIRST in the body of a proposal for the funding of a public health education program?

    A. The specific methods that will be used to meet program objectives-approach, action plan, timeline
    B. Process and outcome measures to be used in evaluating project success
    C. Brief background of the problem in the community, with supporting data
    D. The management plan for the project, including key staff members and their roles

8. At the local high school, a health educator is conducting a workshop on the dangers of certain commonly abused drugs to a group of Asian immigrant parents. The health educator is aware that English is a second language for many of the parents. Each of the following is a strategy that will help the educator overcome this language barrier in presenting information, EXCEPT

    A. speaking more loudly
    B. using images, gestures, and simple written instructions that may be understood by relatives
    C. speaking slowly and enunciating clearly
    D. repeating sentences in the same words if it's been misunderstood

9. A person who takes the structuralist view of behavior and social change will probably focus his or her efforts on the

    A. laws, codes, zoning ordinances, and taxation of the community
    B. sense of shared purpose among community members
    C. biomedical causes of a disease or disorder
    D. individual's motivation for change

10. When defining and organizing a written message for an adult audience with limited reading skills, a health educator's sentences should

    A. include vivid descriptive phrases to add interest
    B. average 8 to 10 words in length
    C. have roughly the same rhythm
    D. be written in the passive voice

11. In researching a community profile, most of the information can be obtained from the data collected by the

    A. local hospitals
    B. state and local social service departments
    C. chambers of commerce
    D. federal Bureau of the Census

12. When deciding whether to use visuals as part of health instruction, the primary consideration should be whether they

   A. enhance the message, rather than compete with it
   B. illustrate key concepts
   C. stimulate learner interest
   D. are culturally appropriate

13. The probability for learning in a health education program is likely to be enhanced when the following principles are used in program design:
   I. Program content is relevant to the learner, and is perceived by the learner to be relevant.
   II. Instructional methods that stimulate the widest variety of senses will generally be most effective.
   III. Concepts should be reviewed and repeated several times during instruction.
   IV. Instruction should move from the unknown to the known.

   A. I and IV
   B. I, II and III
   C. II and III
   D. I, II, III and IV

14. Which of the following is MOST likely to be a kind of formative evaluation used for a health education program?

   A. Studies of public behavior/health change
   B. Assessment of target audience for knowledge gain
   C. Calculation of percentage of target audience participating
   D. Focus group

15. In social marketing theory, the best example of a "channel gatekeeper" would be a

   A. mother of a large urban family
   B. postal carrier
   C. human resources manager at a large corporation
   D. social worker specializing in substance abuse

16. A health agency plans to publish its own nutrition handbook. Guidelines for the visual design of such a publication include
   I. Concepts that belong together or have similarities should be boxed in.
   II. Narrow columns, rather than full-page-wide text, should be used.
   III. When paragraphs are short, do not indent
   IV. If possible, margins should be wider at the bottom than at the top of the page.

   A. I only
   B. I and IV
   C. II and III
   D. I, II, III and IV

17. Which of the following is NOT a risk factor associated with cirrhosis?

   A. Infectious agents
   B. High blood cholesterol

C. Alcohol abuse
D. Biological factors

18. Which of the following types of funding is MOST likely to be awarded for a program that originates with the funding source?

    A. Grant
    B. Public funds
    C. Private funds
    D. Contract

19. The PROCEED model of planning health education programs adds each of the following procedures to the PRECEDE model, EXCEPT assessment of

    A. budgetary and staff resources required
    B. barriers to overcome in delivering health education
    C. predisposing, enabling, and reinforcing factors among community members
    D. policies that can be used to support the program

20. Theatrical or dramatization exercises are sometimes a useful means of instruction in health education. Generally, a disadvantage associated with this activity is that it

    A. may make some participants uncomfortable
    B. stimulates participants' emotions
    C. distracts from the real purpose of the program
    D. may make issues seem artificial or contrived

21. Which of the following questions would be MOST likely to appear in the formative evaluation of a health education program?

    A. Did the media organizations that the agency contacted change their practices to include photos of safe bicycling?
    B. How many agency-sponsored activities received coverage in the local press?
    C. How many members actively monitored the local media on a regular basis?
    D. How many parents were influenced to buy bicycle helmets after reading the agency's press releases?

22. A health educator wants to draw attention to a new program by placing an op-ed piece about AIDS awareness in the local newspaper. The ideal length for such a piece would be about _____ words.

    A. 100
    B. 300
    C. 800
    D. 1200

23. Of the following areas for change, most nationwide initiatives focusing on public health, such as Healthy People 2000, place the highest priority on

    A. alcohol and other drugs
    B. nutrition
    C. maternal and infant health
    D. food and drug safety

24. Problems or shortcomings associated with the client-centered approach to health education include:

    I. Clients tend to overemphasize environmental determinants of health, such as socio-economic conditions and unemployment.
    II. Clients' prior experience may have led them to need and want professional leadership.
    III. Choices of materials and methods usually involve some sort of value judgement on the part of the health educator.
    IV. There may be a conflict between the identified concerns of a client and those of the professional.

    A. I and II
    B. II and IV
    C. III only
    D. I, II, III and IV

25. In conducting a community assessment, advantages associated with focus group interviews include

    I. potential use as a marketing tool
    II. teaching and learning taking place on many levels
    III. possible function as support group for some members
    IV. increased likelihood of candid, unbiased assessments

    A. In only
    B. I, II and III
    C. II and IV
    D. I, II, III and IV

KEY (CORRECT ANSWERS)

1.	C	11.	D
2.	A	12.	A
3.	D	13.	B
4.	A	14.	D
5.	B	15.	C
6.	C	16.	D
7.	C	17.	B
8.	A	18.	D
9.	A	19.	C
10.	B	20.	A

21.	C
22.	C
23.	B
24.	B
25.	B

TEST 3

DIRECTIONS: Each question or incomplete statement is followed by several suggested answers or completions. Select the one the BEST answers the question or completes the statement. *PRINT THE LETTER OF THE CORRECT ANSWER IN THE SPACE AT THE RIGHT.*

1. From a health education perspective, the key to developing strategies for risk reduction in a community is/are the 1.____

    A. receptiveness of the community to intervention
    B. particular health risks generally associated with the community
    C. geographic and hygienic factors in the community
    D. shared values and institutions of the community

2. As a funding source for health education programs, foundations usually 2.____

    A. provide annual reports and funding guidelines on request
    B. provide gifts in kind
    C. don't specify what kind of projects will be funded
    D. don't fund projects requesting 100 percent funding

3. A health educator who takes a holistic approach to service delivery is probably more likely than traditional practitioners to make use of 3.____

    A. existing government structures and programs
    B. translators or community liaisons
    C. secondary health education
    D. natural support systems

4. A health agency has composed a 15-second public service announcement to be aired on local television. The agency wants to learn how and whether the announcement stands out among the clutter of other messages broadcast each day. Assuming adequate resources, the best possible pre-test for the PSA would be 4.____

    A. self-administered questionnaires
    B. focus groups
    C. theater testing
    D. individual interviews

5. At a bare minimum, a comprehensive health promotion program at a major worksite should include each of the following activities, EXCEPT 5.____

    A. group weight loss programs
    B. exercise and fitness programs
    C. nutrition counseling
    D. health risk appraisals

6. A health educator is in the process of recruiting workers at an automobile manufacturing plant for a wellness program. The educator should know that the most effective way to involve blue-collar workers in a worksite program is to avoid 6.____

A. one-on-one counseling or guided self-help
B. setting up screening stations where large numbers of employees work in the production area or the lunchroom, for example
C. a reliance on formal classes for reducing specific health risks
D. attempting to make any changes to the worksite itself

7. In sociology, the _____ theory suggests that society tends toward conservatism and maintenance of the status quo.

    A. exchange
    B. conflict
    C. innovation-diffusion
    D. consensus

8. When evaluating the success of a health education program, an agency should

    A. coordinate the evaluation effort with all phases of the program and all levels of personnel
    B. select the most thorough evaluation possible
    C. opt for sophisticated and complex evaluation approaches
    D. generally ignore subjective inputs from participants

9. Usually, the most effective and efficient way of overcoming a language barrier between a health educator and a group of clients is to

    A. learn the client language in order to interact more personably with them
    B. train and use bilingual community members for use in programs
    C. provide a course in English "survival" skills for clients
    D. seek the help of a health care professional who is fluent in the client language

10. A health educator plans to use headings as an organizational tool in her food safety brochure. Which of the following statements about the use of headings in printed material is generally FALSE?

    A. For competent readers, headings are most effective when used with long paragraphs.
    B. Visuals with headings allow readers to react before more detailed information is given.
    C. One-word headings are more instructional and eye-catching than brief explanatory phrases.
    D. Captions or headings should summarize and emphasize important information.

11. Of the following visual tools for instruction or promotion, which is generally LEAST likely to influence behavior change?

    A. Flipchart
    B. Poster
    C. Talk board
    D. Model

12. In planning a health education program, a group states the goals of its planning process briefly, and then lists in sequence all the steps or activities needed to accomplish the goals. Target data for program implementation is established, and a timetable for each phase of the process is developed. The best way to visually represent this process, in order to illustrate task interde-pendencies, is the

   A. PERT chart
   B. decision tree
   C. Gantt chart
   D. nomograph

13. Each of the following is an example of primary health education, EXCEPT a course in

   A. contraception
   B. quitting smoking
   C. personal relationships
   D. nutrition

14. A correlational study reveals a strong positive relationship between the amount of time subjects spend at their workplace and the incidence of obesity. One researcher, studying the data, raises the possibility that a tendency to spend long hours at work and obesity may both be the result of a certain slowing of the metabolic processes. This is known as

   A. bidirectional causation
   B. a longitudinal relationship
   C. the third-variable problem
   D. a multivariate analysis

15. The main problem or shortcoming associated with the social change approach to health education is the

   A. assumption that "experts" have the "right" answers to complex health problems
   B. political sensitivity of many health issues
   C. lack of community resources available to many clients to reduce health risks
   D. reliance on the value judgements of the health educator

16. When conducting a survey of the community at large, a health educator should

   A. select respondents based on their potential gain from proposed programs
   B. collect as large a sample as possible and use these data to make final program decisions
   C. consider it a way of increasing community awareness
   D. combine results with data obtained from community opinion leaders

17. Guidelines for the use of visuals as part of health instruction include
   I. Images of people in the visuals should look like members of the intended audience
   II. Illustrate both desired and undesired behaviors
   III. Avoid diagrams, graphs, and other complicated visuals
   IV. The number of visuals should be limited to emphasize the most important points

A. I only
B. I, III and IV
C. II and III
D. I, II, III and IV

18. Which of the following is a risk factor associated with diabetes?

    A. Drug abuse
    B. Obesity
    C. Environmental factors
    D. Stress

19. Which of the following questions would be MOST likely to appear in the summative evaluation of a health education program?

    A. How often did staff and members meet with local media representatives to encourage coverage of the agency's breast-feeding classes?
    B. How many times did the agency submit press releases or letters to the editor?
    C. Which other members of the community besides the local press were notified regarding the agency's breast-feeding classes?
    D. How many mothers attended the breast-feeding classes that were offered by the agency?

20. According to the PATCH model of health education planning developed by the Centers for Disease Control and Prevention, the FIRST step in implementing a health education program is

    A. mobilizing the community
    B. choosing health priorities
    C. enhancement of community awareness about the program
    D. developing a comprehensive intervention strategy

21. When making a comparison of mortality rates by race, sex, and age groups, a health educator will need to aggregate _____ of data, unless the community is a large

    A. 6 to 12 months
    B. 12 to 18 months
    C. 3 to 5 years
    D. 5 to 10 years

22. A health educator is asked by the agency director to write a public service announcement to be aired on the radio. The agency has purchased a 20-second spot. The PSA should be about _____ words in length.

    A. 20-25
    B. 30-35
    C. 40-50
    D. 60-75

23. Professional standards for implementing health education programs at the local level include each of the following principles and guidelines, EXCEPT

    A. an emphasis on health outcomes
    B. a fill-in-the-blanks approach to allow communities to establish objectives

C. a focus on professional practice standards, rather than programs
D. the importance of negotiating responsibilities between state and local agencies

24. A health educator decides that in conducting a seminar for elderly Asian-American women on the risk factors associated with osteoporosis, she will adopt a permissive communication style. A potential disadvantage associated with this decision is that clients may

    A. conform to other people's ideas, rather than develop their own
    B. become fearful and reluctant to take independent action
    C. lose self-respect and motivation to change
    D. not receive important advice or information unless they ask for it

25. As a mass media channel for the communication of a health-related message or public service announcement, newspapers

    A. are most likely to reach audiences who do not typically use the health care system
    B. can be used to more specifically target segments of the public
    C. involve strict government regulation concerning the content of public service messages
    D. usually involve the most thorough coverage, but the smallest likelihood of audience attention

KEY (CORRECT ANSWERS)

1.	D	11.	B
2.	A	12.	A
3.	D	13.	B
4.	C	14.	C
5.	A	15.	B
6.	C	16.	C
7.	D	17.	B
8.	A	18.	B
9.	B	19.	D
10.	C	20.	A

21. C
22. C
23. C
24. D
25. D

EXAMINATION SECTION
TEST 1

DIRECTIONS: Each question or incomplete statement is followed by several suggested answers or completions. Select the one the BEST answers the question or completes the statement. *PRINT THE LETTER OF THE CORRECT ANSWER IN THE SPACE AT THE RIGHT.*

1. Among men in their late forties and early fifties, impotence is most often associated with _____ than with any other single factor.

    A. prescription drugs for hypertension
    B. anxiety or stress
    C. alcohol consumption
    D. smoking

2. Physical and physiological effects of cigarette smoking include
    I. increased arterial cholesterol deposits
    II. skin wrinkles
    III. increased blood pressure and heart rate
    IV. impaired liver function

    A. I and III
    B. I, II, and III
    C. III and IV
    D. I, II, III and IV

3. Which of the following is a water-soluble vitamin?

    A. A
    B. C
    C. D
    D. K

4. Overall, the most common method of preventing unwanted pregnancies in the United States is

    A. abstinence
    B. oral contraceptives
    C. the diaphragm
    D. sterilization

5. Mind-altering drugs appear to have their most significant effects on the brain's

    A. limbic system
    B. cerebrum
    C. medulla oblongata
    D. cerebellum

6. Which of the following is the most accurate description of the typical sleep patterns of elderly people?

    A. Longer, more restful periods of sleep.
    B. More wakefulness at night, with missed sleep made up in daytime naps

C. Overall reduced amounts of sleep, achieved in shorter periods of rest.
D. A later bedtime followed by a brief period of deep sleep.

7. Signs of shock include
   I. Staring, lusterless eyes
   II. Hyperventilation
   III. Weak, rapid heartbeat
   IV. Sweating

   A. I and II
   B. I and III
   C. II, III and IV
   D. I, II, III and IV

8. Research has shown that among family-or job-related factors associated with stress-related illness, the most critical factor tends to be the

   A. the degree of physical exertion involved in tasks
   B. the activity level associated with daily routines
   C. overall pressure to perform in individual roles
   D. the person's sense of control over events and circumstances

9. Which of the following valves of the heart allows oxygenated blood to move into the left ventricle from the left atrium?

   A. Tricuspid
   B. Aortic
   C. Mitral
   D. Pulmonary

10. Which of the following activities will be most useful in improving a person's flexibility?

    A. Rowing
    B. Cross-country skiing
    C. Weight lifting
    D. Swimming

11. Which of the following is NOT typically an element of hospice care?

    A. All care decisions are made by a collaborative hospice-care team.
    B. Counseling continues for the patient's family after death.
    C. Care is given in the patient's home or in a home-like environment.
    D. Pain management is used to keep the patient as comfortable and alert as possible.

12. Which of the following substances, found in the urine, may be an indicator of kidney disease?

    A. Albumin
    B. Cortisone
    C. Bilirubin
    D. Hemoglobin

13. Which of the following is NOT an advantage associated with the use of oral contraceptives?

    A. Lighter, more regular periods
    B. Decreased HDL cholesterol
    C. Protection against ovarian cancer
    D. Decreased risk of fibrocystic breast disease

14. The most important risk factor associated with bladder cancer is

    A. Multiple sexual partners
    B. Smoking
    C. Diabetes
    D. Alcoholism

15. What is the term for a deficiency of blood within an organ or part of an organ?

    A. Ischemia
    B. Aneurysm
    C. Infarct
    D. Occlusion

16. Which of the following may cause liver spots on the skin of older people?

    A. A retraction of pigment from the skin
    B. A high-fat diet
    C. Overproduction of liver secretions such as bile
    D. Prolonged overexposure to the sun

17. Which of the following is NOT a body fluid that is considered to be a mode of transmission for human immunodeficiency virus (HIV)?

    A. Semen
    B. Breast milk
    C. Vaginal fluids
    D. Saliva

18. For the purpose of bone maintenance, it is recommended that poslmenopausal women who are not on hormone therapy should increase their daily calcium intake to around _____ mg per day.

    A. 800
    B. 1000
    C. 1500
    D. 2500

19. The most severe form of chronic inflammatory joint disease is

    A. ankylosing spondylitis
    B. osteoarthritis
    C. gout
    D. rheumatoid arthritis

20. A postmenopausal woman should wait about _____ after her last period before she can safely stop using contraceptives.

    A. 8 to 12 weeks
    B. 6 to 8 months
    C. 1 to 2 years
    D. 2 to 3 years

21. The most significant source of radiation exposure in the United States is

    A. radon gas
    B. consumer products
    C. nuclear medicine
    D. chemicals within the human body

22. Which of the following occupations is classified as a "high strain" job-that is, one that is most likely to result in stress-related illness?

    A. Doctor
    B. Janitor
    C. Farmer
    D. Waiter/waitress

23. Of the following, which is NOT a defense against a consumer pleading negligence on the part of a manufacturer?

    A. Disclaimer
    B. Contributory negligence
    C. State of the art in design
    D. Undetectable defect

24. Which of the following should consider taking a calcium supplement?
    I. Adolescents who play contact sports
    II. The elderly
    III. Lactose-intolerant people
    IV. Women and teenage girls

    A. I, II and IV
    B. II and III
    C. II, III and IV
    D. I, II, III and IV

25. It is generally recommended that men _____ and older should undergo a rectal exam and PSA test as part of their regular checkups.

    A. 30
    B. 40
    C. 50
    D. 60

26. Which of the following is/are pancreatic hormones?

   I. Insulin
   II. Corticosteroid
   III. Glucagon
   IV. Globulin

   A. I only
   B. I and III
   C. II and IV
   D. I, III and IV

26.____

27. A person who weighs 180 pounds, walking 2 miles in an hour, will most likely expend about _____ calories.

   A. 80
   B. 140
   C. 210
   D. 450

27.____

28. Which of the following elements of personality is MOST likely to change as a person moves through middle age (40s through 60s)?

   A. Introversion/extroversion
   B. Impulsiveness
   C. Perceived locus of control
   D. Aggression

28.____

29. It is generally believed by health professionals that any diet program that makes a person lose weight at a sustained overall rate of more than _____ pound(s) a week is a possible health risk.

   A. 1
   B. 2
   C. 5
   D. 10

29.____

30. Which of the following metals has the highest toxicity on acute exposures?

   A. Manganese
   B. Lead
   C. Cadmium
   D. Zinc

30.____

31. Which of the following is a pituitary hormone that stimulates the release of breast milk?

   A. Colostrum
   B. Prolactin
   C. Oxytocin
   D. Progesterone

31.____

32. Which of the following is NOT one of the American Cancer Society's warning signs of cancer?

    A. Excessive thirst
    B. Unusual bleeding or discharge
    C. Marked change in bladder or bowel habits
    D. Nagging hoarseness or coughing

33. Withdrawal symptoms from chronic use of marijuana include
    I. diarrhea
    II. vomiting
    III. tremors
    IV. sleep difficulties

    A. I and II
    B. I, II, III and IV
    C. IV only
    D. There are no proven withdrawal symptoms associated with marijuana

34. What is the term for the uterine lining that as sloughed off each month during menstruation is pregnancy does not occur?

    A. Prostaglandin
    B. Placenta
    C. Endometrium
    D. Perinium

35. Which of the following diseases typically breaks out every 10-40 years as a pandemic that affects people all over the world?

    A. Measles
    B. Typhoid fever
    C. Influenza
    D. Scarlet fever

36. Which of the following is a primary symptom of syphilis?

    A. Painless sores on genitals
    B. Soreness and aching in bones and joints
    C. Burning, frequent urination
    D. Vaginal or urethral discharge

37. Which of the following is a symptom of hypoglycemia?

    A. Slowed heart rhythm
    B. Bluish lips and tongue
    C. Extreme thirst
    D. Tingling around the mouth

38. Which of the following statements is TRUE? 38.____

    A. Among adolescents, about three times as many boys as girls suffer from depression.
    B. Across all age groups, males and females suffer from depression at about the same rate.
    C. Among adults, about twice as many women as men suffer from depression
    D. Among the elderly, depression is most likely to be associated with substance abuse.

39. The main consumer advantage to outpatient care is 39.____

    A. greater choice of services
    B. lower cost
    C. professional collaboration on individual cases
    D. supervised recovery

40. A man is 40 years old. Assuming no limiting factors, the target heart rate for his exercise sessions should be about _____ beats per minute. 40.____

    A. 80
    B. 95
    C. 125
    D. 180

41. Which of the following behaviors on the part of the FATHER may affect the well-being of a child at the time of conception? 41.____

    A. Smoking
    B. Heavy caffeine use
    C. Heavy drinking
    D. Moderate exercise

42. The principal site for alcohol absorption by the body is the 42.____

    A. liver
    B. stomach
    C. small intestine
    D. spleen

43. Siderosis is a lung-scarring condition caused by inhalation of 43.____

    A. beryllium
    B. iron oxide
    C. lead oxide
    D. free silica

44. A woman taking oral contraceptives who wants to conceive should switch to another form of birth control for a period of _____ before trying to conceive. 44.____

    A. 8 weeks
    B. 3 months
    C. 6 months
    D. 1 year

45. Which of the following terms is used to describe the abnormal development of a tissue?

    A. Aplastic
    B. Metastasis
    C. Dysplasia
    D. Lithiasis

46. Generally, low-fat or skim milk is recommended over whole milk, EXCEPT for

    A. children under age 2
    B. older people
    C. nursing mothers
    D. people with osteoporosis

47. During the third trimester of a pregnancy, a woman can expect

    A. a slight drop in body temperature
    B. very short, scant bleeding
    C. Braxton-Hicks contractions
    D. a return of energy

48. According to Shontz, a person's first emergency reaction to a diagnosis of a serious illness is marked by each of the following characteristics, EXCEPT

    A. being stunned or bewildered
    B. thinking of alternatives
    C. behaving automatically
    D. feeling a sense of detachment

49. In the first stage of the General Adaptation Syndrome,

    A. the immune system is heavily taxed
    B. a person's resistance suddenly spikes
    C. a disease of adaptation becomes apparent
    D. a person becomes more susceptible to infection and disease

50. What is the term for the class of drugs used to treat allergies, asthma, nausea, motion sickness, nasal congestion, coughing, and itching?

    A. Antihistamines
    B. Salicylates
    C. Analgesics
    D. Corticosteroids

51. A person who has just begun an attempt to quit smoking should expect to experience withdrawal symptoms for a period of

    A. 48-36 hours
    B. 3-10 days
    C. 8-16 days
    D. 14-24 days

52. When a sunscreen has a sun protection factor (SPF) of 45, it means the user

    A. offers 15 times the protection of regular mineral oil
    B. may stay in the sun safely 45 times longer than without sunscreen.
    C. screens out 45% of the sun's harmful ultraviolet (UV) rays
    D. will be protected from the sun for a period of 45 minutes between applications

53. Common signs or symptom of adolescent depression include
    I. Marked loss of interest in activities
    II. Changes in appetite and weight
    III. Gastrointestinal upset
    IV. Hypertension

    A. I only
    B. I and II
    C. I, II and III
    D. I, II, III and IV

54. Which of the following is a condition in which the walls of arteries thicken and harden, sometimes interfering with blood flow?

    A. Angioedema
    B. Arteriosclerosis
    C. Aneurysm
    D. Atherosclerosis

55. Research suggests that the rate of urinary tract infections among uncircumcised infant boys

    A. is slightly higher than that of circumcised infants
    B. is about 10 times higher than that of circumcised infants
    C. is slightly lower than that of circumcised infants
    D. is about 3 times lower than that of circumcised infants

56. Which of the following is NOT typically a physiological response to stress?

    A. Muscle tension
    B. Increased heart rate
    C. Stomach/intestinal upset
    D. Dopamine release

57. Likely mental effects of a regular exercise program include
    I. Improved sleep
    II. Better concentration
    III. Reduced anxiety and stress
    IV. Overall feeling of well-being

    A. I, II and IV
    B. II and III
    C. III and IV
    D. I, II, III and IV

58. Starting at approximately age 20, a woman should examine her breasts

    A. weekly
    B. monthly
    C. every 6 months
    D. annually

59. The first goal in the treatment of most alcoholics is to

    A. separate the alcoholic from all sources of alcohol
    B. separate the alcoholic from all sources of emotional support
    C. penetrate the alcoholic's personal defenses
    D. obtain concrete evidence of the person's alcohol abuse

60. Generally, it is recommended that women refrain from sexual intercourse for a period of _____ after the delivery of a baby.

    A. 24 weeks
    B. 4-6 weeks
    C. 8-12 weeks
    D. 3-6 months

61. A full-scale stroke may be foreshadowed by a(n)

    A. brain aneurysm
    B. coronary thrombosis
    C. transient ischemic attack (TIA)
    D. embolism

62. According to Erikson, the most important issue for people who reach middle age is

    A. whether their lives have had meaning or have been wasted
    B. forming a clear self-image from a complex set of roles
    C. the choice between a preoccupation with self and a concern for others
    D. the ability to share one's self with another without fearing the loss of identity

63. To maintain good health, a person should consume about _____ of polyunsaturated fat in a single day

    A. 1 teaspoon
    B. 1 tablespoon
    C. 3 tablespoons
    D. 1/2 cup

64. Valium, Nembutal, and Quaalude belong to the class of drugs known as

    A. amphetamines
    B. sedative-hypnotics
    C. major tranquilizers
    D. narcotic analgesics

65. Brief, rhythmic cries that intensify over a period of time typically indicate that an infant

    A. is hungry
    B. has colic
    C. is tired
    D. is teething

66. Which of the following is a term for pain in the muscles during exercise, caused by inadequate arterial blood flow?

    A. Claudication
    B. Prolapse
    C. Micturition
    D. Senescence

66._____

67. Other than physiological needs, which of the following is most basic in Maslow's Hierarchy of Needs?

    A. Safety
    B. Self-actualization
    C. Belongingness
    D. Esteem

67._____

68. Which of the following is NOT a risk factor for breast cancer?

    A. Late childbearing
    B. Childlessness
    C. Family history of breast cancer
    D. Formula feeding of children

68._____

69. When talking to children about the death of a friend or family member, it's important to remember that most children don't develop a real understanding of death until around the age of

    A. 5
    B. 7
    C. 9
    D. 11

69._____

70. The central element in the definition of "addiction" is

    A. a loss of control
    B. increased tolerance
    C. denial
    D. impaired functioning

70._____

71. Hormone replacement therapy (HRT) for post-menopausal women

    A. helps to protect women from heart attacks.
    B. alleviates symptoms of cardiovascular problems such as heart disease or asthma.
    C. accelerates the rate at which women acquire the symptoms of osteoporosis.
    D. slows the growth rate of breast cancer.

71._____

72. Which of the following is an example of secondary prevention?

    A. Wearing a seat belt
    B. Getting a mammogram
    C. Exercising
    D. Getting a flu vaccination

72._____

73. After it is fertilized by a sperm cell, an egg is known as a(n)

    A. gamete
    B. dicot
    C. zygote
    D. embryo

74. Which of the following is a symptom of hepatitis?

    A. Aching joints
    B. Hunger
    C. Sweating
    D. Jerky movements

75. For a healthy diet, a person's overall fat intake should generally be limited to _____ % of all calories.

    A. 5
    B. 15
    C. 30
    D. 50

KEY (CORRECT ANSWERS)

1. C	16. D	31. C	46. A	61. C
2. B	17. D	32. A	47. C	62. C
3. B	18. C	33. B	48. C	63. B
4. D	19. D	34. C	49. D	64. B
5. A	20. C	35. C	50. A	65. A
6. B	21. A	36. A	51. B	66. A
7. B	22. D	37. D	52. B	67. A
8. D	23. A	38. C	53. B	68. D
9. C	24. C	39. B	54. B	69. C
10. D	25. B	40. C	55. B	70. A
11. A	26. B	41. C	56. D	71. A
12. A	27. C	42. C	57. D	72. B
13. B	28. C	43. B	58. B	73. C
14. B	29. B	44. B	59. C	74. A
15. A	30. C	45. C	60. B	75. C

TEST 2

DIRECTIONS: Each question or incomplete statement is followed by several suggested answers or completions. Select the one the BEST answers the question or completes the statement. *PRINT THE LETTER OF THE CORRECT ANSWER IN THE SPACE AT THE RIGHT.*

1. Research suggests that postponing a pregnancy until after the age of 35 increases the risk of each of the following, EXCEPT

    A. miscarriage
    B. low birth weight
    C. congenital abnormalities
    D. toxoplasmosis

2. Which of the following mineral nutrients helps to regulate the fluids of the body?

    A. Sodium
    B. Calcium
    C. Potassium
    D. Phosphorus

3. The most common cause of vision loss in older people is

    A. age-related macular degeneration (ARMD)
    B. glaucoma
    C. presbyopia
    D. cataract

4. Which of the following is NOT a physical effect that can be consistently attributed to a regular exercise program?

    A. Muscles require less oxygen
    B. Improved muscle and joint strength/flexibility
    C. For women, improved chance of avoiding osteoporosis
    D. Stronger, more resilient heart

5. The term "platelets" is often used to denote

    A. thrombocytes
    B. leukocytes
    C. erythrocytes
    D. lymphocytes

6. A definition of "mental health" would typically include each of the following, EXCEPT

    A. the ability to sustain relationships with family and friends
    B. the ability to control emotional reactions to conflicts or distressful events until they can be better understood
    C. a realistic perception of the motivations of others
    D. the ability to cope with life's transitions and traumas in a way that allows one's personality to remain intact

7. Effective electrical grounding in a home or other building may be accomplished by use of 7.___

   A. a metal framework or metal structures with negligible resistance to ground or grounding electrodes
   B. three-conductor cords with polarized plug-in receptacles
   C. transformer isolation with a low resistance path to ground
   D. a ground fault interrupter for every circuit with proper cross-connection.

8. Which of the following statements regarding exercise during pregnancy is TRUE? 8.___

   A. Inactive women should start a fitness program while pregnant.
   B. Exercise should be severely limited or avoided altogether after the seventh month.
   C. Active women should increase the length of workouts during the first two trimesters.
   D. Women should avoid exercises done lying on the back after the fourth month.

9. According to the current definition, physical dependence on a drug is characterized by 9.___
   I. tolerance—larger doses to achieve the same high
   II. withdrawal symptoms
   III. cravings for the drug
   IV. interference with daily functioning

   A. I only
   B. I and II
   C. II and III
   D. I, II, III and IV

10. Which of the following methods of contraception has the highest estimated effectiveness? 10.___

    A. Cervical cap
    B. Diaphrarn with spermicide
    C. Vaginal sponge
    D. Condom

11. The leading cause of death among alcoholics is 11.___

    A. cirrhosis of the liver
    B. cancer
    C. Wernicke-Korsakoff's syndrome
    D. cardiovascular disease

12. The largest preventable cause of premature death and disability in the United States is 12.___

    A. workplace accidents
    B. smoking
    C. alcohol abuse
    D. traffic accidents

13. Signs and symptoms of HIV infection include
    I. Chronic diarrhea
    II. Difficulties with speech, memory, or concentration
    III. Soaking night sweats
    IV. Muscular aches and pains

    A. I and IV
    B. I, II, and III
    C. II and III
    D. I, II, III and IV

13.____

14. Which of the following is a NOT a stage of the General Adaptation Syndrome?

    A. appraisal
    B. resistance
    C. exhaustion
    D. alarm reaction

14.____

15. Which of the following methods of contraception may increase a woman's chance of having an ectopic pregnancy?

    A. Cervical cap
    B. Vaginal spermicide
    C. Intrauterine device (IUD)
    D. Tubal ligation

15.____

16. Substitution of a less harmful substance for a toxic material is a practical method of eliminating an industrial health hazard. Substitution should be the primary method of control for which one of the following solvents used in open cleaning?

    A. Hexane
    B. Carbon tetrachloride
    C. Toluene
    D. Xylene

16.____

17. Which of the following is administered as an evaluation of an infant's overall condition immediately after birth?

    A. Apgar score
    B. Foot stick
    C. Tonic reflex
    D. Grant's score

17.____

18. Which of the following is probably a person's best defense against the common cold?

    A. Frequent hand washing
    B. Annual flu shots
    C. Staying warm and dry
    D. High doses of vitamin C

18.____

19. To reduce stress, a patient is taught to concentrate on the self-suggestion of warmth and heavy limbs. This is an example of

    A. biofeedback
    B. hypnosis
    C. autogenic training
    D. meditation

20. Tachycardia is defined as a heart rate that

    A. exceeds 100 beats per minute
    B. is irregular
    C. is lower than 60 beats per minute
    D. is syncopated

21. Which of the following is NOT an opiate?

    A. Heroin
    B. Meperidine
    C. Cocaine
    D. Codeine

22. Which of the following is NOT an arterial pressure point commonly used to stop bleeding?

    A. Beneath the jaw
    B. Inside the elbow
    C. Behind the knee
    D. At the base of the neck

23. To be usable as fuel, carbohydrates must be broken down into

    A. constituent amino acids
    B. lactose
    C. polyunsaturated fats
    D. glucose

24. Within a period of _____ years, a person who quits smoking today will eventually experience a risk of developing heart disease and lung cancer that is equal to that of a nonsmoker.

    A. 1-3
    B. 5-9
    C. 10-15
    D. 15-20

25. At the highest level of Kohlberg's moral development, a person conforms to society's idea of moral behavior in order to

    A. maintain the respect of spectators
    B. avoid self-condemnation
    C. avoid censure and guilt
    D. obtain rewards

26. Hypertension is usually defined as a consistent systolic pressure of at least _____ mm Hg and a consistent diastolic pressure of at least _____ mm Hg.

    A. 60, 150
    B. 80, 120
    C. 110, 75
    D. 140, 90

27. Research suggests that the dietary element most closely related to kidney disease is

    A. carbohydrate
    B. sugar
    C. protein
    D. fat

28. Which of the following conditions should older men expect to encounter regarding their sexuality?
    I. Frequent impotence
    II. Less sexual urgency
    III. Delayed or partial erections
    IV. Less well-defined moment of ejaculation

    A. I and II
    B. I and III
    C. I, III and IV
    D. I, II, III and IV

29. For real benefit, it is important for a person to maintain a schedule of higher-intensity exercise sessions at a rate of

    A. two sessions of at least 40 minutes every week
    B. three sessions of at least 20 minutes every week
    C. five sessions of at least 30 minutes every week
    D. five sessions of at least 45 minutes every week

30. An infant is restless and draws up her legs. She has severe crying spells that do not respond to any efforts to comfort her. The most likely cause of these crying spells is

    A. colic
    B. a soiled diaper
    C. illness
    D. hunger

31. According to Erikson, the most important developmental task for elementary school children is

    A. forming a sense of initiative in deciding on many activities
    B. developing and maintaining an interest in how things work
    C. establishing a sense of autonomy
    D. forming a clear self-image from a complex set of roles

32. In general, the "correct" intensity of exercise requires that a person (who has been exercising for a period of weeks) reach an ideal of _____ percent of his or her maximum heart rate.

    A. 30
    B. 50
    C. 70
    D. 90

33. Most treatment programs for alcoholism make use of each of the following, EXCEPT

    A. aversion therapy
    B. medical treatment
    C. a 12-step or similar program
    D. insistence on abstinence

34. Which of the following is a substance that has a role in stimulating uterine contractions during birth?

    A. Prolactin
    B. Progesterone
    C. Estrogen
    D. Prostaglandin

35. Generally, most cases of multiple sclerosis (MS) begin with a first attack between the ages of

    A. 5 and 8
    B. 12 and 35
    C. 20 and 40
    D. 45 and 65

36. The leading cause of accidental death for people over age 65 is

    A. falling
    B. injury-related infection
    C. traffic accidents
    D. accidental poisoning

37. The main symptom of urinary tract infection (UTI) in women is

    A. blood, pus, or a strong odor in the urine
    B. pain and burning while urinating
    C. pain above the pubic bone
    D. a frequent, urgent need to urinate but with only a small amount fluid passed

38. Risk factors for pancreatic cancer include
    I. smoking
    II. a high-fat diet
    III. regular and heavy use of alcohol
    IV. being over 50

    A. I and II
    B. I, II and III
    C. III and IV
    D. I, II, III and IV

39. A child will typically show signs that he is ready to begin toilet training between _____ months of age

    A. 12 and 18
    B. 18 and 24
    C. 24 and 28
    D. 28 and 32

40. Which of the following is NOT a class A carcinogen, according to the Environmental Protection Agency (EPA)?

    A. Radon
    B. Asbestos
    C. Secondhand cigarette smoke
    D. Dioxin

41. Which of the following neurotransmitters is NOT commonly associated with depression?

    A. Serotonin
    B. Acetylcholine
    C. Norepinephrine
    D. Dopamine

42. The area of the body containing the highest concentration of macrophages is the

    A. lymph nodes
    B. spleen
    C. liver
    D. bone marrow

43. On Monday, a person notices that he has a cough. On Wednesday he concludes that he is ill. On Saturday he decides to seek medical treatment, and on Sunday he sees the doctor. In this example the illness delay is _____ day(s).

    A. 1
    B. 2
    C. 3
    D. 6

44. Typically, a menstrual period that ranges in frequency from _____ days is considered normal

    A. 14 to 40
    B. 18 to 32
    C. 22 to 35
    D. 25 to 45

45. Which of the following activities is likely to expend the greatest number of calories in an hour?

    A. Swimming
    B. Jogging
    C. Tennis
    D. Bicycling

46. Which of the following is a category of blood proteins of which antibodies are formed?

    A. Globulin
    B. Prostaglandin
    C. Bilirubin
    D. Albumin

47. Most psychologists and family therapists suggest that a realistic timetable for a stepfamily to blend comfortably is at least

    A. 6 months
    B. 1 year
    C. 2 years
    D. 4 years

48. Which of the following does NOT occupy the "top" of the Food Guide Pyramid?

    A. Cheese
    B. Oils
    C. Sweets
    D. Fats

49. The class of drugs known as hallucinogens (psychedelics) includes each of the following, EXCEPT

    A. psilocybin
    B. LSD
    C. mescaline
    D. Ecstasy (MDMA)

50. During the first trimester of a pregnancy, a woman can expect

    A. increased blood volume
    B. ankle swelling
    C. leg cramps
    D. heartburn

51. High blood levels of _____ are associated with a lower risk of heart disease.

    A. Triglycerides
    B. High-density lipoprotein (HDL)
    C. Low-density lipoprotein (LDL)
    D. Very low-density lipoprotein (VLDL)

52. The two major problems faced by consumers in the modern health care system are

    A. access and cost
    B. overregulation and generalization
    C. overuse of drug treatments and bias toward surgical interventions
    D. overspecialization and availability

53. Initially, drinking alcohol effects each of the following, EXCEPT   53.____

    A. thoughts
    B. muscle coordination
    C. emotions
    D. judgement

54. Which of the following groups has a higher risk of developing glaucoma than the general   54.____
    population?
          I. Diabetics
         II. Those with a family history of glaucoma
        III. African Americans
        IV. Those with light-colored (blue or green) eyes

    A. I and II
    B. I, II and III
    C. III and IV
    D. I, II, III and IV

55. Tetanus booster shots should generally be administered once every   55.____

    A. 5 years
    B. 10 years
    C. 15 years or every major injury
    D. 20 years

56. "Angina pectoris" is an episodic pain in the chest that is caused by   56.____

    A. inadequate blood supply to the heart
    B. a variation or disruption in the heart's normal rhythm
    C. allergic swelling of the chest's mucous membranes
    D. a sudden rush of blood through the pulmonary vein

57. Which of the following tests/procedures can easily be performed at home by couples who   57.____
    want to assess their fertility?

    A. BBT charting
    B. Postcoital test (PCI)
    C. Semen analysis
    D. Blood tests

58. In recent years, fitness experts have recommended that in addition to regular workout   58.____
    sessions, people should choose moderate-intensity activities that will burn about _____
    calories each day.

    A. 50
    B. 100
    C. 200
    D. 400

59. The main distinction between chest pains caused by a heart attack and those associated with other conditions (heartburn, pulled muscle, etc.) is that chest pain caused by a heart attack

    A. is sharp and burning
    B. radiates from the center of the chest to the jaw, neck, and arms
    C. worsens when the person bends over or lies down
    D. is localized and tender to the touch

59.___

60. Which of the following hormones is an androgen?

    A. Estrogen
    C. Calcitonin
    B. Aldosterone
    D. Testosterone

60.___

61. Hypertension can be alleviated by
    I. stopping smoking
    II. reducing alcohol consumption
    III. regular exercise
    IV. lowering sodium intake

    A. I and II
    B. I and III
    C. II, III, and IV
    D. I, II, III and IV

61.___

62. Which of the following is a bronchodilator?

    A. Digoxin
    B. Lisinopryl
    C. Cephalexin
    D. Theophylline

62.___

63. Biofeedback has proven to be an effective means of accomplishing each of the following, EXCEPT

    A. lowering blood pressure
    B. decreasing blood lactate
    C. slowing metabolism
    D. reducing heart rate

63.___

64. According to researcher Howard Leventhal, one of the basic common sense components of how people think about disease is

    A. health definition
    B. illness history
    C. illness identity
    D. prevalence rates

64.___

65. Around age 45, many people begin to have trouble reading fine print. This is most likely caused by a condition known as

    A. presbyopia
    B. retinopathy
    C. macular degeneration
    D. myopia

65.___

66. Generally, a T-helper cell count of less than _____ is enough to diagnose AIDS.

    A. 100
    B. 200
    C. 500
    D. 750

67. Which of the following is NOT an element of the "relaxation response" designed by Herbert Benson and his associates?

    A. Decreased muscle tension
    B. An active, participatory attitude
    C. A quiet environment
    D. A constant stimulus or mental device

68. Medicare is available to
    I. all persons in a particular state whose income falls below a certain level
    II. all Americans aged 65 or older
    III. some persons with kidney disease
    IV. some handicapped persons

    A. I only
    B. I and II
    C. II, III and IV
    D. I, II, III and IV

69. According to the American Heart Association, a person's daily salt intake should be limited to

    A. 1.5 tablespoons
    B. 3 teaspoons
    C. 1.5 teaspoons
    D. 0.5 teaspoon

70. Which of the following is an antianxiety drug?

    A. Loperamide
    B. Fluoxitine
    C. Lorazepam
    D. Zolpedim

71. Which of the following personality traits is MOST likely to be associated with heart disease or other stress-related illnesses?

    A. Hostility or cynicism
    B. Passivity or hopelessness
    C. Competitiveness
    D. Aggression

72. The period during the heart cycle in which the cardiac muscle relaxes is known as   72.___

    A. sinus rhythm
    B. diastole
    C. discontracture
    D. systole

73. Which of the following statements about Type II (non-insulin-dependent) diabetes is TRUE?   73.___

    A. It comprises 10 percent of all diabetes cases.
    B. The onset is usually sudden and dramatic.
    C. It occurs mainly in adults over the age of 40 who are overweight
    D. Typically, daily insulin injections are required as treatment.

74. The most serious form of hepatitis is   74.___

    A. A
    B. B
    C. C
    D. D

75. Jaundice is a condition caused by an excess of _____ in the blood.   75.___

    A. albumin
    B. gamma globulin
    C. bilirubin
    D. lymph

KEY (CORRECT ANSWERS)

1. D	16. B	31. B	46. A	61. D
2. A	17. A	32. C	47. D	62. D
3. A	18. A	33. A	48. A	63. A
4. A	19. C	34. D	49. D	64. C
5. A	20. A	35. C	50. D	65. A
6. B	21. C	36. A	51. B	66. B
7. A	22. B	37. D	52. A	67. B
8. D	23. D	38. A	53. B	68. C
9. B	24. C	39. B	54. B	69. C
10. D	25. B	40. D	55. B	70. C
11. D	26. D	41. B	56. A	71. A
12. B	27. C	42. B	57. A	72. B
13. B	28. C	43. C	58. C	73. C
14. A	29. B	44. C	59. B	74. B
15. C	30. A	45. D	60. D	75. C

EXAMINATION SECTION
TEST 1

DIRECTIONS: Each question or incomplete statement is followed by several suggested answers or completions. Select the one that BEST answers the question or completes the statement. *PRINT THE LETTER OF THE CORRECT ANSWER IN THE SPACE AT THE RIGHT.*

1. _____ accounts for the LARGEST percentage of personal health care expenditures in the United States.
    A. Physician services
    B. Hospital care
    C. Nursing homes
    D. Drug and medical supplies
    E. Dentist services

2. MOST health care expenses in the United States are paid by
    A government programs
    B. Medicare
    B. Medicaid
    D. private health insurance
    E. out-of-pocket payments

3. A physician is NOT legally required to report
    A. births and deaths
    B. suspected child abuse
    C. gunshot wounds
    D. a child with croup
    E. a child with shigella dysentery

4. Diseases more likely to occur in blacks than whites include all of the following EXCEPT
    A. thalassemia
    B. sickle cell disease
    C. sarcoidosis
    D. tuberculosis
    E. hypertension

5. Among the United States population, what malignant tumor has the greatest incidence?
    A. Breast
    B. Prostate
    C. Lung
    D. Colon
    E. Stomach

6. The MOST frequent cause of chronic obstructive pulmonary disease is

    A. frequent upper respiratory infection
    B. smoking
    C. family member with asthma
    D. drug abuse
    E. infantile paralysis

7. The ultimate legal responsibility for quality of medical care provided in the hospital rests upon the
    A. hospital administrator
    B. chief of nursing staff
    C. director of the hospital
    D. principal nurse
    E. patient's physician

8. Routine screening for diabetes is recommended for all patients EXCEPT those with
   A. family history of diabetes
   B. glucose abnormalities associated with pregnancy
   C. marked obesity
   D. an episode of hypoglycemia as a newborn
   E. physical abnormality, such as circulatory dysfunction and frank vascular impairment

9. Low maternal AFP level is associated with
   A. spina bifida
   B. Down syndrome
   C. meningocele
   D. hypothyroidism
   E. Niemann Pick disease

10. All of the following are skin disorders EXCEPT
    A. psoriasis
    B. eczema
    C. scleroderma
    D. gout
    E. shingles

11. All of the following are true statements regarding osteoporosis EXCEPT:
    A. The reduction of bone mass in osteoporosis causes the bone to be susceptible to fracture.
    B. Bone loss occurs with advancing age in both men and women.
    C. In developing countries, high parity has been associated with decreased bone mass and increased risk of fracture.
    D. Thin women are at higher risk than obese women.
    E. Daughters of women with osteoporosis tend to have lower bone mass than other women of their age.

12. The MOST common type of occupational disease is
    A. hearing loss
    B. dermatitis
    B. pneumoconiosis
    D. pulmonary fibrosis
    E. none of the above

13. The incidence of Down syndrome in the United States is about 1 in ____ births.

    A. 700   B. 1200   C. 1500   D. 2000   E. 10000

14. Lyme disease and Rocky Mountain spotted fever CANNOT be prevented by
    A. door and window screen use
    B. hand washing
    C. wearing protective clothing
    D. using insect repellent
    E. immediate tick removal

15. Individuals with egg allergies can be safely administered all of the following vaccines EXCEPT
    A. MMR (Measles-Mumps-Rubella)
    B. hepatitis B
    C. influenza
    D. DTaP (Diphtheria-Tetanus-Whooping Cough)
    E. none of the above

16. Lifetime prevalence of cocaine use is HIGHER among
    A. Hispanics   B. blacks   C. whites   D. Asians
    E. none of the above

17. The effectiveness of preventive measures against chronic illness is BEST determined from trends in
    A. incidence   B. mortality   C. prevalence   D. frequency of complication
    E. all of the above

18. Primary prevention of congenital heart disease includes all of the following established measures EXCEPT:
    A. Genetic counseling of potential parents and families with congenital heart disease
    B. Avoidance of exposure to viral diseases during pregnancy
    C. Avoidance of all vaccines to all children which eliminate the reservoir of infection
    D. Avoidance of radiation during pregnancy
    E. Avoidance of exposure during first trimester of pregnancy to gas fumes, air pollution, cigarettes, alcohol

19. All of the following are true statements regarding genetic factors associated with congenital heart disease EXCEPT:
    A. The offspring of a parent with a congenital heart disease has a malformation rate ranging from 1.4% to 16.1%.
    B. Identical twins are both affected 25 to 30% of the time.
    C. Single gene disorder accounts for less than 1% of all cardiac congenital anomalies.
    D. Environment does not play a role in cardiac anomalies
    E. Other finding of familial aggregation suggests polygenic factors.

20. MOST likely inadequately supplied in strict vegetarian adults is
    A. vitamin A   B. thiamin   C. vitamin B_{12} D. niacin   E. protein

21. The MOST common reservoir of acquired immune deficiency syndrome is
    A. humans   B. mosquitoes   C. cats   D. dogs   E. monkeys

22. A definitive indicator of active tuberculosis is
    A. chronic persistent cough
    B. positive PPD
    C. night sweats
    D. positive sputum test
    E. hilar adenopathy on chest x-ray

23. Which of the following is NOT a risk factor for development of colorectal carcinoma?
    A. Familial polyposis coli   B. Furcot's syndrome
    C. High fiber diet   D. Increased dietary fat
    E. Villous polyps

24. According to the American Cancer Society, starting at the age of 50, men and women at average risk for developing colorectal cancer should follow which of the following screening regimens?
    A. Colonoscopy every ten years
    B. Flexible sigmoidoscopy every two years
    C. Double-contrast barium enema every two years
    D. CT colonography (virtual colonoscopy) every year
    E. None of the above

25. The MOST common malignancy among women is of the
    A. lung   B. breast   C. ovary   D. rectum   E. vagina

KEY (CORRECT ANSWERS)

1. B
2. D
3. D
4. A
5. D
6. B
7. E
8. D
9. B
10. D

11. C
12. A
13. A
14. B
15. C
16. C
17. C
18. C
19. D
20. C

21. A
22. D
23. C
24. A
25. B

TEST 2

DIRECTIONS: Each question or incomplete statement is followed by several suggested answers or completions. Select the one that BEST answers the question or completes the statement. *PRINT THE LETTER OF THE CORRECT ANSWER IN THE SPACE AT THE RIGHT.*

1. The MOST common cause of death due to malignancy among females in the United States is from
   - A. lung cancer
   - B. ovarian cancer
   - C. skin cancer
   - D. colon and rectum cancer
   - B. leukemia

   1._____

2. Medicare provides health coverage to people
   - A. under 20 years of age
   - B. who work of all ages
   - C. greater than 65 years of age and end-stage renal dialysis patients
   - D. under five years of age who require long-term hospitalization
   - E. who need out-patient care only

   2._____

3. Insurance approaches to contain cost include managed care plans. A popular managed care approach has been
   - A. Medicare
   - B. Medicaid
   - C. HMO's
   - D. institutional reimbursement
   - E. none of the above

   3._____

4. The occupational exposure that may lead to chronic interstitial pulmonary disease is
   - A. silicosis
   - B. pneumoconiosis
   - C. asbestosis
   - D. farmer's lung
   - E. all of the above

   4._____

5. The principal mode of transmission of hepatitis A virus is
   - A. blood transfusion
   - B. droplet nuclei
   - C. fecal and oral route
   - D. mosquitoes
   - E. deer flies

   5._____

6. The leading cause of death among diabetics after 20 years of diabetes is by
   - A. infection
   - B. cerebrovascular accident
   - C. renal and cardiovascular disease
   - D. diabetic ketoacidosis
   - E. malignancy

   6._____

7. A breast-fed infant may require a supplementation of vitamin
   - A. E   B. B_{12} C. K   D. D   E. A

   7._____

8. The MOST common organism associated with chronic active gastritis is
   - A. salmonella
   - B. shigella
   - C. campylobacter pylori
   - D. staphylococcus
   - E. rota virus

   8._____

9. The large proportion of tuberculosis in older persons is due to
    A. recent exposure to tuberculosis
    B. reactivation of latent infection
    C. malnutrition
    D. immunosuppression
    E. substance abuse

9._____

10. The leading vector-borne disease in the United States is
    A. lyme disease
    B. Rocky Mountain spotted fever
    C. ehrlichiosis
    D. Q fever
    E. yellow fever

10._____

11. The malarial species causing the MOST fatal illness is
    A. P. vivax   B. P. falciparum
    C. P. malariae   D. P. cuale
    E. none of the above

11._____

Questions 12-16.

DIRECTIONS: Match the disease in Questions 12 through 16 with the associated animal in Column I.

12. Brucellosis

13. Psittacosis

14. Rabies

15. Tularemia

16. Toxoplasmosis

COLUMN I

A. Bird
B. Swine
C. Rabbit
D. Skunk
E. Cats

12._____

13._____

14._____

15._____

16._____

Questions 17-22.

DIRECTIONS: Match the trade in Questions 17 through 22 with the related occupational cancer in Column I.

17. Pipefitters

18. Rubber industry workers

19. Radiologist

20. Woodworkers

21. Textile workers

22. Chemists

COLUMN I

A. Carcinoma of the bladder
B. Mesothelioma
C. Hodgkin's disease
D. Leukemia
E. Brain cancer
F. Carcinoma of nasal cavity

17.____
18.____
19.____
20.____
21.____
22.____

Questions 23-25.

DIRECTIONS: Match the biostatistical description in Questions 23 through 25 with the related term in Column I.

23. The presence of an event or characteristic at a single point in time

24. Require a long period of observation

25. The occurrence of an event or characteristic over a period of time

COLUMN I

A. Incidence
B. Prevalence
C. Cohort study

23.____
24.____
25.____

KEY (CORRECT ANSWERS)

1. A	11. B
2. C	12. B
3. C	13. A
4. E	14. D
5. C	15. C
6. C	16. E
7. D	17. B
8. C	18. A
9. B	19. D
10. A	20. C

21. F
22. E
23. B
24. C
25. A

EXAMINATION SECTION
TEST 1

DIRECTIONS: Each question or incomplete statement is followed by several suggested answers or completions. Select the one that BEST answers the question or completes the statement. *PRINT THE LETTER OF THE CORRECT ANSWER IN THE SPACE AT THE RIGHT.*

1. The MOST common cause of death before age 65 is 1.____

    A. cerebrovascular disease
    B. malignant neoplasm
    C. heart disease
    D. diabetes mellitus
    E. liver cirrhosis

2. Of the following, the disease NOT transmitted by mosquitoes is 2.____

    A. dengue fever
    B. lymphocytic choriomeningitis
    C. western equine encephalitis
    D. St. Louis encephalitis
    E. yellow fever

3. The single MOST effective measure to prevent hookworm infection is 3.____

    A. washing hands
    B. washing clothes daily
    C. cooking food at high temperatures
    D. wearing shoes
    E. none of the above

4. Transmission of tuberculosis in the United States occurs MOST often by 4.____

    A. fomites
    B. blood transfusion
    C. inhalation of droplet
    D. transplacentally
    E. milk

5. The second MOST common cause of death in the United States is 5.____

    A. accident
    B. cancer
    C. cerebrovascular disease
    D. heart disease
    E. AIDS

6. All of the following bacteria are spread through fecal-oral transmission EXCEPT 6.____

    A. haemophilus influenza type B
    B. campylobacter
    C. escherichia coli
    D. salmonella
    E. shigella

7. Routine immunization is particularly important for children in day care because pre-school-aged children currently have the highest age specific incidence of all of the following EXCEPT 7.____

    A. H-influenzae type B
    B. neisseria meningitis
    C. measles
    D. rubella
    E. pertussis

8. Hand washing and masks are necessary for physical contact with all of the following patients EXCEPT

   A. lassa fever
   B. diphtheria
   C. coxsackie virus disease
   D. varicella
   E. plaque

9. Control measures for prevention of tick-borne infections include all of the following EXCEPT:

   A. Tick-infested area should be avoided whenever possible.
   B. If a tick-infested area is entered, protective clothing that covers the arms, legs, and other exposed area should be worn.
   C. Tick/insect repellent should be applied to the skin.
   D. Ticks should be removed promptly.
   E. Daily inspection of pets and removal of ticks is not indicated.

10. The PRINCIPAL reservoir of giardia lamblia infection is

    A. humans
    B. mosquitoes
    C. rodents
    D. sandflies
    E. cats

11. Most community-wide epidemics of giardia lamblia infection result from

    A. inhalation of droplets
    B. eating infected meats
    C. eating contaminated eggs
    D. drinking contaminated water
    E. blood transfusions

12. Epidemics of giardia lamblia occurring in day care centers are USUALLY caused by

    A. inhalation of droplets
    B. person-to-person contact
    C. fecal and oral contact
    D. eating contaminated food
    E. all of the above

13. Measures of the proportion of the population exhibiting a phenomenon at a particular time is called the

    A. incidence
    B. prevalence
    C. prospective study
    D. cohort study
    E. all of the above

14. The occurrence of an event or characteristic over a period of time is called

    A. incidence
    B. prevalence
    C. specificity
    D. case control study
    E. cohort study

15. All of the following are live attenuated viral vaccines EXCEPT

    A. measles
    B. mumps
    C. rubella
    D. rabies
    E. yellow fever

16. Chlorinating air-cooling towers can prevent 16.____
    A. scarlet fever
    B. impetigo
    C. typhoid fever
    D. mycobacterium tuberculosis
    E. legionnaire's disease

17. Eliminating the disease causing agent may be done by all of the following methods EXCEPT 17.____
    A. chemotherapeutic
    B. cooling
    C. heating
    D. chlorinating
    E. disinfecting

18. Which of the following medications is used to eliminate pharyngeal carriage of neisseria meningitidis? 18.____
    A. Penicillin
    B. Rifampin
    C. Isoniazid
    D. Erythromycin
    E. Gentamicin

19. Post-exposure prophylaxis is recommended for rabies after the bite of all of the following animals EXCEPT 19.____
    A. chipmunks
    B. skunks
    C. raccoons
    D. bats
    E. foxes

20. To destroy the spores of clostridium botulinum, canning requires a temperature of AT LEAST _____ °C. 20.____
    A. 40   B. 60   C. 80   D. 100   E. 120

21. All of the following are killed or fractionated vaccines EXCEPT 21.____
    A. hepatitis B
    B. yellow fever
    C. H-influenza type B
    D. pneumococcus
    E. rabies

22. Of the following, the disease NOT spreadly by food is 22.____
    A. typhoid fever
    B. shigellosis
    C. typhus
    D. cholera
    E. legionellosis

23. In the United States, the HIGHEST attack rate of sheigella infection occurs in children between _____ of age. 23.____
    A. 1 to 6 months
    B. 6 months to 1 year
    C. 1 to 4 years
    D. 6 to 10 years
    E. 10 to 15 years

24. Risk factors for cholera include all of the following EXCEPT 24.____
    A. occupational exposure
    B. lower socioeconomic
    C. unsanitary condition
    D. high socioeconomic
    E. high population density in low income areas

25. The MOST common cause of traveler's diarrhea is 25.___
   A. escherichia coli
   B. shigella
   C. salmonella
   D. cholera
   E. campalobacter

KEY (CORRECT ANSWERS)

1. C
2. B
3. D
4. C
5. B

6. A
7. B
8. C
9. E
10. A

11. D
12. B
13. B
14. A
15. D

16. E
17. B
18. B
19. A
20. E

21. B
22. C
23. C
24. D
25. A

TEST 2

DIRECTIONS: Each question or incomplete statement is followed by several suggested answers or completions. Select the one that BEST answers the question or completes the statement. *PRINT THE LETTER OF THE CORRECT ANSWER IN THE SPACE AT THE RIGHT.*

1. The increased prevalence of entamoeba histolytica infection results from

   A. lower socioeconomic status in endemic area
   B. institutionalized (especially mentally retarded) population
   C. immigrants from endemic area
   D. promiscuous homosexual men
   E. all of the above

   1.____

2. The MOST common infection acquired in the hospital is _____ infection.

   A. surgical wound   B. lower respiratory tract
   C. urinary tract   D. bloodstream
   E. gastrointestinal

   2.____

3. The etiologic agent of Rocky Mountain spotted fever is

   A. rickettsia prowazekii   B. rickettsia rickettsii
   C. rickettsia akari   D. coxiella burnetii
   E. rochalimaena quintana

   3.____

4. The annual death rate for injuries per 100,000 in both sexes is HIGHEST in those _____ years of age.

   A. 1 to 10   B. 10 to 20   C. 30 to 40
   D. 50 to 60   E. 80 to 90

   4.____

5. The death rate per 100,000 population due to motor vehicle accident is HIGHEST among

   A. whites   B. blacks
   C. Asians   D. native Americans
   E. Spanish surnamed

   5.____

6. Among the following, the HIGHEST rate of homicide occurs in

   A. whites   B. blacks
   C. native Americans   D. Asians
   E. Spanish surnamed

   6.____

7. All of the following are true statements regarding coronary heart disease EXCEPT:

   A. About 4.6 million Americans have coronary heart disease.
   B. Men have a greater risk of MI and sudden death.
   C. Women have a greater risk of angina pectoris.
   D. 25% of coronary heart disease death occurs in individuals under the age of 65 years.
   E. White women have a greater risk of MI and sudden death.

   7.____

8. Major risk factors for coronary heart disease include all of the following EXCEPT

   A. smoking
   B. elevated blood pressure
   C. obesity
   D. high level of serum cholesterol
   E. family history of coronary heart disease

9. The MOST common cancer in American men is

   A. stomach   B. lung   C. leukemia
   D. prostate   E. skin

10. The HIGHEST incidence of prostate cancer occurs in _____ Americans.

    A. white   B. black   C. Chinese
    D. Asian   E. Spanish

11. All of the following are risk factors for cervical cancer EXCEPT

    A. smoking
    B. low socioeconomic condition
    C. first coital experience after age 20
    D. multiple sexual partners
    E. contracting a sexually transmitted disease

12. All of the following are independent adverse prognostic factors for lung cancer EXCEPT

    A. female sex
    B. short duration of symptom
    C. small cell histology
    D. metastatic disease at time of diagnosis
    E. persistently elevated CEA

13. Assuming vaccines with 80% efficacy were available in limited quantity, which vaccine among the following should be given to a military recruit?

    A. Polio   B. Pseudomonas
    C. Meningococcus   D. Influenza
    E. None of the above

14. Among the following, the vaccine which should be administered to children with sickle cell disease is

    A. influenza   B. meningococcus
    C. pseudomonas   D. pneumococcal
    E. yellow fever

15. All of the following are correct statements concerning gastric carcinoma in the United States EXCEPT:

    A. The risk for males is 2.2 times greater than for females.
    B. The incidence is increased.
    C. The risk is higher in persons with pernicious anemia than for the general population.

D. City dwellers have an increased risk of stomach cancer.
E. Workers with high levels of exposure to nickle and rubber are at increased risk.

16. During the first year of life, a condition that can be detected by screening is

    A. hypothyroidism
    B. RH incompatibility
    C. phenylketonuria
    D. congenital dislocation of the hip
    E. all of the above

17. The major reservoir of the spread of tuberculosis within a hospital is through

    A. patients   B. custodial staff
    C. doctors   D. nursing staff
    E. undiagnosed cases

18. All of the following statements are true regarding tuberculosis EXCEPT:

    A. Droplet nuclei are the major vehicle for the spread of tuberculosis infection.
    B. The highest incidence is among white Americans.
    C. There is a higher incidence of tuberculosis in prison than in the general population.
    D. HIV infection is a significant independent risk factor for the development of tuberculosis.
    E. A single tubercle bacillus, once having gained access to the terminal air spaces, could establish infection.

19. The human papiloma virus is associated with

    A. kaposi sarcoma
    B. hepatoma
    C. cervical neoplasia
    D. nasopharyngeal carcinoma
    E. none of the above

20. General recommendations for prevention of sexually transmitted diseases include all of the following EXCEPT

    A. contact tracing   B. disease reporting
    C. barrier methods   D. prophylactic antibiotic use
    E. patient education

21. Syphilis remains an important sexually transmitted disease because of all of the following EXCEPT its

    A. public health heritage
    B. effect on perinatal morbidity and mortality
    C. association with HIV transmission
    D. escalating rate among black teenagers
    E. inability to be prevented

22. Which of the following statements about homicide is NOT true? Approximately

   A. forty percent are committed by friends and acquaintances
   B. twenty percent is committed by spouse
   C. fifteen percent is committed by a member of the victim's family
   D. fifteen percent is committed by strangers
   E. fifteen percent are labeled *relationship unknown*

22.____

23. Conditions for which screening has proven cost-effective include

   A. phenylketonuria
   B. iron deficiency anemia
   C. lead poisoning
   D. tuberculosis
   E. all of the above

23.____

24. Suicide is MOST common among

   A. whites
   B. blacks
   C. hispanics
   D. Asians
   E. none of the above

24.____

25. The MOST frequenty used method of suicide is

   A. hanging
   B. poisoning by gases
   C. firearms
   D. drug overdose
   E. drowning

25.____

KEY (CORRECT ANSWERS)

1. E   11. C
2. C   12. A
3. B   13. C
4. E   14. D
5. D   15. B

6. B   16. E
7. E   17. E
8. C   18. B
9. D   19. C
10. B   20. D

21. E
22. B
23. E
24. A
25. C

EXAMINATION SECTION
TEST 1

DIRECTIONS: Each question or incomplete statement is followed by several suggested answers or completions. Select the one that BEST answers the question or completes the statement. *PRINT THE LETTER OF THE CORRECT ANSWER IN THE SPACE AT THE RIGHT.*

1. Which of the following factors contributes MOST to infant mortality?   1.____

    A. Motor vehicle accidents
    B. Congenital cardiac malformation
    C. Prematurity
    D. Acute renal failure
    E. Pneumonia

2. All of the following statements are true regarding tuberculosis in the United States EXCEPT: 2.____

    A. Mortality and morbidity rates increase with age
    B. Mortality rates are higher for males than females
    C. The incidence is much higher among the poor than the rich
    D. In low incidence areas, such as the United States, most tuberculosis is exogenous
    E. In 2015, the reported incidence of clinical disease in the United States was 3.0/100,000 population

3. Tubercle bacilli CANNOT be destroyed by   3.____

    A. heat   B. cold
    C. ultraviolet light   D. phenol
    E. tricresol solution

4. The MOST frequent reservoirs for tuberculosis disease are   4.____

    A. badgers   B. mosquitoes   C. humans
    D. cats   E. deer

5. The LEADING cause of death for people younger than age 65 in the United States is   5.____

    A. heart disease
    B. cerebrovascular disease
    C. chronic obstructive pulmonary disease
    D. diabetes mellitus
    E. chronic liver disease

6. Cooling towers and air conditioning units serve as breeding grounds for   6.____

    A. staphylococcus aureus
    B. klebsiella pneumoniae
    C. streptococcus pneumoniae
    D. L. pneumophilia
    E. histoplasma capsulatum

7. Diseases transmitted by mosquitoes, mites, and ticks can be prevented by all of the following precautions EXCEPT

    A. protective clothing
    B. mask and gloves
    C. insect repellents
    D. door and window screens
    E. more than one but not all of the above

8. The PRINCIPAL area of study in injury control is

    A. epidemiology
    B. prevention
    C. treatment
    D. rehabilitation
    E. all of the above

9. Benzene is MOST likely to be associated with _____ cancer.

    A. blood
    B. kidney
    C. liver
    D. brain
    E. bone

10. A _____ test is used when the patient's wishes can be inferred from his or her known religious, ethical, and/or lifestyle beliefs.

    A. subjective
    B. relative
    C. limited objective
    D. pure objective
    E. none of the above

11. It is NOT true that standard deviation

    A. is the positive square root of variance
    B. is the most useful measure of dispersion
    C. standardizes extreme values
    D. decreases when the sample size increases
    E. of a small size in a sample causes the sample mean to be close to each individual value

12. The difference between the highest and lowest values in a series is called the

    A. range
    B. variance
    C. standard deviation
    D. coefficient of variation
    E. none of the above

13. The ratio of the standard deviation of a series to the arithmetic mean of the series is known as the

    A. coefficient of variation
    B. range
    C. variance
    D. frequency
    E. prevalence

14. In a disease which is usually of acute onset, lasts a couple of weeks, and has a case fatality rate of 75 to 85%, the

    A. prevalence is always higher than that of annual incidence
    B. incidence is always higher than the prevalence
    C. prevalence and annual incidence are always equal
    D. mortality rate will be consistently high in all countries where the disease occurs
    E. none of the above

15. A random sample of 20,000 men is screened for a history of excessive sugar consumption and the presence of diabetes.
    This is called a _____ study.

    A. prospective
    B. historical
    C. cross-sectional population
    D. retrospective-prospective
    E. case control retrospective

16. Five hundred young adults who are known cocaine users are assembled together with a control group. Recognizable psychotics are excluded, and the remainder are followed for 3 years to see whether any psychoses develop in them.
    This is a _____ study.

    A. retrospective
    B. case control retrospective
    C. cross-sectional population
    D. cohort
    E. none of the above

17. The FIRST and most important thing for the epidemiologist to do during the investigation of a patient with a communicable disease is to investigate

    A. the first source of infection
    B. the mode of transmission
    C. how many people have been infected
    D. the accuracy of the diagnosis
    E. preventive control of the disease

18. The single MOST important measure for the prevention of typhoid fever in a community is

    A. a ceftriaxon prophylaxis for all persons who are exposed to the disease
    B. washing hands
    C. immunization of the high risk population
    D. hospitalization and treatment of all known carriers
    E. water purification

19. Diseases more likely to occur in women than in men include all of the following EXCEPT

    A. Raynaud's disease
    B. sarcoidosis
    C. gout
    D. systemic lupus erythematosus
    E. secondary hypothyroidism

20. Over the past 50 years, which of the following chronic conditions has experienced the greatest decline in mortality rate?

    A. Heart disease
    B. Stroke
    C. Cancer
    D. Pneumonia
    E. Influenza

21. The population having the HIGHEST frequency of thalassemia is the   21____

    A. Jews   B. Italians   C. Chinese
    D. Japanese   E. Americans

22. Over the past ten years, the majority of individuals who were initially diagnosed with   22____
    diabetes mellitus were in what age group?

    A. 18-29   B. 30-39
    C. 50-59   D. 70-79
    E. 80-89

23. Of the following, the disease LARGELY confined to people born in temperate climate   23____
    zones and manifested in early adult life is

    A. diabetes   B. multiple sclerosis
    C. thalassemia   D. hypertension
    E. prostate cancer

24. Hepatitis A has the highest incidence rate in individuals in which age group?   24____

    A. 0-9   B. 10-19   C. 20-29
    D. 30-39   E. 50-59

25. Recurrent episodes of low grade fever and arthralgia FREQUENTLY affect workers in   25____

    A. slaughter houses   B. cotton mills
    C. coal mines   D. hospital laboratories
    E. none of the above

KEY (CORRECT ANSWERS)

1. C	11. C
2. D	12. A
3. B	13. A
4. C	14. B
5. A	15. C
6. D	16. D
7. B	17. D
8. E	18. E
9. A	19. C
10. C	20. B

21. B
22. C
23. B
24. C
25. A

TEST 2

DIRECTIONS: Each question or incomplete statement is followed by several suggested answers or completions. Select the one that BEST answers the question or completes the statement. *PRINT THE LETTER OF THE CORRECT ANSWER IN THE SPACE AT THE RIGHT.*

1. Risk factors for malignancies of the liver and intra-hepatic biliary tract may include all of the following EXCEPT

    A. alpha-1 antitrypsin deficiency
    B. aflatoxin
    C. gentamicin
    D. alcohol
    E. steroids

1____

2. The parasite associated with an increased risk for developing carcinoma of the biliary tree is

    A. ascaris lumbricoides   B. balantidium coli
    C. cryptoporidium   D. colonorchis sinensis
    E. enterobias vermicular is

2____

3. Of the following, the immunization that should NOT be given to an individual who has received immune globulin within the previous 3 months is

    A. IPV   B. DTP   C. MMR
    D. HBIG   E. none of the above

3____

4. Which of the following is the LEADING cause of maternal death among pregnancies with abortive outcomes?

    A. Rubella   B. Ectopic pregnancy
    C. Teratoma   D. Defective germ cell
    E. Herpes simplex II

4____

5. All of the following are leading causes of maternal mortality in the United States EXCEPT

    A. anesthesia complication
    B. embolism
    C. hypertensive disease of pregnancy
    D. hemorrhage
    E. maternal age between 20 and 30

5____

6. _____ is NOT a reportable disease.

    A. Pulmonary tuberculosis   B. Mumps
    C. Measles   D. Choriomeningitis
    E. Meningococcal sepsis

6____

7. The scientific field dealing with the collection, classification, description, analysis, interpretation, and presentation of data is called

    A. distributions   B. statistics
    C. standard deviation   D. median
    E. cohort study

7____

77

8. What type of treatment regimen should be administered to an infant born to a mother with active gonorrhea?

   A. Single IM dose of ceftriaxone
   B. Single oral dose of azithromycin
   C. Dual therapy of ceftriaxone and azithromycin
   D. Dual therapy of ceftriaxone and spectinomycin
   E. None of the above

9. A precaution necessary for children in day care who have pneumococcal disease is _____ isolation.

   A. strict   B. contact   C. enteric
   D. respiratory   E. none of the above

10. Children who have ever had a life-threatening allergic reaction to _____ should not get the polio vaccine.

    A. gluten   B. peanuts   C. eggs
    D. antibiotics   E. pollen

11. Stillbirths or perinatal death is a result of _____ % of pregnancies in women with untreated early syphilis.

    A. 5   B. 10   C. 25   D. 40   E. 80

12. Strongyloidiasis is endemic in the tropics and subtropics, including the southern and southwestern United States. The single MOST important control measure is

    A. purification of water
    B. food cooked at a higher temperature
    C. sanitary disposal measure for human waste
    D. mass vaccination of exposed population
    E. detection and treatment of all infected persons

13. In a large population, the mode of transmission MOST difficult to prevent is _____ spread.

    A. vector   B. person to person
    C. airborne   D. droplet
    E. none of the above

14. Of the following, the factor contributing the MOST to infant mortality is

    A. seizures   B. prematurity   C. hypothyroidism
    D. congenital heart disease E. birth trauma

15. Point prevalence studies tend to have an over-representation of

    A. chronic cases   B. fatal cases   C. short-term cases
    D. healthy persons   E. all of the above

16. The PRIMARY function of the federal government in the Medicaid program is to

    A. set standards
    B. provide services in their own institutions *only*
    C. investigate *only* services rendered
    D. pay for services
    E. pay for nursing care *only*

Questions 17-21.

DIRECTIONS: In Questions 17 through 21, match the numbered description with the appropriate lettered term listed in Column I. Place the letter of the correct answer in the space at the right.

COLUMN I
A. Sensitivity
B. Specificity
C. Screening
D. Median
E. Mode

17. The MOST commonly occurring value in a series of values   17.____

18. The initial examination of an individual whose disease is not yet under medical care   18.____

19. May be calculated in an ongoing longevity study   19.____

20. The ability of a screening test to identify correctly those individuals who truly have the disease   20.____

21. The ability of a test to identify correctly those individuals who truly do not have the disease   21.____

Questions 22-25.

DIRECTIONS: In Questions 22 through 25, match the numbered definition with the appropriate lettered term listed in Column I. Place the letter of the correct answer in the space at the right.

COLUMN I
A. Efficiency
B. Validity
C. Reliability
D. Bias
E. Causality

22. The extent to which a test provides the same result on the same subject on two or more occasions   22.____

23. The extent to which the results of a test agree with the results of another test that is accepted as more accurate or closer to the truth   23.____

24. A systematic error that is unintentionally made   24.____

25. Denotes direct effect   25.____

KEY (CORRECT ANSWERS)

1.	C	11.	D
2.	D	12.	C
3.	C	13.	C
4.	B	14.	B
5.	E	15.	C
6.	D	16.	D
7.	B	17.	E
8.	C	18.	C
9.	E	19.	D
10.	D	20.	A

21. B
22. C
23. B
24. D
25. E

EXAMINATION SECTION
TEST 1

DIRECTIONS: Each question or incomplete statement is followed by several suggested answers or completions. Select the one that BEST answers the question or completes the statement. *PRINT THE LETTER OF THE CORRECT ANSWER IN THE SPACE AT THE RIGHT.*

1. Multiphasic screening, now adopted by many health departments, is BEST defined as a   1._____

    A. new method of testing vision
    B. case finding procedure combining tests for several diseases
    C. combined vision and hearing test
    D. new method of cancer detection

2. Of the following statements that a nurse might make to a patient ill with cancer who says, *I don't think I'll ever get better. When the pain comes, I'm afraid I'll die before anyone gets here,* the one which would be MOST appropriate is: 2._____

    A. I wouldn't worry about that. People do not die because of pain.
    B. Of course you'll get better. You look much better than you did the last time I was here.
    C. You should try to have someone here with you and not be alone. Then you won't be afraid.
    D. I think I understand how you feel, but why do you think you won't get better?

3. In an epidemiological study of a disease, the one of the following steps which would usually NOT be included is   3._____

    A. collecting and compiling data on the incidence, prevalence, and trends of the disease
    B. reviewing the *natural history* of the disease
    C. making a sociological study of the community in which the disease is prevalent
    D. defining gaps in knowledge and developing hypotheses on which to base further investigation

4. Adequate lighting in the school is an important part of the sight conservation program. The school nurse familiar with standards for classroom lighting should know that the RECOMMENDED illumination on each desk for ordinary classroom work is _____ candles.   4._____

    A. 20-foot   B. 35-foot   C. 50-foot   D. 75-foot

5. The relation of fluorine to dental health has been the subject of extensive study for many years.
Of the following statements concerning the relation of fluorine to dental caries, the one which is CORRECT is that   5._____

    A. mass medication by fluorine is now accepted as the best means of treating and curing dental caries
    B. fluoridation of water supplies, though effective, is too expensive for wide usage
    C. fluoridation is effective only in children born in areas in which fluoridation exists
    D. fluoridation prevents dental caries but does not treat or cure it

6. There are measures which are effective in the prevention of diabetes in those with an hereditary disposition.
Of the following, the one which has the GREATEST value as a preventive measure is

   A. preventing acute infection
   B. preventing obesity
   C. avoidance of emotional stress
   D. avoidance of marriage with a known diabetic

7. The basis of a program of *natural childbirth* is to

   A. prevent or dispel fear through education in the physiology of pregnancy
   B. reduce premature births and the complications of pregnancy
   C. reduce the maternal and neonatal mortality rates
   D. prepare the mother's body for the muscular activity of delivery

8. The one of the following statements which is CORRECT concerning retrolental fibroplasia is that it is a

   A. blood dyscrasia
   B. condition occurring in Rh negative infants whose mothers are Rh positive
   C. condition causing blindness in premature infants
   D. complication of congenital syphilis

9. Of the following factors, the one which is MOST important in maintaining optimum health in the older age group is

   A. regular medical supervision for early recognition and treatment of minor symptoms
   B. economic independence which gives a feeling of security
   C. avoidance of all emotional tensions
   D. adjustment of the environment to prevent physical and mental strain

10. The MOST outstanding result of antibiotic therapy in the treatment of syphilis has been to

    A. reduce the toxic effect of treatment
    B. shorten the treatment period
    C. prevent a relapse
    D. prevent late complications

11. To achieve the most effective and economical case finding for tuberculosis, mass examinations should be conducted PRIMARILY for

    A. infants under one year
    B. industrial workers
    C. elementary school students
    D. pre-school age group

12. Though tuberculosis occurs in all age groups, there is a certain period of life when individuals have the greatest resistance to the infection.
That period is

    A. under one year of age
    B. between 3 years and puberty
    C. between 15 and 35 years of age
    D. between 25 and 40 years of age

13. Drug therapy for tuberculosis has proven to be an important tool in the control of the disease in its active stage.
    Of the following, the one which has had the MOST satisfactory results to date in that fewer patients develop resistance to the drug and the incidence of drug toxicity is reduced is

    A. para-amino-salicylic acid (P.A.S.) in combination with streptomycin
    B. dihydro-streptomycin
    C. streptomycin in combination with promine
    D. penicillin

13._____

14. Studies have indicated that the use of streptomycin in the treatment of tuberculosis has GREATEST value in

    A. recently developed pneumonic or exudative lesions
    B. long standing infections which have been resistant to other therapies
    C. military T.B.
    D. meningeal T.B.

14._____

15. The PARTICULAR effectiveness of chemotherapeutic agents in the treatment of pulmonary tuberculosis is that they

    A. are important adjuncts to surgery
    B. inhibit the growth of the bacillus
    C. heal lesions rapidly
    D. render the patient non-infectious

15._____

KEY (CORRECT ANSWERS)

1. B
2. D
3. C
4. A
5. D

6. B
7. A
8. C
9. A
10. B

11. B
12. B
13. A
14. A
15. B

TEST 2

DIRECTIONS: Each question or incomplete statement is followed by several suggested answers or completions. Select the one that BEST answers the question or completes the statement. *PRINT THE LETTER OF THE CORRECT ANSWER IN THE SPACE AT THE RIGHT.*

1. The CHIEF shortcoming of chemotherapeutic agents in the treatment of pulmonary tuberculosis is

    A. their prohibitive cost in any long-term treatment
    B. the toxic effects which follow their use
    C. that their use is limited to early cases
    D. the development of bacterial resistance by the host

    1.____

2. Though precise knowledge concerning the optimum duration of chemotherapy in treating pulmonary tuberculosis is lacking, the present APPROVED practice is

    A. continued uninterrupted treatment until the sputum is negative
    B. short courses of treatment with rest periods in between
    C. continued treatment for a minimum of 12 months
    D. continued treatment for one year after a negative sputum and cultures are obtained

    2.____

3. A community program for the control of tuberculosis must include school children and school personnel if it is to be a success.
Of the following statements, the one which BEST represents expert opinion on the use of B.C.G. vaccine in the school program for tuberculosis control is that

    A. through immunization of all school children it serves as an important control measure
    B. its chief value is that it is an inexpensive and rapid method of case finding
    C. it would nullify the subsequent use of the tuberculin test which is the best case finding method for schools
    D. it is a valuable diagnostic method which would reduce the evidence of contact with active cases

    3.____

4. Nutritional deficiencies are a common problem in geriatrics.
The dietary adjustment usually necessary to maintain PROPER nutrition for the average person in the older age group is

    A. increased proteins and vitamins
    B. elimination of fats
    C. increased carbohydrates
    D. elimination of roughage

    4.____

5. The death rate from cancer can be reduced by early diagnosis and treatment. It is important, therefore, for the nurse to assist in case finding.
She should know that, of the following sites, the one which the GREATEST incidence of cancer in women occurs is the

    A. mouth   B. skin   C. breast   D. rectum

    5.____

6. Many cancers appear to develop when pre-existing abnormal conditions and changes in the tissue are present.
   Of the following, the one which is at present considered PRECANCEROUS is

   A. fibroid tumor
   B. chronic cervicitis
   C. fat tissue tumor
   D. sebaceous cyst

7. The diagnosis of cancer by examination of isolated cells in body secretions is known as

   A. biopsy
   B. aspiration technique
   C. histological diagnosis
   D. Papanicolaou smear

8. Of the following statements concerning our present knowledge of the etiology of human cancer, the one which is TRUE is that

   A. there is definite evidence that some cancers are caused by a virus
   B. some types of cancer are definitely contagious
   C. there is a strong possibility that cancer is transmitted from mother to baby in utero
   D. so many factors are involved that the discovery of a single cause is unlikely

9. The National Venereal Disease Control Program carried on by the Public Health Service of the U.S. Government is concerned PRIMARILY with

   A. promoting medical programs to provide early effective treatment of infected individuals
   B. a national program of education in the prevention of venereal diseases
   C. distribution of free drugs to physicians for the treatment of venereal disease
   D. providing funds for the education of physicians and nurses in the treatment and care of venereal disease

10. Of the following, the one which is of GREATEST importance in the prevention of poliomyelitis is to

    A. build up resistance with proper diet
    B. keep away from crowds during periods when the disease is prevalent
    C. immunize with gamma globulin
    D. adopt general public health measures for the protection of food and water

11. Of the following statements concerning the present status of chemotherapy in the treatment of cancer, the one which is TRUE is:

    A. Results to date indicate it may soon surpass radiation and surgery as an effective cure
    B. It has not proven effective except in cases where early diagnosis was made
    C. It must be used in conjunction with radiation or surgery
    D. It inhibits the growth of certain types of cancer and prolongs life but is not effective as a cure

12. The W.H.O. Regional Organization for Europe has set up a long-term plan for European health needs.
    Of the following activities, the one which is NOT planned as a major activity is

A. coordinating health policies in European countries
B. promoting improved service through demonstration of an ideal health program in one country
C. promoting professional and technical education for health workers in the member countries
D. providing for exchange of services among member nations

13. A health problem becomes the concern of public health authorities when the incidence is great and the mortality rate high.
In terms of this statement, of the following problems, the one which should be a PRIMARY concern is

    A. venereal diseases in young adults
    B. tuberculosis
    C. tropical diseases among ex-servicemen and their families
    D. degenerative diseases of middle and later life

14. Of the following, the one which is now considered to be the MOST common mode of transmission of poliomyelitis is

    A. infected insects   B. contaminated water
    C. personal contact   D. infected food

15. The incubation period for infantile paralysis is

    A. usually 7 to 14 days, but may vary from 3 to 35 days
    B. not known
    C. one week
    D. usually 48 hours, but may vary from 1 to 7 days

KEY (CORRECT ANSWERS)

1.	D	6.	B
2.	C	7.	D
3.	C	8.	D
4.	A	9.	A
5.	C	10.	B

11. D
12. B
13. D
14. C
15. A

EXAMINATION SECTION
TEST 1

DIRECTIONS: Each question or incomplete statement is followed by several suggested answers or completions. Select the one that BEST answers the question or completes the statement. *PRINT THE LETTER OF THE CORRECT ANSWER IN THE SPACE AT THE RIGHT.*

1. A specialist is meeting with a panel of local community leaders to determine their perceptions about the effectiveness of a recent outreach program. The leaders seem unresponsive to the specialist's questions, looking at the floor or each other without directly answering the specialist's questions.
   One strategy that might work to elicit the desired information would be to
   A. try to discern the hidden meaning of their silence
   B. adopt a mildly confrontational tone and remind them of what's at stake in the community
   C. keep asking open-ended questions and wait patiently for responses
   D. tell them to come back when they're ready to tell you their opinions

   1.____

2. Each of the following statements about maintaining a community's attention is true, EXCEPT:
   A. The more challenging it is to pay attention to a message, the more likely it is that it will be attended to
   B. Listeners will be more motivated to pay attention if a speech is personally meaningful
   C. People will be more likely to attend if a speaker pauses to suggest natural transitions in a speech
   D. Listeners will attend to messages that stand out

   2.____

3. Each of the following is a key strategy to integrative bargaining among community members in conflict, EXCEPT
   A. focusing on positions, rather than interests
   B. separating the people from the problem
   C. aiming for an outcome based on an objectively identified standard
   D. using active listening skills, such as rephrasing and questioning

   3.____

4. Which of the following is NOT one of the major variables to take into account when considering a community needs assessment?
   A. State of program development   B. Resources available
   C. Demographics   D. Community attitudes

   4.____

5. Which of the following groups would probably be formed specifically for, or be involved in, the purpose of addressing a specific unmet community need?
   A. An existing consumer group
   B. A council of community representatives
   C. A committee
   D. An existing community organization

   5.____

6. If a public outreach campaign designed to mobilize a community fails, the MOST likely reason for this failure is that the campaign
    A. was not specific about what it wanted people to do
    B. was overly serious and did not appeal to people's sense of humor
    C. offered no incentive for the audience to make a change
    D. did not use language that appealed to the audience's emotions

7. Nationwide, the rate of involvement of elderly people in community-based programs demonstrates that they are
    A. under-served when compared to other age groups
    B. served at about the same rate as other age groups
    C. over-served when compared to other age groups
    D. hardly served at all

8. In projecting the likelihood of an education program's success, a domestic violence specialist identifies every single event that must occur to complete the project. The specialist then arranges these events in sequential order and allocates time requirements for each. Finally, the total time is calculated and a model showing all their events and timelines is charted.
    The specialist has used
    A. a PERT chart
    B. a simulation
    C. a Markov model
    D. the critical path method

9. When working with members of a predominantly African-American community, specialists from other cultural backgrounds should be aware that African-Americans tend to express thoughts and feelings through descriptions of
    A. physically tangible sensations
    B. problems to be analyzed
    C. corresponding analogies
    D. spiritual issues

10. Local nonprofessionals should be considered useful to a specialist who is looking to undertake a community outreach or educational initiative.
    Which of the following is LEAST likely to be a characteristic or role demonstrated by these community members?
    A. Undertaking support functions at the agency
    B. Serving as a communication channel between the agency and clients
    C. Encouraging greater agency acceptance and credibility within the community
    D. Helping the agency to accomplish meaningful change

11. In working with Native American groups or clients, it is important to recognize that the GREATEST health problem facing their communities today is
    A. domestic violence
    B. depression and suicide
    C. alcoholism
    D. tuberculosis

12. A specialist is facilitating a cooperative conflict resolution session between community members who have different opinions about what kinds of intervention services should be offered by the local adult protective services agency.
    Which of the following is NOT a guideline that should be followed in this process?
    A. Early in the negotiations, ask each party to name the issues on which they will positively not yield.
    B. Try to get the parties to view the issue from other points of view, beside the two or three conflicting ones.
    C. Have each side volunteer what it would be willing to do to resolve the conflict.
    D. At the end of the session, draw up a formal agreement with agreed-upon actions for both parties.

13. A specialist wants to evaluate the effectiveness of a local women's shelter. The shelter has suffered from lax participation, given the number of women who have been abused in the surrounding area. The specialist wants to speak with the women in the community who did not follow up on referrals to the shelter, and begins by visiting some of these women. After gaining the trust of these women, the specialist asks for the names of women they know who might be in need of help with a domestic violence situation.
    The specialist's approach in this case is _____ sampling.
    A. maximum variation   B. snowball
    C. convenience   D. typical case

14. When it comes to perceiving messages, people typically DON'T
    A. tend to simplify causal connections and sometimes even seek a single cause to explain what may be a highly complex effect
    B. tend to perceive messages independently of a categorical framework, especially if the message may be distorted by such an interpretation
    C. have a predisposition toward accepting any pattern that a speaker offers to explain seemingly unconnected facts
    D. tend to interpret things in the way they are viewed by their reference group

15. The elder members of Native American communities, regardless of kinship, are MOST commonly referred to as
    A. the ancients   B. father or mother
    C. grandfather or grandmother   D. chiefs

16. Each of the following is typically an objective of community mobilization, EXCEPT:
    A. To convince existing community resources to alter their services or work together to address an unmet need
    B. To gather and distribute information to consumers and agencies about unmet needs

C. To publicize existing community resources and make them more accessible
D. To bring an unmet community need to public attention in order to achieve acceptance of and support for fulfilling the need

17. Research in community outreach shows that women often build friendships through shared positive feelings, whereas men often build friendships through
   A. metacommunication
   B. catharsis
   C. impression management
   D. shared activities

17.____

18. Typically, the FIRST step in a community-needs assessment is to
   A. identify community's strengths
   B. explore the nature of the neighborhood
   C. get to know the area and its residents
   D. talk to people in the community

18.____

19. Most public relations experts agree that _____ exposure(s) to a message is the minimum just to get the message noticed. If the aim of a public outreach campaign is action or a change in behavior, the agency budget must plan for more exposures.
   A. one   B. two   C. three   D. four

19.____

20. In the program development/community liaison model of community work and public outreach, the PRIMARY constituency is considered to be
   A. community representatives and the service agency board or administrators
   B. elected officials, social agencies, and interagency organizations
   C. marginalized or oppressed population groups in a city or region
   D. residents of a neighborhood, parish or rural county

20.____

21. Social or interpersonal problems in many African-American communities have their roots in
   A. personality deficits
   B. unresolved family conflicts
   C. poor communication
   D. external stressors

21.____

22. A public outreach campaign should
   I. focus on short-term, measurable goals, rather than ultimate outcomes
   II. try to alter entrenched attitudes within a short time, with powerfully worded messages
   III. proceed in steps or phases, each of which lays out a mechanism that leads to the desired effect
   IV. ignore causes that led to a problem, and instead focus on solutions

   The CORRECT answer is:
   A. I and II   B. II and III   C. III only   D. I, II, III and IV

22.____

23. Research findings indicate that in listing preferences for helping professional attributes, individuals from culturally diverse groups are MOST likely to consider _____ as more important than _____.
    A. personality similarity; either race/ethnic similarity or attitude similarity
    B. therapist experience; any kind of similarity
    C. race/ethnic similarity; attitude similarity
    D. attitude similarity; race/ethnic similarity

24. Each of the following is considered to be an objective of community organization EXCEPT
    A. effecting changes in the distribution of decision-making power
    B. helping people develop and strengthen the traits of self-direction and cooperation
    C. effecting and maintaining the balance between needs and resources in a community
    D. helping people deal with their problems by developing alternative behaviors

25. A specialist is helping the adult protective services agency to design a public outreach campaign. The topic to be addressed is complex, public understanding is low, and most professionals at the agency feel that having more complete information might change the opinions of community members. Which method of pre-campaign research is probably MOST appropriate?
    A. Deliberative polling
    B. Attitude scales
    C. Surveys or questionnaires
    D. Focus groups

KEY (CORRECT ANSWERS)

1.	C		11.	C
2.	A		12.	A
3.	A		13.	B
4.	C		14.	B
5.	C		15.	C
6.	A		16.	B
7.	A		17.	D
8.	D		18.	B
9.	C		19.	C
10.	A		20.	A

21.	D
22.	C
23.	D
24.	D
25.	A

TEST 2

DIRECTIONS: Each question or incomplete statement is followed by several suggested answers or completions. Select the one that BEST answers the question or completes the statement. *PRINT THE LETTER OF THE CORRECT ANSWER IN THE SPACE AT THE RIGHT.*

1. A specialist has been called in to resolve a dispute between two community leaders who have been arguing about the level of service needed within the community. The discussion has been going on for several hours when the specialist arrives, and both people seem to be upset.
After calming the two down and getting each of them to agree on a statement of the problem, the specialist should ask each person to
    A. summarize his or her argument in three main points
    B. explain why he or she became so upset
    C. clearly state, in objective terms, the position of the other in a form that meets with the other's approval
    D. identify the best alternative outcome, other than their presumed ideal

2. In evaluating the impact of a public outreach campaign, the _____ model can be used early in the campaign to address first impressions.
    A. exposure or advertising
    B. expert interview
    C. impact monitoring or process
    D. experimental or quasi-experimental

3. When trying to motivate an older population to take action on a community problem, it is helpful to remember that older people
    A. are more self-reliant in their decision-making than other members of the same family
    B. often need more time to decide than younger people
    C. are more likely than younger people to view community problems self-referentially
    D. tend to take a pragmatic, rather than philosophical, view of life

4. The method of group or community decision-making that is normally MOST time-consuming is
    A. majority opinion   B. consensus
    C. expert opinion   D. authority rule

5. A local adult protective services agency has identified one of the goals of its recent public outreach campaign to be the mobilization of activists.
The campaign should probably
    A. target neutral audiences
    B. home in on supporters
    C. stick to purely factual information
    D. try to persuade community fence-sitters

6. Research of Native American youths' perceptions of family concerns for their well-being has generally found that these youths
   A. have a high degree of uncertainty about their families' feelings toward them
   B. believe their families don't care about them
   C. believe that their mothers care a great deal about them, but their fathers don't
   D. believe their families care a great deal about them

7. A domestic violence specialist is developing a new outreach program for the local community. The specialist has defined the target problem, set program goals, and planned the actions that will take place as a result of the program. Most likely, the next step will be to
   A. evaluate the resources available to achieve program goals
   B. define and sequence the steps that will be taken to achieve program goals
   C. determine how the program will be evaluated
   D. decide how the program will operate

8. Elder: *I'm so glad to have someone to talk to, someone who really understands my problem.*
   Specialist: *It is nice to be able to talk to someone who will listen.*
   Elder: *That's for sure.*
   In the above exchange, what listening skill is evident in the underlined statement?
   A. Verbatim response
   B. Paraphrasing
   C. Advising
   D. Evaluation

9. Which of the following activities is involved in the specialist's task of mobilizing?
   A. Meeting individuals in the community with problems and assisting them in finding help
   B. Identifying unmet community needs
   C. Speaking out against an unjust policy or procedure
   D. Developing new services or linking presently available services to meet community needs

10. The preliminary research associated with a public outreach campaign should FIRST be aimed at determining
    A. the budget
    B. the message's ultimate audience
    C. what media to use
    D. the short-term behavioral goals of the campaign

11. A specialist in a low-income community wants to plan programs that will deal with the influence of unemployment on domestic disturbances. The specialist needs to know not only how many unemployed people are in the community now, but also how many people will be unemployed at any particular tie in the future, and how those numbers will vary given certain conditions.

Probably the BEST way to trace employment rates over time and within differing conditions is through the use of
A. the critical path
B. linear programming
C. difference equations
D. the Markov model

12. Generally, public outreach programs—whatever their stated goal—should
    I. create a sense of urgency about a problem
    II. decline to identify opponents of the issue or idea
    III. propose concrete, easily understandable solutions
    IV. urge a specific action

    The CORRECT answer is:
    A. I only
    B. I, III and IV
    C. II and III
    D. I, II, III and IV

13. Which of the following methods of community needs assessment relies to the GREATEST degree on existing public records?
    A. Social indicators
    B. Field study
    C. Rates under treatment
    D. Key informant

14. During an interview with a Native American client, a specialist is careful to maintain close and nearly constant eye contact.
    The client is MOST likely to interpret this as a(n)
    A. show of high concern
    B. sign of disrespect
    C. uncomfortable assumption of intimacy
    D. attempt to intimidate

15. The BEST strategy for addressing an audience that is known to be captive, or even hostile, is to
    A. refer to experiences in common
    B. flatter the audience
    C. joke about things in or near the audience
    D. plead for fairness

16. Integrative conflict resolution is characterized by
    A. an overriding concern to maximize joint outcomes
    B. one side's interests opposing the other's
    C. a fixed and limited amount of resources to be divided, so that the more one group gets, the less another gets
    D. manipulation and withholding information as negotiation strategies

17. A specialist wants to learn how to interact with the members of a largely Latino community in a more culturally sensitive way.
    Which of the following is NOT a guideline for interacting with members of a Latino community?
    A. Efforts to foster independence and self-reliance may be interpreted by many Latinos as a lack of concern for others.
    B. Efforts to deal one-on-one with an adolescent client may serve to alienate the parents, especially the mother.

C. A nonverbal gesture, such as lowering the eyes, is interpreted by many Latinos as a sign of respect and deference to authority.
D. In much of Latino culture, the focus of control for problems tends to be much more external than internal.

18. Each of the following is a supporting assumption of community organization, EXCEPT:
    A. Democracy requires cooperative participation.
    B. In order for communities to change, it is necessary for each individual in the community to be willing to change.
    C. Communities often need help with organization and planning.
    D. Holistic approaches work better than fragmented or ad-hoc programs.

19. Helping professionals often have difficulty to bring community resources together to fulfill unmet community needs.
    Which of the following is NOT usually a reason for this?
    A. Some community groups resist assistance when it is offered.
    B. Few community groups make their needs known.
    C. Community resources frequently change the type of services they offer.
    D. Often, community resources prefer to work alone.

20. When dealing with groups or populations of elderly clients, specialists should be mindful that about _____ of the nation's elderly suffer from mental health problems.
    A. a tenth   B. a quarter   C. a third   D. half

21. In an African-American community, a specialist from another culture should recognize that church participation, for most African-Americans, is viewed as a
    A. method for maintaining control and communicating competency
    B. way of depersonalizing problems or troubles
    C. way to divert attention away from problems
    D. means of cathartic emotional release

22. Adult protective service programs supported by state statutes protect elderly people from abuse and neglect under the doctrine of
    A. parens patriae   B. habeas corpus
    C. in loco parentis   D. volenti non fit injuria

23. In terms of public outreach, which of the following statements about an audience is NOT generally true?
    A. The more heterogeneous the audience, the more necessary it will be to use specific examples and appeals to certain types of people.
    B. The smaller the audience, the more likely that its members will share assumptions and values.
    C. When the speaker does not know the status of an audience, it is best to assume that they are captive rather than voluntary.
    D. The larger an audience, the more formal a presentation is likely to be.

24. A specialist often spends time in the places frequented by community residents. She listens carefully to what residents seem most concerned about, and engages many in conversations, asking them how they see the problems in the community. During these conversations, she makes mental notes about whether the statements of the problems are the same things that are mentioned in their conversations. From these conversations, the worker determines what she thinks the unmet needs of the community are.
    Which of the key issues in identifying unmet needs has the worker neglected to address?
    A. The different points of view regarding the issues, and whether there is any common ground
    B. Whether the stated problems and conversations with community residents reflect the same concerns
    C. How community residents define the issues
    D. What the residents talk about with one another in a community

25. Which of the following political styles should be used to promote an issue that could become controversial if it is perceived to involve major reforms?
    A. High-conflict, polarized
    B. High-conflict, consensual
    C. Moderate conflict, compromise-oriented
    D. Low-conflict, technical

KEY (CORRECT ANSWERS)

1.	C		11.	D
2.	A		12.	B
3.	B		13.	A
4.	B		14.	B
5.	B		15.	A
6.	D		16.	A
7.	A		17.	D
8.	B		18.	B
9.	D		19.	C
10.	B		20.	B

21.	D
22.	A
23.	A
24.	A
25.	D

PREPARING WRITTEN MATERIAL

PARAGRAPH REARRANGEMENT
COMMENTARY

The sentences that follow are in scrambled order. You are to rearrange them in proper order and indicate the letter choice containing the correct answer at the space at the right.

Each group of sentences in this section is actually a paragraph presented in scrambled order. Each sentence in the group has a place in that paragraph; no sentence is to be left out. You are to read each group of sentences and decide upon the best order in which to put the sentences so as to form a well-organized paragraph.

The questions in this section measure the ability to solve a problem when all the facts relevant to its solution are not given.

More specifically, certain positions of responsibility and authority require the employee to discover connection between events sometimes, apparently, unrelated. In order to do this, the employee will find it necessary to correctly infer that unspecified events have probably occurred or are likely to occur. This ability becomes especially important when action must be taken on incomplete information.

Accordingly, these questions require competitors to choose among several suggested alternatives, each of which presents a different sequential arrangement of the events. Competitors must choose the MOST logical of the suggested sequences.

In order to do so, they may be required to draw on general knowledge to infer missing concepts or events that are essential to sequencing the given events. Competitors should be careful to infer only what is essential to the sequence. The plausibility of the wrong alternatives will always require the inclusion of unlikely events or of additional chains of events which are NOT essential to sequencing the given events.

It's very important to remember that you are looking for the best of the four possible choices, and that the best choice of all may not even be one of the answers you're given to choose from.

There is no one right way to solve these problems. Many people have found it helpful to first write out the order of the sentences, as they would have arranged them, on their scrap paper before looking at the possible answers. If their optimum answer is there, this can save them some time. If it isn't, this method can still give insight into solving the problem. Others find it most helpful to just go through each of the possible choices, contrasting each as they go along. You should use whatever method feels comfortable and works for you.

While most of these types of questions are not that difficult, we've added a higher percentage of the difficult type, just to give you more practice. Usually there are only one or two questions on this section that contain such subtle distinctions that you're unable to answer confidently. And you then may find yourself stuck deciding between two possible choices, neither of which you're sure about.

PREPARING WRITTEN MATERIAL
PARAGRAPH REARRANGEMENT
EXAMINATION SECTION
TEST 1

DIRECTIONS: The following groups of sentences need to be arranged in an order that makes sense. Select the letter preceding the sequence that represents the best sentence order. *PRINT THE LETTER OF THE CORRECT ANSWER IN THE SPACE AT THE RIGHT.*

1. I.   The ostrich egg shell's legendary toughness makes it an excellent substitute for certain types of dishes or dinnerware, and in parts of Africa ostrich shells are cut and decorated for use as containers for water.
    II. Since prehistoric times, people have used the enormous egg of the ostrich as a part of their diet, a practice which has required much patience and hard work—to hard boil an ostrich egg takes about four hours.
    III. Opening the egg's shell, which is rock hard and nearly an inch thick, requires heavy tools, such as a saw or chisel; from inside, a baby ostrich must use a hornlike projection on its beak as a miniature pick-axe to escape from the egg.
    IV. The offspring of all higher-order animals originate from single egg cells that are carried by mothers, and most of these eggs are relatively small, often microscopic.
    V.   The egg of the African ostrich, however, weighs a massive thirty pounds, making it the largest single cell on earth, and a common object of human curiosity and wonder.

    The BEST order is:
    A. V, IV, I, II, III   B. I, IV, V, III, II   C. IV, II, III, V, I   D. IV, V, II, III, I

    1.____

2. I.   Typically only a few feet high on the open sea, individual tsunami have been known to circle the entire globe two or three times if their progress is not interrupted, but are not usually dangerous until they approach the shallow water that surrounds land masses.
    II. Some of the most terrifying and damaging hazards caused by earthquakes are tsunami, which were once called "tidal waves"—a poorly chosen name, since these waves have nothing to do with tides.
    III. Then a wave, slowed by the sudden drag on the lower part of its moving water column, will pile upon itself, sometimes reaching a height of over 100 feet.
    IV. Tsunami (Japanese for "great harbor wave") are seismic waves that are caused by earthquakes near oceanic trenches, and once triggered, can travel up to 600 miles an hour on the open ocean.
    V.   A land-shoaling tsunami is capable of extraordinary destruction; some tsunami have deposited large boats miles inland, washed out two-foot-thick seawalls, and scattered locomotive trains over long distances.

    The BEST order is:
    A. IV, I, III, II, V   B. I, III, IV, II, V   C. V, I, III, II, IV   D. II, IV, I, III, V

    2.____

3. I. Soon, by the 1940s, jazz was the most popular type of music among American intellectuals and college students.
    II. In the early days of jazz, it was considered "lowdown" music, or music that was played only in rough, disreputable bars and taverns.
    III. However, jazz didn't take too long to develop from early ragtime melodies into more complex, sophisticated forms, such as Charlie Parker's "bebop" style of jazz.
    IV. After charismatic band leaders such as Duke Ellington and Count Basie brought jazz to a larger audience, and jazz continued to evolve into more complicated forms, white audiences began to accept and even to enjoy the new American art form.
    V. Many white Americans, who then dictated the tastes of society, were wary of music that was played almost exclusively in black clubs in the poorer sections of cities and towns.
    The BEST order is:
    A. V, IV, III, II, I   B. II, V, III, IV, I   C. IV, V, III, I, II   D. I, II, IV, III, V

4. I. Then, hanging in a windless place, the magnetized end of the needle would always point to the south.
    II. The needle could then be balanced on the rim of a cup, or the edge of a fingernail, but this balancing act was hard to maintain, and the needle often fell off.
    III. Other needles would point to the north, and it was important for any traveler finding his way with a compass to remember which kind of magnetized needle he was carrying.
    IV. To make some of the earliest compasses in recorded history, ancient Chinese "magicians" would rub a needle with a piece of magnetized iron called a lodestone.
    V. A more effective method of keeping the needle free to swing with its magnetic pull was to attach a strand of silk to the center of the needle with a tiny piece of wax.
    The BEST order is:
    A. IV, II, V, I, III   B. IV, III, V, II, I   C. IV, V, II, I, III   D. IV, I, III, V, II

5. I. The now-famous first mate of the *H.M.S. Bounty*, Fletcher Christian, founded one of the world's most peculiar civilizations in 1790.
    II. The men knew they had just committed a crime for which they could be hanged, so they set sail for Pitcairn, a remote, abandoned island in the far eastern region of the Polynesian archipelago, accompanied by twelve Polynesian women and six men.
    III. In a mutiny that has become legendary, Christian and the others forced Captain Bligh into a lifeboat and set him adrift off the coast of Tonga in April of 1789.
    IV. In early 1790, the *Bounty* landed at Pitcairn Island, where the men lived out the rest of their lives and founded an isolated community which to this day includes direct descendants of Christian and the other Crewmen.

V. The *Bounty*, commanded by Captain William Bligh, was in the middle of a global voyage, and Christian and his shipmates had come to the conclusion that Bligh was a reckless madman who would lead them to their deaths unless they took the ship from him.

The BEST order is:
A. IV, V, III, II, I   B. I, III, V, II, IV   C. I, V, III, II, IV   D. III, I, V, IV, II

6.
I. But once the vines had been led to make orchids, the flowers had to be carefully hand-pollinated, because unpollinated orchids usually lasted less than a day, wilting and dropping off the vine before it had even become dark.
II. The Totonac farmers discovered that looping a vine back around once it reached a five-foot height on its host tree would cause the vine to flower.
III. Though they knew how to process the fruit pods and extract vanilla's flavoring agent, the Totonacs also knew that a wild vanilla vine did not produce abundant flowers or fruit.
IV. Wild vines climbed along the trunks and canopies of trees, and this constant upward growth diverted most of the vine's energy to making leaves instead of the orchid flowers that once pollinated, would produce the flavorful pods.
V. Hundreds of years before vanilla became a prized food flavoring in Europe and the Western World, the Totonac Indians of the Mexican Gulf Coast were skilled cultivators of the vanilla vine, whose fruit they literally worshipped as a goddess.

The BEST order is:
A. II, III, IV, I, V   B. II, IV, III, I, V   C. V, III, IV, II, I   D. III, IV, I, II, V

6._____

7.
I. Once airborne, the spider is at the mercy of the air currents—usually the spider takes a brief journey, traveling close to the ground, but some have been found in air samples collected as high as 10,000 feet, or been reported landing on ships far out at sea.
II. Once a young spider has hatched, it must leave the environment into which it was born as quickly as possible, in order to avoid competing with its hundreds of brothers and sisters for food.
III. The silk rises into warm air currents, and as soon as the pull feels adequate the spider lets go and drifts up into the air, suspended from the silk strand in the same way that a person might parasail.
IV. To help young spiders do this, many species have adapted a practice known as "aerial dispersal," or, in common speech, "ballooning."
V. A spider that wants to leave its surroundings quickly will climb to the top of a grass system or twig, face into the wind, and aim its back end into the air, releasing a long stream of silk from the glands near the tip of its abdomen.

The BEST order is:
A. V, IV, II, III, I   B. V, II, IV, I, III   C. II, V, IV, III, I   D. II, IV, V, III, I

7._____

8. I. For about a year, Tycho worked at a castle in Prague with a scientist named Johannes Kepler, but their association was cut short by another argument that drove Kepler out of the castle, to later develop, on his own, the theory of planetary orbits.
    II. Tycho found life without a nose embarrassing, so he made a new nose for himself out of silver, which reportedly remained glued to his face for the rest of his life.
    III. Tycho Brahe, the 17th-century Danish astronomer, is today more famous for his odd and arrogant personality than for any contribution he has made to our knowledge of the stars and planets.
    IV. Early in his career, as a student at Rostock University, Tycho got into an argument with another student about who was the better mathematician, and the two became so angry that the argument turned into a sword fight, during which Tycho's nose was sliced off.
    V. Later in his life, Tycho's arrogance may have kept him from playing a part in one of the greatest astronomical discoveries in history: the elliptical orbits of the solar system's planets.

    The BEST order is:
    A. I, IV, II, III, V   B. IV, II, III, V, I   C. IV, II, I, III, V   D. III, IV, II, V, I

9. I. The processionaries are so used to this routine that if a person picks up the end of a silk line and brings it back to the origin—creating a closed circle—the caterpillars may travel around and around for days, sometimes starving or freezing, without changing course.
    II. Rather than relying on sight or sound, the other caterpillars, who are lined up end-to-end behind the leader, travel to and from their nests by walking on this silk line, and each will reinforce it by laying down its own marking line as it passes over.
    III. In order to insure the safety of individuals, the processionary caterpillar nests in a tree with dozens of other caterpillars, and at night, when it is safest, they all leave together in search of food.
    IV. The processionary caterpillar of the European continent is a perfect illustration of how much some inspect species rely on instinct in their daily routines.
    V. As they leave their nests, the processionaries form a single-file line behind a leader who spins and lays out a silk line to mark the chosen path.

    The BEST order is:
    A. IV, III, V, II, I   B. III, V, IV, II, I   C. III, V, II, I, IV   D. IV, V, III, I, II

10. I. Often, the child is also given a handcrafted walker or push cart, to provide support for its first upright explorations.
    II. In traditional Indian families, a child's first steps are celebrated as a ceremonial event, rooted in ancient myth.
    III. These carts are often intricately designed to resemble the chariot of Krishna, an important figure in Indian mythology.
    IV. The sound of these anklet bells is intended to mimic the footsteps of the legendary child Rama, who is celebrated in devotional songs throughout India.

V. When the child's parents see that the child is ready to begin walking, they will fit it with specially designed ankle bracelets, adorned with gently ringing bells.

The BEST order is:
A. II, III, IV, I, V   B. II, V, III, I, IV   C. V, IV, I, III, II   D. V, III, II, I, IV

11. I. The settlers planted Osage oranges all across Middle America, and today long lines and rectangles of Osage orange trees can still be seen on the prairies, running along the former boundaries of farms that no longer exist.
    II. After trying sod walls and water-filled ditches with no success, American farmers began to look for a plant that was adaptable to prairie weather, and that could be trimmed into a hedge that was "pig-tight, horse-high, and bull-strong."
    III. The tree, so named because it bore a large (but inedible) fruit the size of an orange, was among the sturdiest and hardiest of American trees, and was prized among Native Americans for the strength and flexibility of bows which were made from its wood.
    IV. The first people to practice agriculture on the American flatlands were faced with an important problem: what would they use to fence their land in a place that was almost entirely without trees or rocks?
    V. Finally, an Illinois farmer brought the settlers a tree that was native to the land between the Red and Arkansas rivers, a tree called the Osage orange.

    The BEST order is:
    A. II, I, V, III, IV   B. I, II, III, IV, V   C. IV, II, V, III, I   D. IV, II, I, III, V

11.____

12. I. After about ten minutes of such spirited and complicated activity, the head dancer is free to make up his or her own movements while maintaining the interest of the New Year's crowd.
    II. The dancer will then perform a series of leg kicks, while at the same time operating the lion's mouth with his own hand and moving the ears and eyes by means of a string which is attached to the dancer's own mouth.
    III. The most difficult role of this dance belongs to the one who controls the lion's head; this person must lead all the other "parts" of the lion through the choreographed segments of the dance.
    IV. The head dancer begins with a complex series of steps. alternately stepping forward with the head raised, and then retreating a few steps while lowering the head, a movement that is intended to create the impression that the lion is keeping a watchful eye for anything evil.
    V. When performing a traditional Chinese New Year's lion dance, several performers must fit themselves inside a large lion costume and work together to enact different parts of the dance.

    The BEST order is:
    A. V, III, IV, II, I   B. III, IV, II, V, I   C. III, I, V, IV, II   D. IV, II, III, V, I

12.____

13. I. For many years the shell of the chambered nautilus was treasured in Europe for its beauty and intricacy, but collectors were unaware that they were in possession of the structure that marked a "missing link" in the evolution of marine mollusks.
    II. The nautilus, however, evolved a series of enclosed chambers in its shell, and invented a new use for the structure: the shell began to serve as a buoyancy device.
    III. Equipped with this new flotation device, the nautilus did not need the single, muscular foot of its predecessors, but instead developed flaps, tentacles, and a gentle form of jet propulsion that transformed it into the first mollusk able to take command of its own density and explore a three-dimensional world.
    IV. By pumping and adjusting air pressure into the chambers, the nautilus could spend the day resting on the bottom, and then rise toward the surface at night in search of food.
    V. The nautilus shell looks like a large snail shell, similar to those of its ancestors, who used their shells as protective coverings while they were anchored to the sea floor.
    The BEST order is:
    A. V, II, IV, I, III   B. V, I, II, III, IV   C. I, II, V, III, IV   D. I, V, II, IV, III

13._____

14. I. While France and England battled for control of the region, the Acadiens prospered on the fertile farmland, which was finally secured by England in 1713.
    II. Early in the 17th century, settlers from Western France founded a colony called Acadie in what is now the Canadian province of Nova Scotia.
    III. At this time, English officials feared the presence of spies among the Acadiens who might be loyal to their French homeland, and the Acadiens were deported to spots along the Atlantic and Caribbean shores of America.
    IV. The French settlers remained on this land, under English rule, for around forty years, until the beginning of the French and Indian War, another conflict between France and England.
    V. As the Acadien refugees drifted toward a final home in Southern Louisiana, neighbors shortened their name to "Cadien," and finally "Cajun," the name which the descendants of early Acadiens still call themselves.
    The BEST order is:
    A. I, IV, II, III, V   B. II, I, III, V, IV   C. II, I, IV, III, V   D. V, II, III, IV, I

14._____

15. I. Traditional households in the Eastern and Western regions of Africa serve two meals a day—one at around noon, and the other in the evening.
    II. The starch is then used in the way that Americans might use a spoon, to scoop up a portion of the main dish on the person's plate.
    III. The reason for the starch's inclusion in every meal has to do with taste as well as nutrition; African food can be very spicy, and the starch is known to cool the burning effect of the main dish.
    IV. When serving these meals, the main dish is usually served on individual plates, and the starch is served on a communal plate, from which diners break off a piece of bread or scoop rice or fufu in their fingers.

15._____

V. The typical meals usually consist of a thick stew or soup as the main course, and an accompanying starch—either bread, rice, or *fufu*, a starchy grain paste similar in consistency to mashed potatoes.

The BEST order is:

A. V, II, III, IV, I B. V, I, IV, III, II C. I, IV, V, III, II D. I, V, IV, II, III

16.
   I. In the early days of the American Midwest, Indiana settlers sometimes came together to hold an event called an apple peeling, where neighboring settlers gathered at the homestead of a host family to help prepare the hosts' apple crop for cooking, canning, and making apple butter.
   II. At the beginning of the event, each peeler sat down in front of a ten- or twenty-gallon stone jar and was given a crock of apples and a paring knife.
   III. Once a peeler had finished with a crock, another was placed next to him; if the peeler was an unmarried man, he kept a strict count of the number of apples he had peeled, because the winner was allowed to kiss the girl of his choice.
   IV. The peeling usually ended by 9:30 in the evening, when the neighbors gathered in the host family's parlor for a dance social.
   V. The apples were peeled, cored, and quartered, and then placed into the jar.

   The BEST order is:

   A. I, V, III, IV, II B. II, V, III, IV, I C. I, II, V, III, IV D. II, I, V, IV, III

16._____

17.
   I. If your pet turtle is a land turtle and is native to temperate climates, it will stop eating some time in October, which should be your cue to prepare the turtle for hibernation.
   II. The box should then be covered with a wire screen, which will protect the turtle from any rodents or predators that might want to take advantage of a motionless and helpless animal.
   III. When your turtle hasn't eaten for a while and appears ready to hibernate, it should be moved to its winter quarters, most likely a cellar or garage, where the temperature should range between 40° and 45°F.
   IV. Instead of feeding the turtle, you should bathe it every day in warm water, to encourage the turtle to empty its intestines in preparation for its long winter sleep.
   V. Here the turtle should be placed in a well-ventilated box whose bottom is covered with a moisture-absorbing layer of clay beads, and then filled three-fourths full with almost dry peat moss or wood chips, into which the turtle will burrow and sleep for several months.

   The BEST order is:

   A. I, IV, III, V, II B. III, IV, II, V, I C. III, II, IV, I, V D. IV, V, II, III, I

17._____

18.
   I. Once he has reached the nest, the hunter uses two sturdy bamboo poles like huge chopsticks to pull the next away from the mountainside, into a large basket that will be lowered to people waiting below.
   II. The world's largest honeybees colonize the Nealese mountainsides, building honeycombs as large as a person on sheer rock faces that are often hundreds of feet high.

18._____

III. In the remote mountain country of Nepal, a small band of "honey hunters" carry out a tradition so ancient that 10,000 year-old drawings of the practice have been found in the caves of Nepal.
IV. To harvest the honey and beeswax from these combs, a honey hunter climbs above the nests, lowers a long bamboo-fiber ladder over the cliff, and then climbs down.
V. Throughout this dangerous practice, the hunter is stung repeatedly, and only the veterans, with skin that has been toughened over the years, are able to return from a hunt without the painful swelling caused by stings.

The BEST order is:
  A. II, IV, III, V, I   B. II, IV, I, V, III   C. V, III, II, IV, I   D. III, II, IV, I, V

19. I. After the Romans left Britain, there were relentless attacks on the islands from the barbarian tribes of northern Germany—the Angles, Saxons, and Jutes.
II. As the empire weakened, Roman soldiers withdrew from Britain, leaving behind a country that continued to practice the Christian religion that had been introduced by the Romans.
III. Early Latin writings tell of a Christian warrior named Arturius (Arthur, in English) who led the British citizens to defeat these barbarian invades, and brought an extended period of peace to the lands of Britain.
IV. Long ago, the British Isles were part of the far-flung Roman Empire that extended across most of Europe and into Africa and Asia.
V. The romantic legend of King Arthur and his knights of the Round Table, one of the most popular and widespread stories of all time, appears to have some foundation in history.

The BEST order is:
  A. V, IV, III, II, I   B. V, IV, II, I, III   C. IV, V, II, III, I   D. IV, III, II, I, V

19.____

20. I. The cylinder was allowed to cool until it could stand on its own, and then it was cut from the tube and split down the side with a single straight cut.
II. Nineteenth-century glassmakers, who had not yet discovered the glazier's modern techniques for making panes of glass, had to create a method for converting their blown gas into flat sheets.
III. The bubble was then pierced at the end to make a hole that opened up while the glassmaker gently spun it, creating a cylinder of glass.
IV. Turned on its side and laid on a conveyor belt, the cylinder was strengthened, or tempered, by being heated again and cooled very slowly, eventually flattening out into a single rectangular of glass.
V. To do this, the glassmaker dipped the end of a long tube into melted glass and blew into the other end of the tube, creating an expanding bubble of glass.

The BEST order is:
  A. II, V, III, IV, I   B. II, IV, V, III, I   C. III, V, II, IV, I   D. III, I, IV, V, II

20.____

21. I. The splints are almost always hidden, but horses are occasionally born whose splinted toes project from the leg on either side, just above the hoof.
    II. The second and fourth toes remained, but shrank to thin splints of bone that fused invisibly to the horse's leg bone.
    III. Horses are unique among mammals, having evolved feet that each end in what is essentially a single toe, capped by a large, sturdy hoof.
    IV. Julius Caesar, an emperor of ancient Rome, was said to have owned one of these three-toed horses, and considered it so special that he would not permit anyone else to ride it.
    V. Though the horse's earlier ancestors possessed the traditional mammalian set of five toes on each foot, the horse has retained only its third toe; its first and fifth toes disappeared completely as the horse evolved.
    The BEST order is:
    A. III, V, II, I, IV   B. V, III, II, IV, I   C. III, II, V, I, IV   D. V, II, III, I, IV

21._____

22. I. The new building materials—some of which are twenty feet long, and weigh nearly six tons—were transported to Pohnpei on rafts, and were brought into their present position by using hibiscus fiber ropes and leverage to move the stone columns upward along the inclined trunks of coconut palm trees.
    II. The ancestors built great fires to heat the stone, and then poured cool seawater on the columns, which caused the stone to contract and split along natural fracture lines.
    III. The now-abandoned enclave of Nan Madol, a group of 92 man-made islands off the shore of the Micronesian island of Pohnpei, is estimated to have been built around the year 500 A.D.
    IV. The islanders say their ancestors quarried stone columns from a nearby island, where large basalt columns were formed by the cooling of molten lava.
    V. The structures of Nan Madol are remarkable for the sheer size of some of the stone "longs" or columns that were used to create the walls of the offshore community, and today anthropologists can only rely on the information of existing local people for clues about how Nan Madol was built.
    The BEST order is:
    A. V, IV, III, II, I   B. V, III, I, IV, II   C. III, V, IV, II, I   D. III, I, IV, II, V

22._____

23. I. One of the most easily manipulated substances on earth, glass can be made into ceramic tiles that are composed of over 90% air.
    II. NASA's space shuttles are the first spacecraft ever designed to leave and re-enter the earth's atmosphere while remaining intact.
    III. These ceramic tiles are such effective insulators that when a tile emerges from the oven in which it was fired, it can be held safely in a person's hand by the edges while its interior still glows at a temperature well over 2000°F.
    IV. Eventually, the engineers were led to a material that is as old as our most ancient civilization.
    V. Because the temperature during atmospheric re-entry is so incredibly hot, it took NASA's engineers some time to find a substance capable of protecting the shuttles.

22._____

The BEST order is:
A. V, II, I, II, IV   B. II, V, IV, I, III   C. II, III, I, IV, V   D. V, IV, III, I, II

24. I. The secret to teaching any parakeet to talk is patience, and the understanding that when a bird talks," it is simply imitating what it hears, rather than putting ideas into words.
    II. You should stay just out of sight of the bird and repeat the phrase you want it to learn, for at least fifteen minutes every morning and evening.
    III. It is important to leave the bird without any words of encouragement or farewell; otherwise it might combine stray remarks or phrases, such as "Good night," with the phrase you are trying to teach it.
    IV. For this reason, to train your bird to imitate your words you should keep it free of any distractions, especially other noises, while you are giving it "lesson."
    V. After your repetition, you should quietly leave the bird alone for a while, to think over what it has just heard.
    The BEST order is:
    A. I, IV, II, V, III   B. I, II, IV, III, V   C. III, II, I, V, IV   D. III, I, V, IV, II

25. I. As a school approaches, fishermen from neighboring communities join their fishing boats together as a fleet, and string their gill nets together to make a huge fence that is held up by cork floats.
    II. At a signal from the party leaders, or *nakura*, the family members pound the sides of the boats or beat the water with long poles, creating a sudden and deafening noise.
    III. The fishermen work together to drag the trap into a half-circle that may reach 300 yards in diameter, and then the families move their boats to form the other half of the circle around the school of fish.
    IV. The school of fish flee from the commotion into the awaiting trap, where a final wall of net is thrown over the open end of the half-circle, securing the day's haul.
    V. Indonesian people from the area around the Sulu islands live on the sea, in floating villages made of lashed-together or stilted homes, and make much of their living by fishing their home waters for migrating schools of snapper, scad, and other fish.
    The BEST order is:
    A. I, V, III, IV, II   B. I, II, IV, III, V   C. V, I, II, III, IV   D. V, I, III, II, IV

KEY (CORRECT ANSWERS)

1.	D	11.	C
2.	D	12.	A
3.	B	13.	D
4.	A	14.	C
5.	C	15.	D
6.	C	16.	C
7.	D	17.	A
8.	D	18.	D
9.	A	19.	B
10.	B	20.	A
21.	A		
22.	C		
23.	B		
24.	A		
25.	D		

PREPARING WRITTEN MATERIAL
EXAMINATION SECTION
TEST 1

DIRECTIONS: Each short paragraph below is followed by four restatements or summaries of the information contained within it. Select the one that most completely and accurately states the information or opinion given in the paragraph. *PRINT THE LETTER OF THE CORRECT ANSWER IN THE SPACE AT THE RIGHT.*

1. Australia's koalas live solely on a diet of the leaves of the eucalyptus tree, a low-protein food that requires a koala to eat about three or four pounds of leaves a day. For most mammals, these strong-smelling leaves, saturated with toxins such as phenols and the oily compound known as cineole, are among the least digestible foods on the planet. However, the koala is equipped with a digestive system that is able to handle these toxins, trapping the tiniest leaf particles for as much as eight days while the sugars, proteins, and fats are extracted. 1.____
    A. Because eucalyptus leaves contain a large amount of toxins and oils, it takes a long time for koalas to digest them.
    B. Koalas have to eat three or four pounds of eucalyptus leaves a day, because the leaves are so poor in nutrients.
    C. Koalas have a unique digestive system that allows them to exist solely on a diet of eucalyptus leaves, which are generally toxic and inedible.
    D. The digestive system of the koala illustrates the unique evolutionary palette of the Australian continent.

2. Norway's special geopolitical position—it was the only NATO country to share a border with Russia—drove it to adopt much more cautious policies than other European countries during the Cold War. Its decision to join NATO led to strong protests from Russia, and in order to avoid provocation, Norway's foreign policy had to balance the need for ensuring defense capability with the need to keep tensions at the lowest possible level. Norway's low-tension "base policy" made clear the nation's refusal to allow foreign military forces on Norwegian territory as long as the country is not attacked or threatened with an attack. 2.____
    A. Norway's "base policy," in spite of its shared border with Russia, is the work of a pacifist nation that should serve as a model for foreign diplomacy everywhere.
    B. When Norway joined NATO, Russia feared a ground invasion over their shared border.
    C. The "base policy" of Norway is a perfect illustration on how much of Europe during the Cold War was a powder keg ready to explode at the slightest provocation.
    D. As the only member of the NATO alliance to border on Russia, Norway was forced to adopt a more conciliatory foreign policy than other members of the alliance.

3. During the women's suffrage movement of the early twentieth century, it was typical of many psychologists and anti-suffragists to automatically associate feminism with mental illness. In 1918, H.W. Frink wrote of feminists: "A certain proportion of at least the most militant suffragists are neurotics who in some instances are compensating for masculine trends, in others, are more or less successfully sublimating sadistic and homosexual ones." In the United States, anti-suffragists, finding comfort in psychology, concluded that suffragists all bordered hysteria and, thus, their arguments could not be taken seriously,

3.____

   A. The relationship between suffragism and feminism led many scientists to conclude that suffragists were afflicted with some kinds of mental illness.
   B. During the women's suffrage movement, anti-suffragists such as H.W. Frink tended to label women who fought for voting rights as mentally ill in order to dismiss their arguments.
   C. Responses to the women's suffrage movement are indicative of the tendency to label those who challenge the status quo as "Crazy" than to comfort their arguments.
   D. Most of the women who fought for suffrage during the early twentieth century were feminists who were mentally ill.

4. All of the earth's early plant life lived in the ocean, and most of these plants were concentrated in the shallow coastal waters, where the sun's energy could be easily absorbed. Because of the constant advance and retreat of tides in these regions, the plants—mostly algae—were repeatedly exposed to the atmosphere, and were forced to adapt to life out of water. It took millions of years before plant species had evolved that could survive out of the sea altogether, with stems that drew water from the ground, and a waxy covering to keep them from drying in the sun.

4.____

   A. After spending millions of years underwater, the earth's plants finally evolved ways of surviving on land.
   B. Most algaes today, because of evolutionary advances, are able to survive for extended periods of time out of water.
   C. Despite the fact that plants began as purely underwater organisms, they have always needed the sun's energy to survive.
   D. Land plants evolved from sea plants after millions of years in response to the gradual warming of the earth's atmosphere.

5. Because of the unique convergence of mild temperature and abundant rain (17 feet a year), British Columbia's temperate coastal rainforest is the most biologically productive ecosystem on earth. It's also an increasingly rare and vulnerable ecosystem: in its Holocene heyday, it covered only 0.2 percent of the earth's land surface. Today, logging and other development have consumed more than half this original range.

5.____

   A. The uniquely productive ecosystem of British Columbia's coastal rainforest has always been small, and has been reduced by human activity.
   B. Despite the fact that it is the most biologically productive ecosystem on earth, the coastal rainforest of British Columbia has been largely ignored by environmental activists.

C. The coastal rainforests of British Columbia have been nearly devastated by logging and other development.
D. British Columbia's coastal rainforest originated during the Holocene Era, but has declined steadily ever since.

6. The Roman Empire, which ruled much of the Western world for hundreds of years, was led by an aristocratic class famous for its tendency to drink large amounts of wine. Recently, an American medical researcher theorized that this taste for wine was eventually what caused the decline and fall of the empire—not the drinking of the wine itself, but a gradual poisoning from the lead that was used to line and seal Roman wine casks. The researcher, Dr. S.C. Gilfillan, argues that this lead poisoning specifically affected members of the Empire's ruling class, because they were the Romans most likely to consume wine and other products, like preserved fruits, that were stored in lead-lined jars.

6.____

A. The Roman aristocracy's taste for wine and dried fruits, according to one researcher, is a cautionary tale about the consequences of overindulgence.
B. While the Roman Empire's ruling class suffered from widespread lead poisoning, most commoners remained in good health throughout the empire.
C. One of the most far-fetched theories about the fall of the Roman Empire concerns itself with the lead used to line the wine casks and fruit jars of the ruling class.
D. An American medical researcher has theorized that the fall of the Roman Empire was caused by slow poisoning from the lead used to line and seal Roman wine casks and fruit jars.

7. In the second century B.C., King Hiero of Syracuse called upon the renowned scientist, Archimedes, to find a way to see if his crown was made of pure gold or a combination of metals. Archimedes came upon the solution some time later, as he was entering a tub full of hot water and noticed that the weight of his body displaced a certain amount of water. Realizing that this same principle could be used on the crown, he forgot himself with excitement, jumping out of the tub and running naked through the town, yelling "Eureka! Eureka!"

7.____

A. Archimedes, in making his famous discovery, unknowingly contributed the word "Eureka!" to the English vocabulary.
B. The relative purity of gold can be determined by the amount of water it displaces when submerged.
C. Archimedes, after discovering the solution to a scientific problem while stepping into his tub, became so excited that he ran through the town naked.
D. The word "Eureka" has become a part of the English language because of an interesting story involving the ancient scientist, Archimedes.

8. In the nineteenth century most Americans had never heard of, let alone tasted, an abalone, the marine mollusk considered to be a delicacy by many Asians, and undisturbed abalone populations thrived all along the west coast. When the California Gold Rush of the 1840s and 1850s brought thousands of Asian

8.____

immigrants to America, many of these people began to harvest the dense beds of abalone that inhabited the state's intertidal zone. The Asian harvests eventually brought in annual catches of over 4 million pounds of abalone, and as a result, some county governments passed ordinances making it illegal to dive for abalone in waters less than twenty feet deep.
  A. The Asians who immigrated to California during the Gold Rush harvested so much abalone from intertidal waters that some governments were compelled to limit abalone diving.
  B. Abalone diving was unheard of in California before the Gold Rush, when many Asians immigrated to the state and began to harvest abalone from the intertidal zone.
  C. The extreme shortage of abalone in California's intertidal waters can be traced to the Asians who immigrated during the Gold Rush.
  D. The abalone of California's coastal waters generally live in waters less than twenty feet deep, where they are not protected by most county governments.

9. Maria Tallchief, the daughter of a full-blood Osage Indian from Oklahoma, was America's first internationally celebrated prima ballerina, rising to stardom at a time when classical American ballet was still struggling to gain international acceptance and acclaim. Her innovative interpretations of such classics as "Swan Lake" and "The Nutcracker" helped convince critics worldwide that American ballet was a force to be reckoned with, and her glamorous beauty helped popularize ballet in America at a time when very few people took it seriously.
  A. As ballet grew more popular in America, Maria Tallchief became a phenomenon in Europe, helping to secure a worldwide reputation for excellence for American ballet.
  B. Nobody in America took ballet seriously until the beautiful Maria Tallchief became an international star.
  C. With her beauty and technical innovations, Maria Tallchief gained unprecedented critical and popular success for American ballet.
  D. Before the success of Maria Tallchief, there were not many ballet dancers in the United States worth noticing.

10. Early in the Constitutional Convention of 1787, the idea of a two-tiered legislature was agreed upon by the framers of the Constitution. The final form of each of the resulting houses, however, was an issue that was debated openly, and which was finally resolved by the "great compromise" of the Constitutional Convention. While the House of Representatives was intended to be a large, politically sensitive body, the Senate was designed to be a moderating influence that would check the powers of the House.
  A. The framers of the Constitution could not agree on whether the nation's legislature should be bicameral, or two-tiered, at first, but after the "great compromise," they devised a House and Senate.
  B. The Constitutional Convention of 1787 ended with the "great compromise" that gave the nation its two-tiered legislature.

C. After much behind-the-scenes dealmaking, the two-tiered legislature of the United States was devised by the framers of the Constitution.
D. The framers of the Constitution, after some debate, decided on a two-tiered legislature made up of a House of Representatives and a Senate that was less susceptible to regional politics.

11. Although scientists have succeeded in creating robots able to process huge amounts of information, they are still struggling to create one whose reasoning ability matches that of a human baby. The main challenge facing these scientists is the difficulty of understanding and imitating the complex process of human perception and reasoning, which involve the ability to register and analyze even the smallest changes in the external environment, and then to act on those changes.   11.____
    A. Even the most sophisticated robot is unable to imitate innate human abilities such as learning to walk, converse, or perceive depth.
    B. Because of their inability to process large amounts of information, robots have yet to achieve even the most fundamental level of reasoning.
    C. Despite considerable technological advances, scientists have as yet been unable to produce a robot that can respond intelligently to changes in its environment.
    D. Because robots cannot automatically filter out all extraneous information and focus on the most important details of a given situation, they are unable to reason as well as humans.

12. Thor Heyerdahl, a Norwegian anthropologist, had long held the opinion that the Polynesian inhabitants of South Pacific islands such as Samoa, Tonga, and Fiji had actually been migrants from South America. To prove that this was possible, in 1947 Heyerdahl made a crude raft out of balsa wood, which he named after an Incan sun god, *Kon-Tiki*, and sailed from the coast of Peru to the islands east of Tahiti.   12.____
    A. Thor Heyerdahl's 1947 voyage on the *Kon-Tiki* proved that Polynesians probably had common ancestors in South America.
    B. While Thor Heyerdahl's *Kon-Tiki* voyage suggested a South American origin for Polynesians, most experts today believe the great migrations were launched from somewhere near Indonesia.
    C. To support the idea that Polynesians could have sailed from South America to the Pacific Islands, Thor Heyerdahl sailed the *Kon-Tiki* from Peru to Tahiti in 1947.
    D. Thor Heyerdahl's famous raft, the *Kon-Tiki*, was named for an Incan sun god, and was so well-made that it made it from Peru to Tahiti.

13. During the Age of Exploration, after thousands of miles of open sea, ships entered the bays of the Azore Islands, west of Portugal, with tattered sails, battered hulls, crewmen weakened from scurvy, and cargo holds laden with the treasure they had gained on their long trading journeys. Spanish, English, and Dutch warships prowled the waters around the Azores to protect this treasure, sometimes even sinking their own ships to keep it from falling into enemy   13.____

hands. During these fierce battles, many ships filled with treasure were sent to the ocean floor, where they still remain, preserved by the cold saltwater and centuries of rest.
- A. Although they are now sparsely populated, the Azore Islands were once a resting place for every ship returning from a long journey to the Americas.
- B. Many treasure hunters and archaeologists believe the sea floor around the Azores, a group of islands west of Portugal, still harbors some of the richest sunken treasure in the world.
- C. Economic competition between the European powers was so intense during the Age of Exploration that captains would rather sink their own ships rather than let their treasure fall into enemy hands.
- D. The rich history of the Azore Islands has deposited a large amount of sunken treasure in their surrounding waters.

14. The Whigs, a short-lived American political party, were wary of a domineering president, and many of them believed that the legislative branch should govern the nation. In particular, Whig leader Henry Clay often attempted to bully and belittle President John Tyler into submission. Tyler's resistance to Clay's high-handed tactics strengthened the office of the presidency, and in particular gave greater credibility to all later vice presidents who happened to succeed to the office.
    - A. While U.S. politics was at first dominated by the legislature, President John Tyler shifted the center of power to the presidency, while laying the groundwork for the downfall of the Whig Party.
    - B. President John Tyler, a failure by almost any other measure, can at least be credited with contributing to the strength of the presidency.
    - C. Henry Clay, who believed in a strong legislature, failed to win much influence over presidents who were not from the Whig Party.
    - D. President John Tyler, in resisting Henry Clay's bullying tactics, strengthened the U.S. presidency and lent credibility to the authority of vice presidential successors to the presidency.

14.____

15. By far the richest city on earth, Tokyo, Japan is also one of the most over-crowded; most of its people are only able to afford living in extremely small houses and apartments. In addition to cramped housing, Tokyo's overpopulation has created a commuter problem so grim that a corps of "pushers" has been hired by the city, to stand outside crowded commuter trains and help pack people inside. Problems such as these are so severe in Tokyo that there has been serious talk in recent years of moving Japan's capital elsewhere.
    - A. Despite the example of Tokyo, there is no evidence to suggest that economic wealth and overpopulation are related variables.
    - B. Tokyo's prosperity has led to such overcrowding that the country of Japan has recently begun to consider moving its capital to another location.
    - C. Despite being the richest city on earth, Tokyo, Japan is seriously overcrowded.
    - D. The small houses and apartments in Tokyo, along with its overcrowded transit system, are a perfect example of how economic wealth does not always improve a society's quality of life.

15.____

16. One of the greatest, and least publicized, legacies of Native American culture has been the worldwide cultivation of food staples through careful farming methods. Over centuries, tribes throughout North and South America domesticated the wild plants that have come to produce over half of the vegetables the world eats today. Corn, or maize, was first cultivated in the Mexican highlands almost seven thousand years ago, from a common wild grass called teosinte, and both potatoes and tomatoes were originally domesticated by the Peruvian Incas from native plants that still grow throughout Peru and Bolivia.

    A. Explorers of the Americas carried many native vegetables back to Europe, where they continued to adapt and flourish over the centuries.
    B. Today's common corn is a descendent of the wild Mexican teosinte plant, and potatoes and tomatoes were originally grown by the Incas.
    C. Without the agricultural knowledge and skill of early Native Americans, much of the world today would be in danger of famine.
    D. Foods that are today grown and eaten almost worldwide, such as corn, tomatoes, and potatoes, were first cultivated by the natives of North and South Americas.

16._____

17. America's transportation sector—95 percent of it driven by oil—consumes two-thirds of the petroleum used in the United States. With the 400 million cars now on the world's roads expected to grow to 1 billion by the year 2020, oil-foreign or not and other finite fossil-fuel resources will some day be conversation pieces for the nostalgic, rather than components of the nation's energy mix.

    A. In the future, most motor vehicles in the United States will be powered by an alternative energy source such as hydrogen or solar power.
    B. The continued growth of the oil-dependent transportation sector is outpacing the capacity of fossil-fuel energy resources.
    C. Our nation's dependence on foreign oil is a serious vulnerability that can only be corrected by increased domestic production.
    D. In the future, 1 billion cars across the world will be competing for oil and gasoline.

17._____

18. Althea Gibson, the first African-American to win the Wimbledon Tennis Championship, began her career by riding the subway out of her neighborhood in Harlem to 143rd Street, where she played paddle tennis against anyone who dared to challenge her. Since the Wimbledon tournament was played on grass, Gibson knew she would have to prepare herself by training on a surface that returned balls as quickly as a grass court. She found the solution to this problem in the gyms of Harlem, whose wood floors allowed her to perfect the rapid volley that helped her win two Wimbledon championships.

    A. Althea Gibson's tennis skills, including her famous volley, were developed in and around the inner-city neighborhood of Harlem.
    B. Althea Gibson had to leave her neighborhood to learn tennis, but to perfect her game, she had to return home to Harlem.
    C. Without the wood floors in the gyms of her Harlem neighborhood, Althea Gibson probably wouldn't have developed a volley that would help her win two Wimbledon tennis championships.

18._____

8 (#1)

D. Although Althea Gibson achieved international fame as the first African-American to win the Wimbledon Tennis Championship, the path she followed to that championship was as unorthodox as the champion herself.

19. The greenhouse effect is a naturally occurring process that aids in heating the Earth's surface and atmosphere. It results from the fact that certain atmospheric gases, such as carbon dioxide, water vapor, and methane, are able to change the energy balance of the planet by being able to absorb longwave radiation from the Earth's surface. Without the greenhouse effect, life on this planet would probably not exist, as the average temperature of the Earth would be a chilly 5 degrees, rather than the present 59 degrees.   19.____
    A. The naturally-occurring greenhouse effect, by which atmospheric air is warmed, enables life to exist on earth.
    B. The greenhouse effect is a completely natural phenomenon that has nothing to do with human activity, and in fact it is beneficial to the planet's ecosystems.
    C. Human contributions to the increases in the greenhouse effect threaten life on Earth.
    D. In order for life to exist on Earth there must be some kind of greenhouse effect.

20. The religious and scientific communities have for centuries been at odds with each other, and held opposing viewpoints concerning the origin and nature of life. Progressive thinkers from both groups, however, claim that the two communities, in their ways of seeking answers to humanity's most important questions, share a common set of goals and procedures that would benefit greatly from a cooperative effort.   20.____
    A. Scientists and theologians will probably never agree on the origin and nature of life, though some progressive thinkers are trying to change the way the two communities talk about these issues.
    B. Though most scientists do not believe in God, progressive religious thinkers are continually trying to persuade them otherwise.
    C. Progressive religious and scientific thinkers have identified shared goals and questions that the two communities can work together to achieve and solve.
    D. Religious thinkers, who usually scorn such scientific theories as evolution, have begun to acknowledge the usefulness of science in answering important questions.

21. The administrations of Presidents Richard Nixon and Jimmy Carter oversaw an Export-Import Bank that was increasingly active in trade promotion, with expanding programs and lending authority. During this period, expenditures for program activities expanded to five times their 1969 rate, but the bank's net income dropped sharply—the low interest rates at which the bank financed its loan programs were lowering its profits.   21.____
    A. During the Nixon and Carter administrations, the budget of the Export-Import Bank grew to five times its 1969 expenditures.

9 (#1)

  B. Though the Export-Import Bank was very active during the Nixon and Carter administrations, its profits were reduced by its low interest rates.
  C. Both the Nixon and Carter administrations demonstrated a lack of fiscal discipline that led to a declining net income at the Export-Import Bank.
  D. Presidents Nixon and Carter both favored an activist Export-Import Bank, but while Nixon emphasized the function of trade promotion, Carter was more focused on making loans.

22. The Kombai and Korawai tribes of eastern Indonesia are known as the "tree people" for their custom of living in large tree houses, built as high as 150 feet above ground to avoid attacks from their enemies. These houses are built mostly from the fronds of the sago palm, a plant that also serves to produce one of the tree people's primary food sources—the larvae, or grub, of the scarab beetle. The tree people cultivate grubs by cutting a stretch of sago forest and then, after splitting and tying the palms together, leaving the palms to rot.   22.____
    A. The food-gathering methods of the Kombai and Korawai illustrate that deforestation is not a contemporary problem.
    B. The Kombai and Korawai people of eastern Indonesia relay on the sago palm for both food and housing.
    C. The Kombai and Korawai fears of enemy attacks have led them to build their trees high in the forest canopy
    D. Among the world's least-tamed native cultures are the Kombai and Korawai of Irian Jaya, the easternmost region of Indonesia.

23. It's no secret that corporate and federal information networks continue to deal with increasing bandwidth needs. The appetite for data—whether it's for internet access, file delivery, or the integration of digital voice applications—isn't likely to level off any time soon, and most information technology professionals allow that there is cause for concern. But emerging technologies for increasing raw bandwidth, accompanied by the streaming and maturing of transfer and switching protocols, are a good bet to accommodate the hunger for bandwidth, at least into the near future.   23.____
    A. There are two ways to decrease the demand for more bandwidth over computer networks: either increase the "raw" amount of bandwidth over an infrastructure, or devise more efficient transfer and switching protocols.
    B. Emerging technologies, aimed at the constantly increasing demand for bandwidth, are some day likely to result in virtually unlimited bandwidth for computer networks.
    C. Many different applications contribute to the demand for bandwidth over a computer network, and so the technologies that are devised to meet this demand must be many-faceted.
    D. While there is always a need for more bandwidth on large computer networks, newer technologies promise to increase the supply in the near term.

24. In the year 805, a Japanese Buddhist monk named Dengyo Daishi returned from his studies in China with some tea seeds, which he planted on a Japanese mountainside. In China, tea had long been the favorite drink of monks, because it helped them stay awake and attentive during their long periods of meditation, and Dengyo Daishi wanted to bring this practice to Japan. Over the centuries, tea-drinking would prove to be a custom that would influence nearly every aspect of Japanese culture, and Dengyo Daishi has long been considered a sort of saint among the Japanese.

24.____

   A. Because of the cultural similarities between China and Japan, it was only a matter of time before the ritual of tea-drinking made its way from the mainland to the island empire.
   B. Dengo Daishi, the first person to plant tea seeds in Japan, is revered among today's Japanese.
   C. The Japanese tea-drinking custom was begun in 805 by a Buddhist monk who brought tea seeds from China.
   D. Without the shared cultural traditions of Buddhism, it is unlikely that tea ever would have been imported from China to Japan.

25. Aztec women held a position in society that was far more respected than that of women in most Western civilizations of the time. For example, an Aztec wife was free to divorce a man who failed to provide for their children, or who was physically abusive, and once divorced, a woman was free to remarry whomever she chose. Perhaps the unusually high regard for Aztec women is best illustrated by the traditional Aztec religious belief that a special, elevated status in the afterlife was reserved for only two types of Aztec citizens-warriors who had died defending their tribe, and woman who had died during childbirth.

25.____

   A. The rights and privileges of Aztec women demonstrate that they were more respected by their societies than women of many cultures of the time.
   B. In the Aztec culture, women had the same rights and status as the most exalted men.
   C. Though the rights of Aztec women were still generally inferior to those of men, most Aztec women were granted a high degree of independence due to their service to the community.
   D. The relatively high position that Aztec women held in their society reveals the Aztec culture to be well ahead of its time.

KEY (CORRECT ANSWERS)

1.	C	11.	C
2.	D	12.	C
3.	B	13.	D
4.	A	14.	D
5.	A	15.	B
6.	D	16.	D
7.	C	17.	B
8.	A	18.	A
9.	C	19.	A
10.	D	20.	C

21. B
22. B
23. D
24. C
25. A

HERE'S TO YOUR HEALTH
HEALTHY PEOPLE 2010

Contents

Introduction 1

A Systematic Approach to Health Improvement 7
    Healthy People 2010 Goals 8
    Objectives 17
    Determinants of Health 18
    Health Status 21

Leading Health Indicators 24
    Physical Activity 26
    Overweight and Obesity 28
    Tobacco Use 30
    Substance Abuse 32
    Responsible Sexual Behavior 34
    Mental Health 36
    Injury and Violence 38
    Environmental Quality 40
    Immunization 42
    Access to Health Care 44

Appendix:
    Short Titles for Healthy People 2010 Objectives

Introduction

Healthy People 2010 presents a comprehensive, nationwide health promotion and disease prevention agenda. It is designed to serve as a roadmap for improving the health of all people in the United States during the first decade of the 21st century.

Like the preceding Healthy People 2000 initiative—which was driven by an ambitious, yet achievable, 10-year strategy for improving the Nation's health by the end of the 20th century—Healthy People 2010 is committed to a single, overarching purpose: promoting health and preventing illness, disability, and premature death.

The History Behind the Healthy People 2010 Initiative

Healthy People 2010 builds on initiatives pursued over the past two decades. In 1979, *Healthy People: The Surgeon General's Report on Health Promotion and Disease Prevention* provided national goals for reducing premature deaths and preserving independence for older adults. In 1980, another report, *Promoting Health/Preventing Disease: Objectives for the Nation*, set forth 226 targeted health objectives for the Nation to achieve over the next 10 years.

Healthy People 2000: National Health Promotion and Disease Prevention Objectives, released in 1990, identified health improvement goals and objectives to be reached by the year 2000. The Healthy People 2010 initiative continues in this tradition as an instrument to improve health for the first decade of the 21st century.

> **Healthy People 2010 is grounded in science, built through public consensus, and designed to measure progress.**

The Development of Healthy People 2010 Goals and Objectives

Healthy People 2010 represents the ideas and expertise of a diverse range of individuals and organizations concerned about the Nation's health. The Healthy People Consortium—an alliance of more than 350 national organizations and 250 State public health, mental health, substance abuse, and environmental agencies—conducted three national meetings on the development of Healthy People 2010. In addition, many individuals and organizations gave testimony about health priorities at five Healthy People 2010 regional meetings held in late 1998.

On two occasions—in 1997 and in 1998—the American public was given the opportunity to share its thoughts and ideas. More than 11,000 comments on draft materials were received by mail or via the Internet from individuals in every State, the District of Columbia, and Puerto Rico. All the comments received during the development of Healthy People 2010 can be viewed on the Healthy People Web site: http://www.health.gov/healthypeople/.

The final Healthy People 2010 objectives were developed by teams of experts from a variety of Federal agencies under the direction of Health and Human Services Secretary Donna Shalala, Assistant Secretary for Health and Surgeon General David Satcher, and former Assistant Secretaries for Health. The process was coordinated by the Office of Disease Prevention and Health Promotion, U.S. Department of Health and Human Services.

The Goals of Healthy People 2010

Healthy People 2010 is designed to achieve two overarching goals:

- Increase quality and years of healthy life.
- Eliminate health disparities.

These two goals are supported by specific objectives in 28 focus areas (see page 17). Each objective was developed with a target to be achieved by the year 2010. A full explanation of the two goals can be found in the next section of this document: "A Systematic Approach to Health Improvement."

The Relationship Between Individual and Community Health

Over the years, it has become clear that individual health is closely linked to community health—the health of the community and environment in which individuals live, work, and play. Likewise, community health is profoundly affected by the collective beliefs, attitudes, and behaviors of everyone who lives in the community.

Indeed, the underlying premise of Healthy People 2010 is that the health of the individual is almost inseparable from the health of the larger community and that the health of every community in every State and territory determines the overall health status of the Nation. That is why the vision for Healthy People 2010 is "Healthy People in Healthy Communities."

> **Community health is profoundly affected by the collective beliefs, attitudes, and behaviors of everyone who lives in the community.**

How Healthy People 2010 Will Improve the Nation's Health

One of the most compelling and encouraging lessons learned from the Healthy People 2000 initiative is that we, as a Nation, can make dramatic progress in improving the Nation's health in a relatively short period of time. For example, during the past decade, we achieved significant reductions in infant mortality. Childhood vaccinations are at the highest levels ever recorded in the United States. Fewer teenagers are becoming parents. Overall, alcohol, tobacco, and illicit drug use is leveling off. Death rates for coronary heart disease and stroke have declined. Significant advances have been made in the diagnosis and treatment of cancer and in reducing unintentional injuries.

But we still have a long way to go. Diabetes and other chronic conditions continue to present a serious obstacle to public health. Violence and abusive behavior continue to ravage homes and communities across the country. Mental disorders continue to go undiagnosed and untreated. Obesity in adults has increased 50 percent over the past two decades. Nearly 40 percent of adults engage in no leisure time physical activity. Smoking among adolescents has increased in the past decade. And HIV/AIDS remains a serious health problem, now disproportionately affecting women and communities of color.

Healthy People 2010 will be the guiding instrument for addressing these and emerging health issues, reversing unfavorable trends, and expanding past achievements in health.

The Key Role of Community Partnerships

Community partnerships, particularly when they reach out to nontraditional partners, can be among the most effective tools for improving health in communities.

For the past two decades, Healthy People has been used as a strategic management tool for the Federal Government, States, communities, and many other public- and private-sector partners. Virtually all States, the District of Columbia, and Guam have developed their own Healthy People plans modeled after the national plan. Most States have tailored the national objectives to their specific needs.

Partnerships are effective tools for improving health in communities.

Businesses; local governments; and civic, professional, and religious organizations also have been inspired by Healthy People to print immunization reminders, set up hotlines, change cafeteria menus, begin community recycling, establish worksite fitness programs, assess school health education curriculums, sponsor health fairs, and engage in myriad other activities.

Everyone Can Help Achieve the Healthy People 2010 Objectives

Addressing the challenge of health improvement is a shared responsibility that requires the active participation and leadership of the Federal Government, States, local governments, policymakers, health care providers, professionals, business executives, educators, community leaders, and the American public itself. Although administrative responsibility for the Healthy People 2010 initiative rests in the U.S. Department of Health and Human Services, representatives of all these diverse groups shared their experience, expertise, and ideas in developing the Healthy People 2010 goals and objectives.

Healthy People 2010, however, is just the beginning. The biggest challenges still stand before us, and we all have a role in building a healthier Nation.

Regardless of your age, gender, education level, income, race, ethnicity, cultural customs, language, religious beliefs, disability, sexual orientation, geographic location, or occupation, Healthy People 2010 is designed to be a valuable resource in determining how you can participate most effectively in improving the Nation's health. Perhaps you will recognize the need to be a more active participant in decisions affecting your own health or the health of your children or loved ones. Perhaps you will assume a leadership role in promoting healthier behaviors in your neighborhood or community. Or perhaps you will use your influence and social stature to advocate for and implement policies and programs that can improve dramatically the health of dozens, hundreds, thousands, or even millions of people.

Whatever your role, this document is designed to help you determine what *you* can do—in your home, community, business, or State—to help improve the Nation's health.

Other Information Is Available About Healthy People 2010

Healthy People 2010: Understanding and Improving Health is the first of three parts in the Healthy People 2010 series. The second part, *Healthy People 2010*, contains detailed descriptions of 467 objectives to improve health. These objectives are organized into 28 specific focus areas. The third part, *Tracking Healthy People 2010*, provides a comprehensive review of the statistical measures that will be used to evaluate progress.

Healthy People 2010 contains 467 objectives to improve health, organized into 28 focus areas.

Healthy People in Healthy Communities

A Systematic Approach to Health Improvement

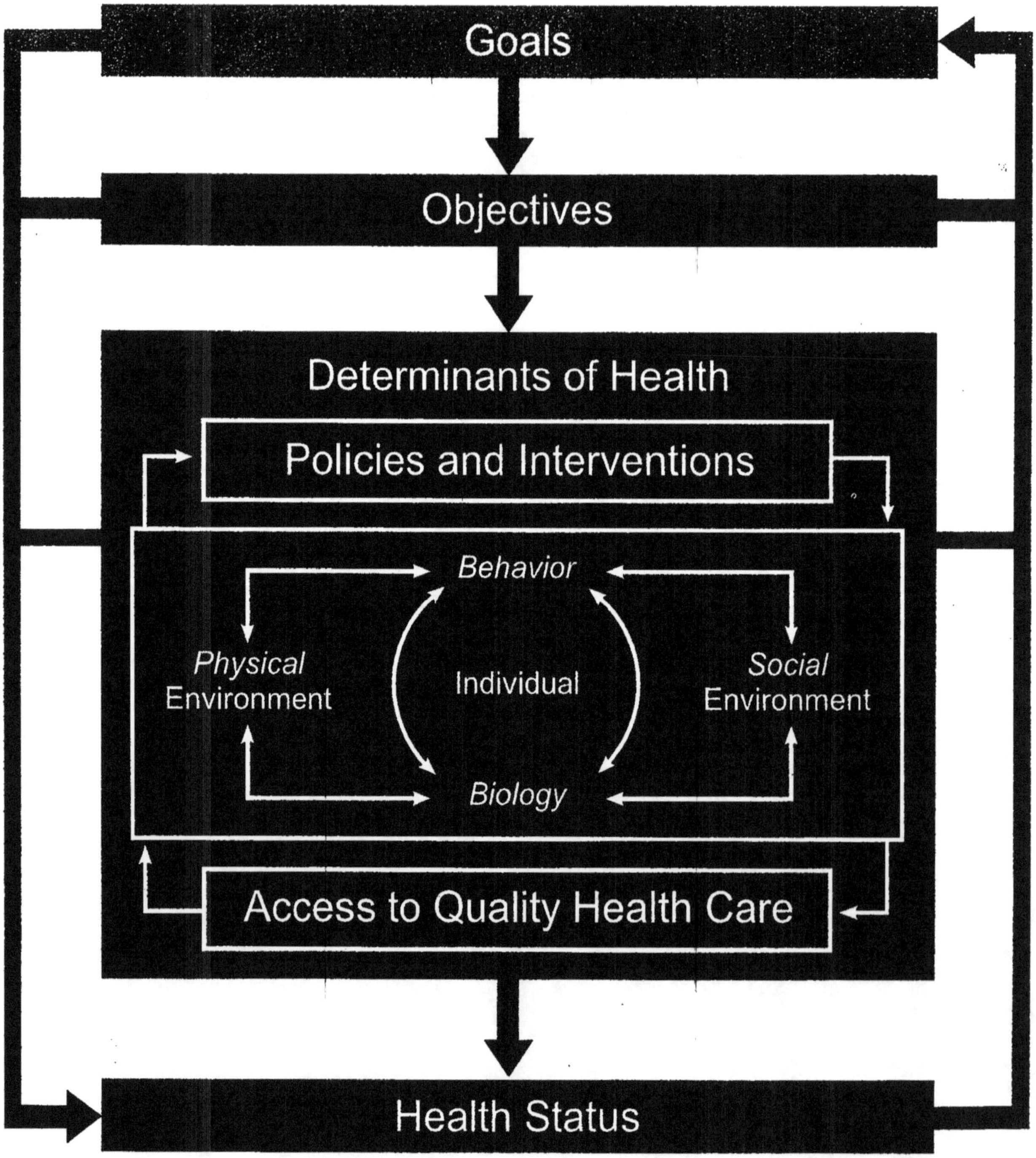

A Systematic Approach to Health Improvement

Healthy People 2010 is about improving health—the health of each individual, the health of communities, and the health of the Nation. However, the Healthy People 2010 goals and objectives cannot by themselves improve the health status of the Nation. Instead, they need to be recognized as part of a larger, systematic approach to health improvement.

This systematic approach to health improvement is composed of four key elements:

- Goals
- Objectives
- Determinants of health
- Health status

Whether this systematic approach is used to improve health on a national level, as in Healthy People 2010, or to organize community action on a particular health issue, such as promoting smoking cessation, the components remain the same. The goals provide a general focus and direction. The goals, in turn, serve as a guide for developing a set of objectives that will measure actual progress within a specified amount of time. The objectives focus on the determinants of health, which encompass the combined effects of individual and community physical and social environments and the policies and interventions used to promote health, prevent disease, and ensure access to quality health care. The ultimate measure of success in any health improvement effort is the health status of the target population.

Successful community partnerships use a systematic approach to health improvement.

Healthy People 2010 is built on this systematic approach to health improvement.

Healthy People 2010 Goals

Goal 1: Increase Quality and Years of Healthy Life

The first goal of Healthy People 2010 is to help individuals of all ages increase life expectancy *and* improve their quality of life.

Life Expectancy

Life expectancy is the average number of years people born in a given year are expected to live based on a set of age-specific death rates. At the beginning of the 20th century, life expectancy at birth was 47.3 years. Fortunately, life expectancy has increased dramatically over the past 100 years (see figure 1). Today, the average life expectancy at birth is nearly 77 years.

Life expectancy for persons at every age group also has increased during the past century. Based on today's age-specific death rates, individuals aged 65 years can be expected to live an average of 18 more years, for a total of 83 years. Those aged 75 years can be expected to live an average of 11 more years, for a total of 86 years.

Differences in life expectancy between populations, however, suggest a substantial need and opportunity for improvement. At least 18 countries with populations of 1 million or more have life expectancies greater than the United States for both men and women (see figure 2).

Figure 1. Past and projected female and male life expectancy at birth, United States, 1900—2050.

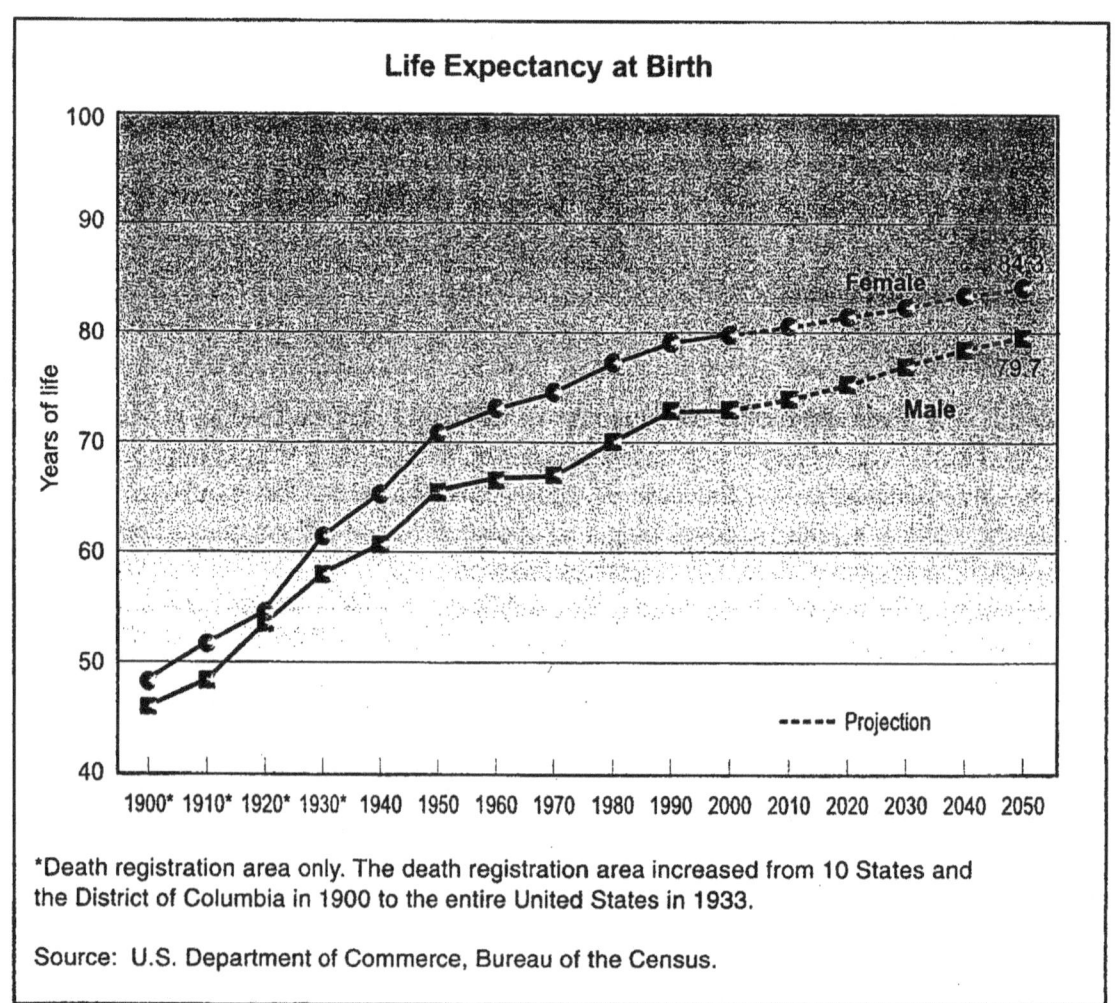

*Death registration area only. The death registration area increased from 10 States and the District of Columbia in 1900 to the entire United States in 1933.

Source: U.S. Department of Commerce, Bureau of the Census.

Healthy People 2010 Goals

Figure 2. Life expectancy at birth by gender and ranked by selected countries, 1995.

Life Expectancy by Country

Female Country	Years of Life Expectancy	Male Country	Years of Life Expectancy
Japan	82.9	Japan	76.4
France	82.6	Sweden	76.2
Switzerland	81.9	Israel	75.3
Sweden	81.6	Canada	75.2
Spain	81.5	Switzerland	75.1
Canada	81.2	Greece	75.1
Australia	80.9	Australia	75.0
Italy	80.8	Norway	74.9
Norway	80.7	Netherlands	74.6
Netherlands	80.4	Italy	74.4
Greece	80.3	England and Wales	74.3
Finland	80.3	France	74.2
Austria	80.1	Spain	74.2
Germany	79.8	Austria	73.5
Belgium	79.8	Singapore	73.4
England and Wales	79.6	Germany	73.3
Israel	79.3	New Zealand	73.3
Singapore	79.0	Northern Ireland	73.1
United States	**78.9**	Belgium	73.0
		Cuba	73.0
		Costa Rica	73.0
		Finland	72.8
		Denmark	72.8
		Ireland	72.5
		United States	**72.5**

Sources: World Health Organization; United Nations; Centers for Disease Control and Prevention; National Center for Health Statistics; National Vital Statistics System 1990–95 and unpublished data.

Healthy People 2010 Goals

There are substantial differences in life expectancy among different population groups within the United States. For example, women outlive men by an average of 6 years. White women currently have the greatest life expectancy in the United States. The life expectancy for African American women has risen to be higher today than that for white men. People from households with an annual income of at least $25,000 live an average of 3 to 7 years longer, depending on gender and race, than do people from households with annual incomes of less than $10,000.

Quality of Life

Quality of life reflects a general sense of happiness and satisfaction with our lives and environment. General quality of life encompasses all aspects of life, including health, recreation, culture, rights, values, beliefs, aspirations, and the conditions that support a life containing these elements. *Health-related quality of life* reflects a personal sense of physical and mental health and the ability to react to factors in the physical and social environments. Health-related quality of life is more subjective than life expectancy and therefore can be more difficult to measure. Some tools, have been developed to measure health-related quality of life.

Global assessments, in which a person rates his or her health as "poor," "fair," "good," "very good," or "excellent," can be reliable indicators of one's perceived health. In 1996, 90 percent of people in the United States reported their health as good, very good, or excellent.

Healthy days is another measure of health-related quality of life that estimates the number of days of poor or impaired physical and mental health in the past 30 days. In 1998, adults averaged 5.5 days during the past month when their physical or mental health was not good—including 1.8 days when they were not able to do their usual activities. However, 52 percent of adults reported having good physical and mental health for the entire month in contrast with 10 percent of adults who were unhealthy for all 30 days. Typically, younger adults report more mentally unhealthy days while older adults report more physically unhealthy days.

Years of healthy life is a combined measure developed for the Healthy People initiative. The difference between life expectancy and years of healthy life reflects the average amount of time spent in less than optimal health because of chronic or acute limitations. Years of healthy life increased in 1996 to 64.2 years, a level that was only slightly above the 64.0 years at the beginning of the decade. During the same period, life expectancy increased a full year.

As with life expectancy, various population groups can show dramatic differences in quality of life. For example, people in the lowest income households are five times more likely to report their health as fair or poor than people in the highest income households (see figure 3). A higher percentage of women report their health as fair or poor compared to men. Adults in rural areas are 36 percent more likely to report their health status as fair or poor than are adults in urban areas.

Achieving a Longer and Healthier Life—the Healthy People Perspective

Healthy People 2010 seeks to increase life expectancy and quality of life over the next 10 years by helping individuals gain the knowledge, motivation, and opportunities they need to make informed decisions about their health. At the same time, Healthy People 2010 encourages local and State leaders to develop communitywide and statewide efforts that promote healthy behaviors, create healthy environments, and increase access to high-quality health care. Because individual and community health are virtually inseparable, both the individual and the community need to do their parts to increase life expectancy and improve quality of life.

Figure 3. Percentage of persons with perceived fair or poor health status by household income, United States, 1995.

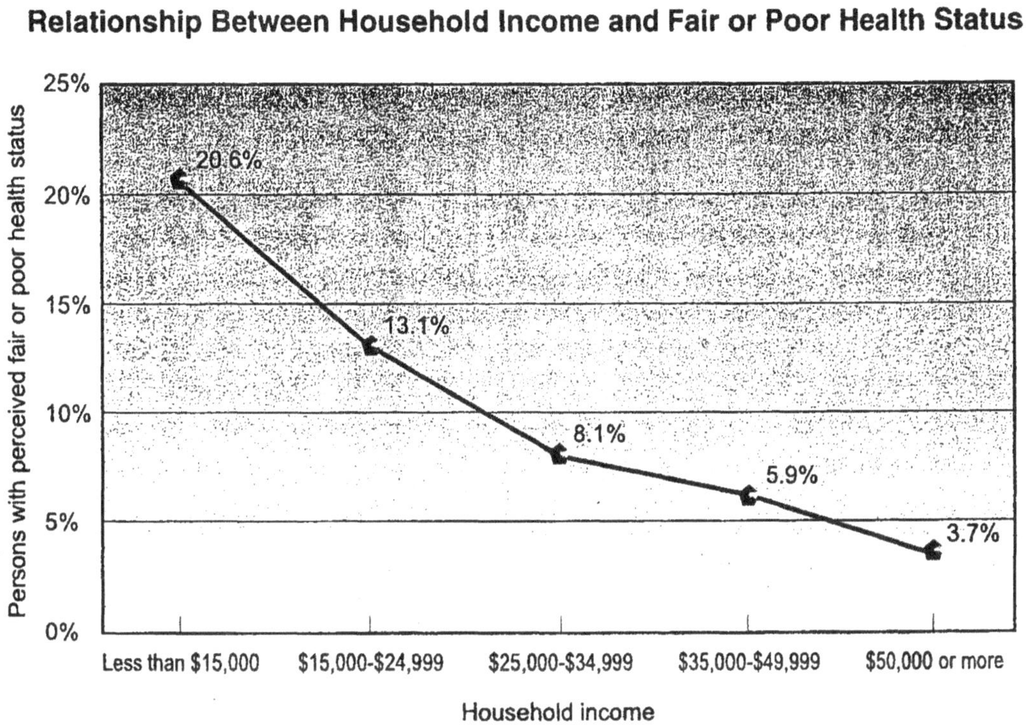

Relationship Between Household Income and Fair or Poor Health Status

- Less than $15,000: 20.6%
- $15,000–$24,999: 13.1%
- $25,000–$34,999: 8.1%
- $35,000–$49,999: 5.9%
- $50,000 or more: 3.7%

Source: Centers for Disease Control and Prevention, National Center for Health Statistics. National Health Interview Survey. 1995.

Goal 2: Eliminate Health Disparities

The second goal of Healthy People 2010 is to eliminate health disparities among segments of the population, including differences that occur by gender, race or ethnicity, education or income, disability, geographic location, or sexual orientation. This section highlights ways in which health disparities can occur among various demographic groups in the United States.

Gender

Whereas some differences in health between men and women are the result of biological differences, others are more complicated and require greater attention and scientific exploration. Some health differences are obviously gender specific, such as cervical and prostate cancers.

Overall, men have a life expectancy that is 6 years less than that of women and have higher death rates for each of the 10 leading causes of death. For example, men are two times more likely than women to die from unintentional injuries and four times more likely than women to die from firearm-related injuries. Although overall death rates for women may currently be lower than for men, women have shown increased death rates over the past decade in areas where men have experienced improvements, such as lung cancer. Women are also at greater risk for Alzheimer's disease than men are and twice as likely as men to be affected by major depression.

Healthy People 2010 Goals

Race and Ethnicity

Current information about the biologic and genetic characteristics of African Americans, Hispanics, American Indians, Alaska Natives, Asians, Native Hawaiians, and Pacific Islanders does not explain the health disparities experienced by these groups compared with the white, non-Hispanic population in the United States. These disparities are believed to be the result of the complex interaction among genetic variations, environmental factors, and specific health behaviors.

Even though the Nation's infant mortality rate is down, the infant death rate among African Americans is still more than double that of whites. Heart disease death rates are more than 40 percent higher for African Americans than for whites. The death rate for all cancers is 30 percent higher for African Americans than for whites; for prostate cancer, it is more than double that for whites. African American women have a higher death rate from breast cancer despite having a mammography screening rate that is nearly the same as the rate for white women. The death rate from HIV/AIDS for African Americans is more than seven times that for whites; the rate of homicide is six times that for whites.

Hispanics living in the United States are almost twice as likely to die from diabetes as are non-Hispanic whites. Although constituting only 11 percent of the total population in 1996, Hispanics accounted for 20 percent of the new cases of tuberculosis. Hispanics also have higher rates of high blood pressure and obesity than non-Hispanic whites. There are differences among Hispanic populations as well. For example, whereas the rate of low birth weight infants is lower for the total Hispanic population compared with that of whites, Puerto Ricans have a low birth weight rate that is 50 percent higher than the rate for whites.

American Indians and Alaska Natives have an infant death rate almost double that for whites. The rate of diabetes for this population group is more than twice that for whites. The Pima of Arizona have one of the highest rates of diabetes in the world. American Indians and Alaska Natives also have disproportionately high death rates from unintentional injuries and suicide.

Asians and Pacific Islanders, on average, have indicators of being one of the healthiest population groups in the United States. However, there is great diversity within this population group, and health disparities for some specific segments are quite marked. Women of Vietnamese origin, for example, suffer from cervical cancer at nearly five times the rate for white women. New cases of hepatitis and tuberculosis are also higher in Asians and Pacific Islanders living in the United States than in whites.

Income and Education

Inequalities in income and education underlie many health disparities in the United States. Income and education are intrinsically related and often serve as proxy measures for each other (see figure 4). In general, population groups that suffer the worst health status are also those that have the highest poverty rates and the least education. Disparities in income and education levels are associated with differences in the occurrence of illness and death, including heart disease, diabetes, obesity, elevated blood lead level, and low birth weight. Higher incomes permit increased access to medical care, enable people to afford better housing and live in safer neighborhoods, and increase the opportunity to engage in health-promoting behaviors.

Healthy People 2010 Goals

Figure 4. Relationship between education and median household income among adults aged 25 years and older, by gender, United States, 1996.

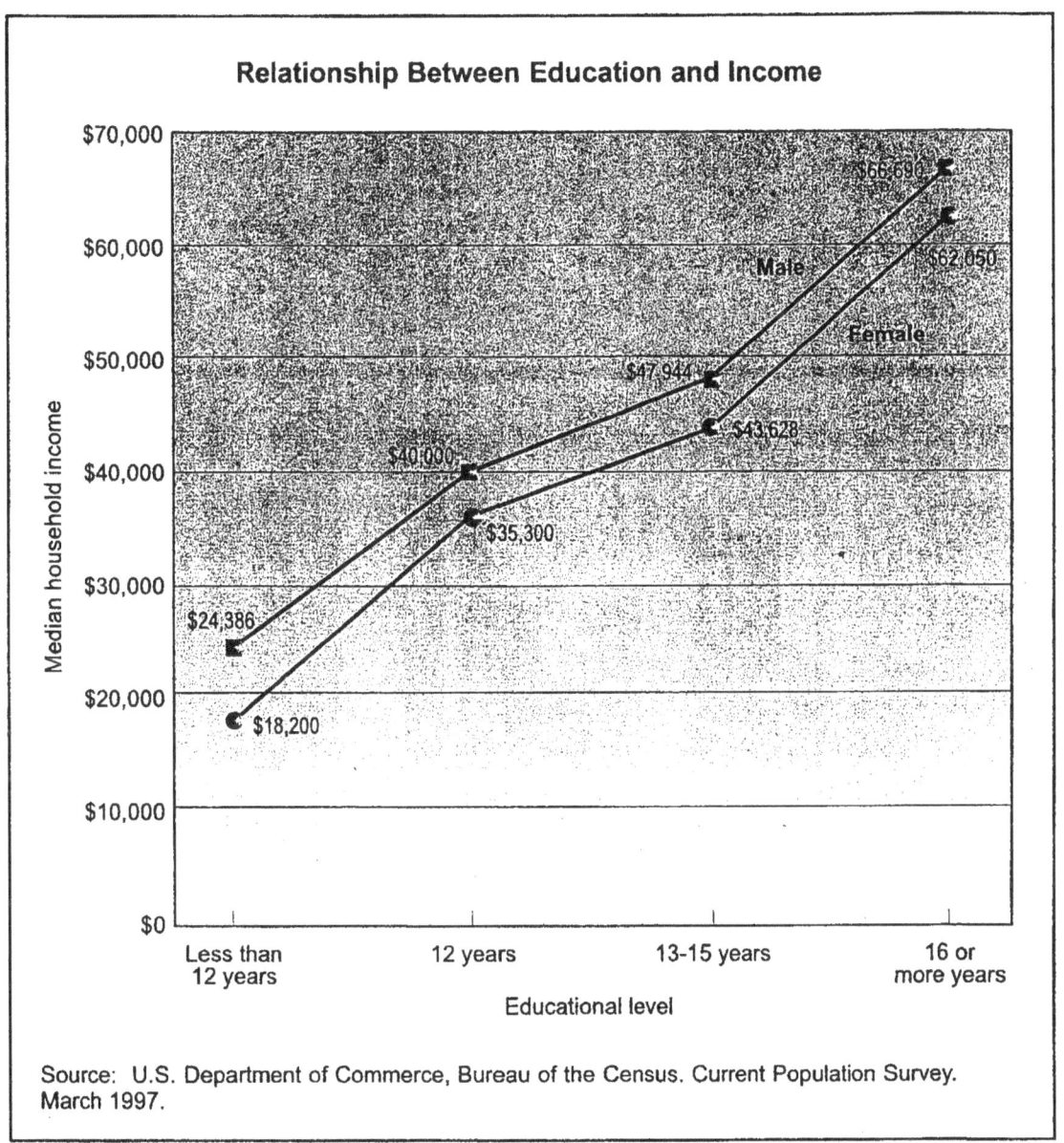

Source: U.S. Department of Commerce, Bureau of the Census. Current Population Survey. March 1997.

Income inequality in the United States has increased over the past three decades. There are distinct demographic differences in poverty by race, ethnicity, and household composition (see figure 5) as well as geographical variations in poverty across the United States. Recent health gains for the U.S. population as a whole appear to reflect achievements among the higher socioeconomic groups; lower socioeconomic groups continue to lag behind.

Healthy People 2010 Goals

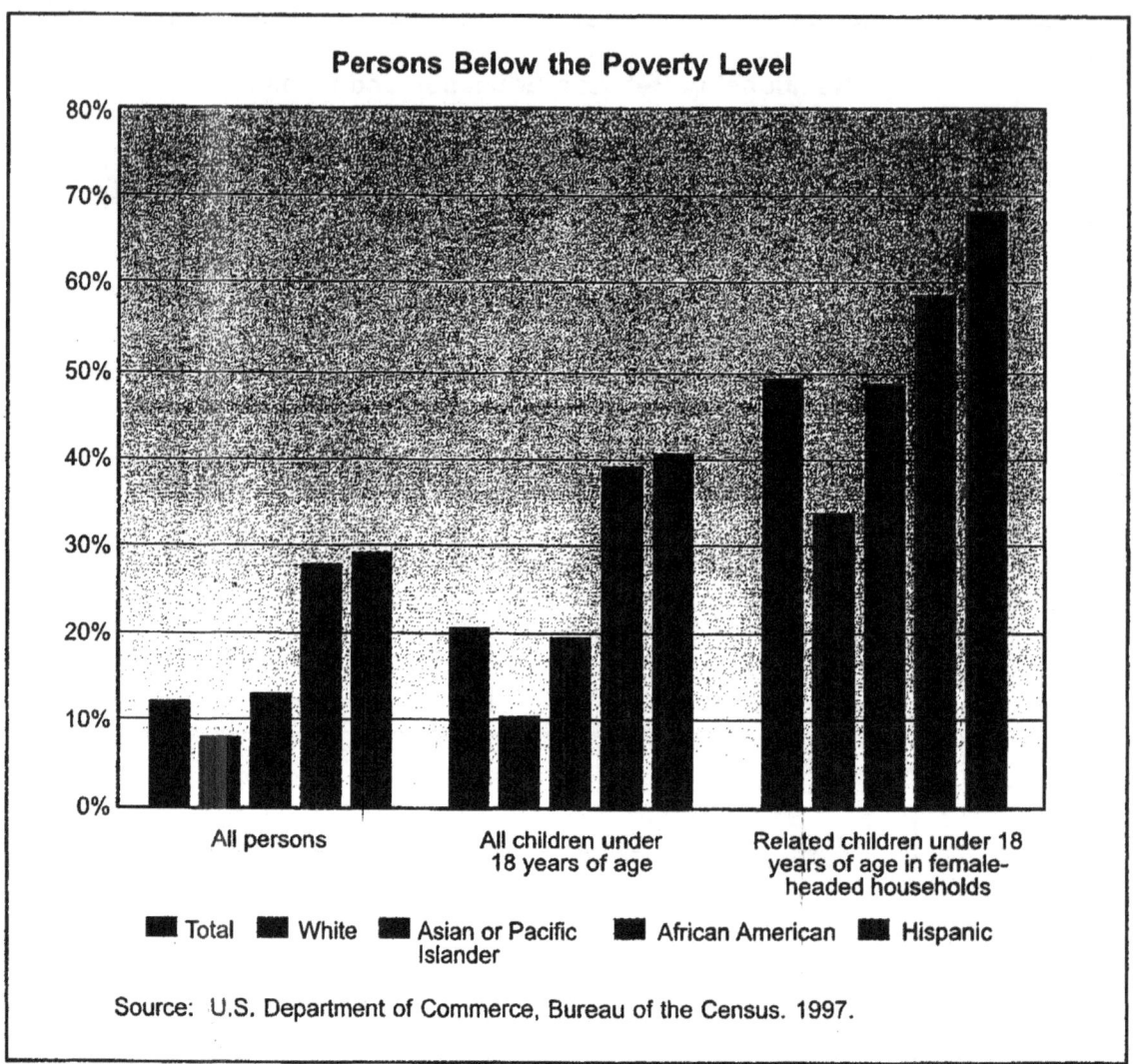

Figure 5. Percentage of persons below the poverty level by race and ethnicity and type of household, United States, 1996.

Source: U.S. Department of Commerce, Bureau of the Census. 1997.

Overall, those with higher incomes tend to fare better than those with lower incomes. For example, among white men aged 65 years, those in the highest income families could expect to live more than 3 years longer than those in the lowest income families. The percentage of people in the lowest income families reporting limitation in activity caused by chronic disease is three times that of people in the highest income families.

The average level of education in the U.S. population has increased steadily over the past several decades—an important achievement given that more years of education usually translate into more years of life. For women, the amount of education achieved is a key determinant of the welfare and survival of their children. Higher levels of education also may increase the likelihood of obtaining or understanding health-related information needed to develop health-promoting behaviors and beliefs in prevention. But again, educational attainment differs by race and ethnicity (see figure 6). Among people aged 25 to 64 years in the United States, the overall death rate for those with less than 12 years of education is more than twice that for people with 13 or more years of education. The infant mortality rate is almost double for infants of mothers with less than 12 years of education compared with those with an educational level of 13 or more years.

Figure 6. Percentage of adults aged 25 to 64 years by educational level and race and ethnicity, United States, 1996.

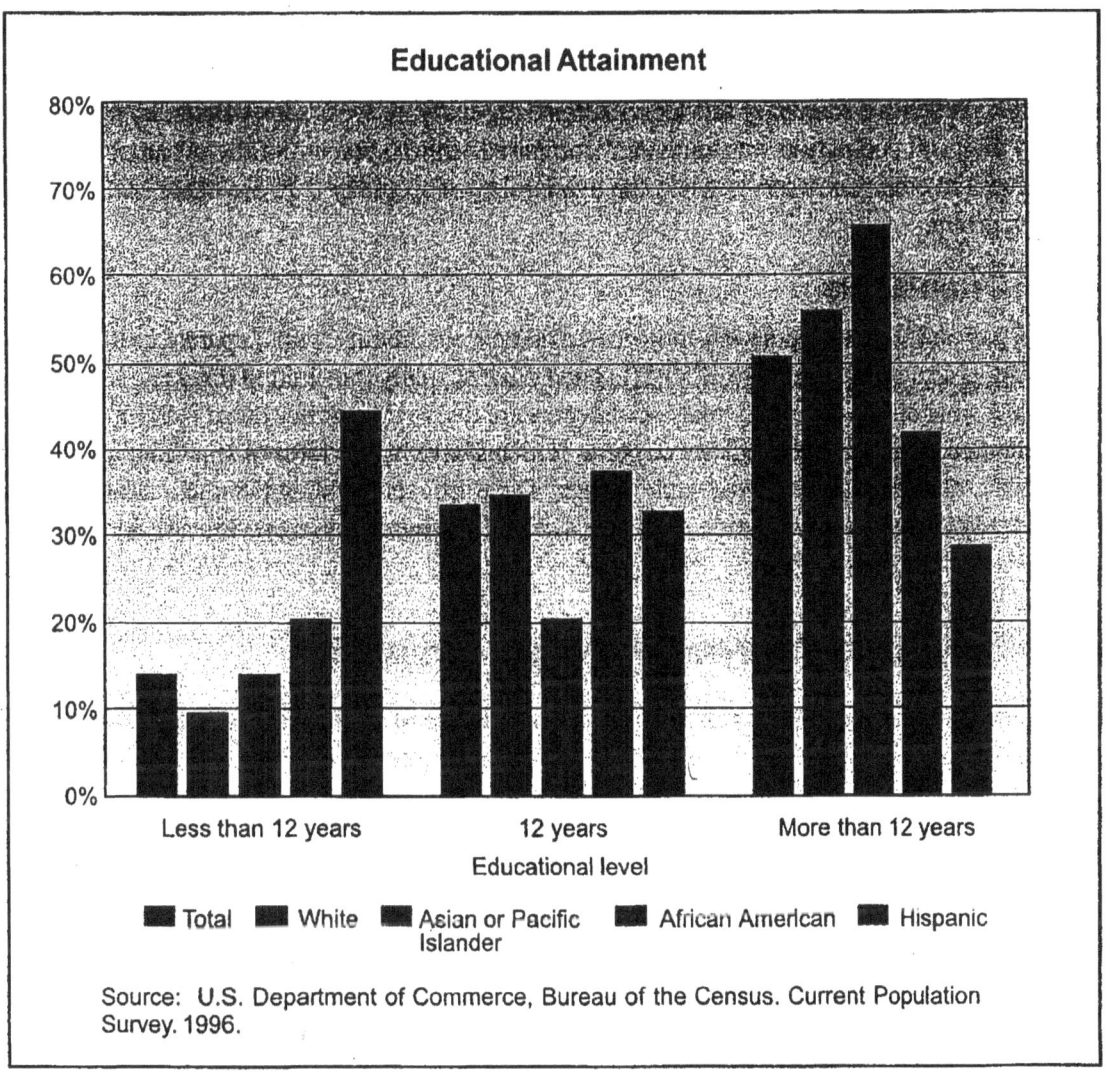

Source: U.S. Department of Commerce, Bureau of the Census. Current Population Survey. 1996.

Disability

People with disabilities are identified as persons having an activity limitation, who use assistance, or who perceive themselves as having a disability. In 1994, 54 million people in the United States, or roughly 21 percent of the population, had some level of disability. Although rates of disability are relatively stable or falling slightly for people aged 45 years and older, rates are on the rise among the younger population. People with disabilities tend to report more anxiety, pain, sleeplessness, and days of depression and fewer days of vitality than do people without activity limitations. People with disabilities also have other disparities, including lower rates of physical activity and higher rates of obesity. Many people with disabilities lack access to health services and medical care.

Healthy People 2010 Goals

Geographic Location

Twenty-five percent of Americans live in rural areas, that is, places with fewer than 2,500 residents. Injury-related death rates are 40 percent higher in rural populations than in urban populations. Heart disease, cancer, and diabetes rates exceed those for urban areas. People living in rural areas are less likely to use preventive screening services, exercise regularly, or wear safety belts. In 1996, 20 percent of the rural population was uninsured compared with 16 percent of the urban population. Timely access to emergency services and the availability of specialty care are other issues for this population group.

Sexual Orientation

America's gay and lesbian population comprises a diverse community with disparate health concerns. Major health issues for gay men are HIV/AIDS and other sexually transmitted diseases, substance abuse, depression, and suicide. Gay male adolescents are two to three times more likely than their peers to attempt suicide. Some evidence suggests lesbians have higher rates of smoking, overweight, alcohol abuse, and stress than heterosexual women. The issues surrounding personal, family, and social acceptance of sexual orientation can place a significant burden on mental health and personal safety.

Achieving Equity—The Healthy People Perspective

Although the diversity of the American population may be one of the Nation's greatest assets, it also represents a range of health improvement challenges—challenges that must be addressed by individuals, the community and State in which they live, and the Nation as a whole.

Healthy People 2010 recognizes that communities, States, and national organizations will need to take a multidisciplinary approach to achieving health equity—an approach that involves improving health, education, housing, labor, justice, transportation, agriculture, and the environment, as well as data collection itself. In fact, current data collection methods make it impossible to assess accurately the health status for some populations, particularly relatively small ones. However, the greatest opportunities for reducing health disparities are in empowering individuals to make informed health care decisions and in promoting communitywide safety, education, and access to health care.

Healthy People 2010 is firmly dedicated to the principle that—regardless of age, gender, race or ethnicity, income, education, geographic location, disability, and sexual orientation—every person in every community across the Nation deserves equal access to comprehensive, culturally competent, community-based health care systems that are committed to serving the needs of the individual and promoting community health.

Objectives

The Nation's progress in achieving the two goals of Healthy People 2010 will be monitored through 467 objectives in 28 focus areas. Many objectives focus on interventions designed to reduce or eliminate illness, disability, and premature death among individuals and communities. Others focus on broader issues, such as improving access to quality health care, strengthening public health services, and improving the availability and dissemination of health-related information. Each objective has a target for specific improvements to be achieved by the year 2010.

Together, these objectives reflect the depth of scientific knowledge as well as the breadth of diversity in the Nation's communities. More importantly, they are designed to help the Nation achieve Healthy People 2010's two overarching goals and realize the vision of healthy people living in healthy communities.

A list of the short titles of all Healthy People 2010 objectives by focus area can be found in the Appendix. In addition, *Healthy People 2010* provides an overview of the issues, trends, and opportunities for action in each of the 28 focus areas. It also contains detailed language of each objective, underlying rationale, target for the year 2010, and national data tables of its measures.

Healthy People 2010 Focus Areas

1. Access to Quality Health Services
2. Arthritis, Osteoporosis, and Chronic Back Conditions
3. Cancer
4. Chronic Kidney Disease
5. Diabetes
6. Disability and Secondary Conditions
7. Educational and Community-Based Programs
8. Environmental Health
9. Family Planning
10. Food Safety
11. Health Communication
12. Heart Disease and Stroke
13. HIV
14. Immunization and Infectious Diseases
15. Injury and Violence Prevention
16. Maternal, Infant, and Child Health
17. Medical Product Safety
18. Mental Health and Mental Disorders
19. Nutrition and Overweight
20. Occupational Safety and Health
21. Oral Health
22. Physical Activity and Fitness
23. Public Health Infrastructure
24. Respiratory Diseases
25. Sexually Transmitted Diseases
26. Substance Abuse
27. Tobacco Use
28. Vision and Hearing

Determinants of Health

Topics covered by the objectives in Healthy People 2010 reflect the array of critical influences that determine the health of individuals and communities.

For example, individual behaviors and environmental factors are responsible for about 70 percent of all premature deaths in the United States. Developing and implementing policies and preventive interventions that effectively address these determinants of health can reduce the burden of illness, enhance quality of life, and increase longevity.

Individual *biology* and *behaviors* influence health through their interaction with each other and with the individual's *social* and *physical environments.* In addition, *policies and interventions* can improve health by targeting factors related to individuals and their environments, including *access to quality health care* (see figure 7).

Figure 7. Determinants of health.

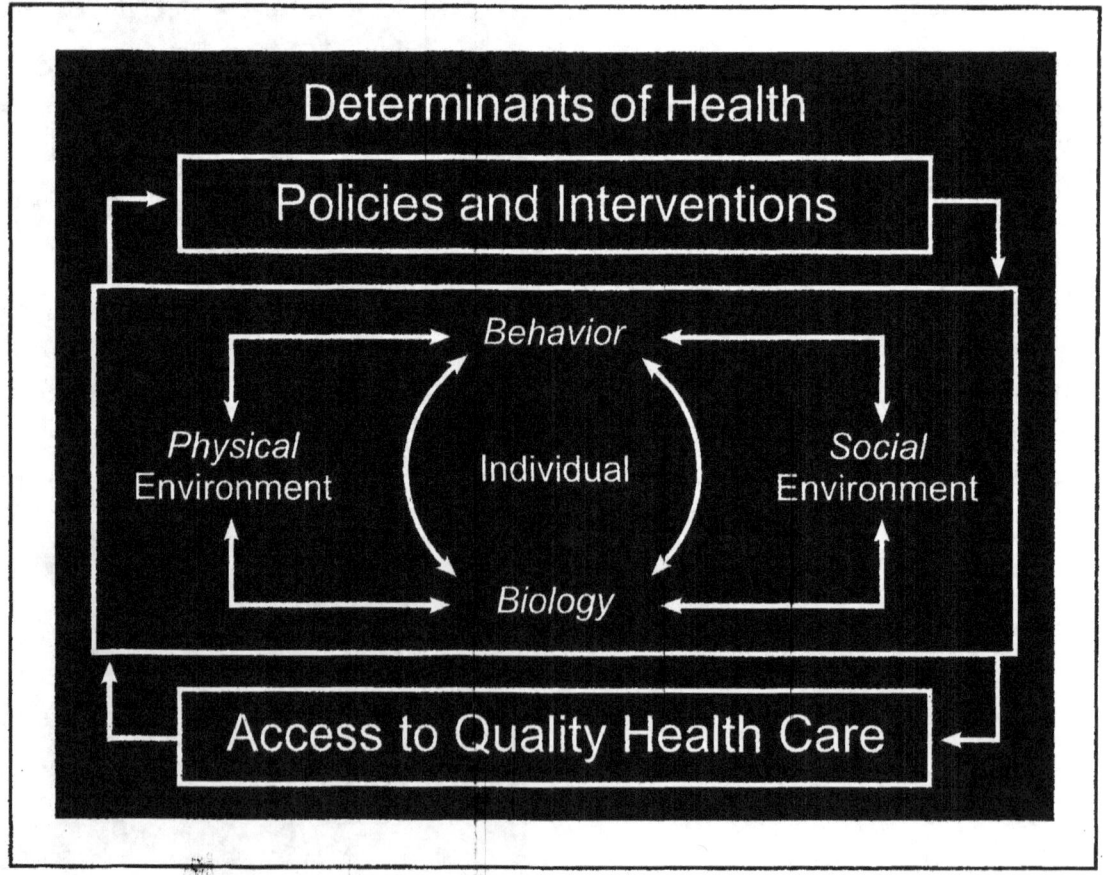

Determinants of Health

Biology refers to the individual's genetic makeup (those factors with which he or she is born), family history (which may suggest risk for disease), and the physical and mental health problems acquired during life. Aging, diet, physical activity, smoking, stress, alcohol or illicit drug abuse, injury or violence, or an infectious or toxic agent may result in illness or disability and can produce a "new" biology for the individual.

Behaviors are individual responses or reactions to internal stimuli and external conditions. Behaviors can have a reciprocal relationship to biology; in other words, each can react to the other. For example, smoking (behavior) can alter the cells in the lung and result in shortness of breath, emphysema, or cancer (biology) that then may lead an individual to stop smoking (behavior). Similarly, a family history that includes heart disease (biology) may motivate an individual to develop good eating habits, avoid tobacco, and maintain an active lifestyle (behaviors), which may prevent his or her own development of heart disease (biology).

Personal choices and the social and physical environments surrounding individuals can shape behaviors. The social and physical environments include all factors that affect the life of individuals, positively or negatively, many of which may not be under their immediate or direct control.

Social environment includes interactions with family, friends, coworkers, and others in the community. It also encompasses social institutions, such as law enforcement, the workplace, places of worship, and schools. Housing, public transportation, and the presence or absence of violence in the community are among other components of the social environment. The social environment has a profound effect on individual health, as well as on the health of the larger community, and is unique because of cultural customs; language; and personal, religious, or spiritual beliefs. At the same time, individuals and their behaviors contribute to the quality of the social environment.

Physical environment can be thought of as that which can be seen, touched, heard, smelled, and tasted. However, the physical environment also contains less tangible elements, such as radiation and ozone. The physical environment can harm individual and community health, especially when individuals and communities are exposed to toxic substances; irritants; infectious agents; and physical hazards in homes, schools, and worksites. The physical environment also can promote good health, for example, by providing clean and safe places for people to work, exercise, and play.

Policies and interventions can have a powerful and positive effect on the health of individuals and the community. Examples include health promotion campaigns to prevent smoking; policies mandating child restraints and safety belt use in automobiles; disease prevention services, such as immunization of children, adolescents, and adults; and clinical services, such as enhanced mental health care. Policies and interventions that promote individual and community health may be implemented by a variety of agencies, such as transportation, education, energy, housing, labor, justice, and other venues, or through places of worship, community-based organizations, civic groups, and businesses.

Determinants of Health

The health of individuals and communities also depends greatly on **access to quality health care**. Expanding access to quality health care is important to eliminate health disparities and to increase the quality and years of healthy life for all people living in the United States. Health care in the broadest sense not only includes services received through health care providers but also health information and services received through other venues in the community.

The determinants of health—individual biology and behavior, physical and social environments, policies and interventions, and access to quality health care—have a profound effect on the health of individuals, communities, and the Nation. An evaluation of these determinants is an important part of developing any strategy to improve health.

Our understanding of these determinants and how they relate to one another, coupled with our understanding of how individual and community health affects the health of the Nation, is perhaps the most important key to achieving our Healthy People 2010 goals of increasing the quality and years of life and of eliminating the Nation's health disparities.

Health Status

To understand the health status of a population, it is essential to monitor and evaluate the consequences of the determinants of health.

The health status of the United States is a description of the health of the total population, using information representative of most people living in this country. For relatively small population groups, however, it may not be possible to draw accurate conclusions about their health using current data collection methods. The goal of eliminating health disparities will necessitate improved collection and use of standardized data to identify correctly disparities among select population groups.

Health status can be measured by birth and death rates, life expectancy, quality of life, morbidity from specific diseases, risk factors, use of ambulatory care and inpatient care, accessibility of health personnel and facilities, financing of health care, health insurance coverage, and many other factors. The information used to report health status comes from a variety of sources, including birth and death records; hospital discharge data; and health information collected from health care records, personal interviews, physical examinations, and telephone surveys. These measures are monitored on an annual basis in the United States and are reported in a variety of publications, including *Health, United States* and *Healthy People Reviews.*

The leading causes of death are used frequently to describe the health status of the Nation. Over the past 100 years, the Nation has seen a great deal of change in the leading causes of death (see figure 8). At the beginning of the 1900s, infectious diseases ran rampant in the United States and worldwide and topped the leading causes of death. A century later, with the control of many infectious agents and the increasing age of the population, chronic diseases top the list.

A very different picture emerges when the leading causes of death are viewed for various population groups. Unintentional injuries, mainly motor vehicle crashes, are the fifth leading cause of death for the total population, but they are the leading cause of death for people aged 1 to 44 years. Similarly, HIV/AIDS is the 14th leading cause of death for the total population but the leading cause of death for African American men aged 25 to 44 years (see figure 9).

The leading causes of death in the United States generally result from a mix of behaviors; injury, violence, and other factors in the environment; and the unavailability or inaccessibility of quality health services. Understanding and monitoring behaviors, environmental factors, and community health systems may prove more useful to monitoring the Nation's *true* health, and in driving health improvement activities, than the death rates that reflect the cumulative impact of these factors. This more complex approach has served as the basis for developing the Leading Health Indicators.

Health Status

Figure 8. The leading causes of death as a percentage of all deaths in the United States, 1900 and 1997.

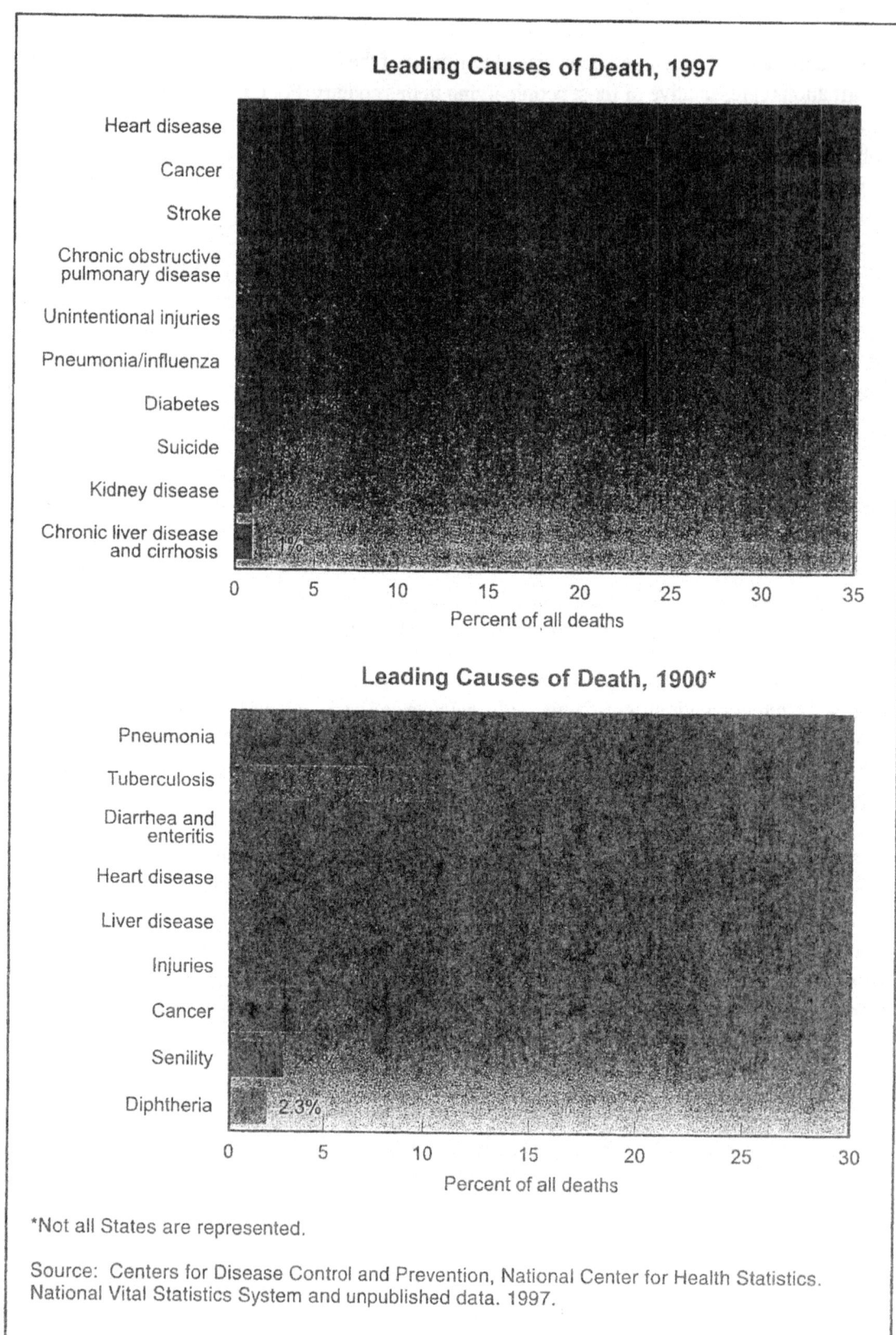

*Not all States are represented.

Source: Centers for Disease Control and Prevention, National Center for Health Statistics. National Vital Statistics System and unpublished data. 1997.

Health Status

Figure 9. The three leading causes of death by age group, United States, 1997.

Leading Causes of Death by Age Group

Under 1 Year	Number of Deaths
Birth defects	6,178
Disorders related to premature birth	3,925
Sudden infant death syndrome	2,991
1-4 Years	
■ Unintentional injuries	2,005
Birth defects	589
■ Cancer	438
5-14 Years	
■ Unintentional injuries	3,371
■ Cancer	1,030
Homicide	457
15-24 Years	
■ Unintentional injuries	13,367
Homicide	6,146
■ Suicide	4,186
25-44 Years	
■ Unintentional injuries	27,129
■ Cancer	21,706
■ Heart disease	16,513
45-64 Years	
■ Cancer	131,743
■ Heart disease	101,235
■ Unintentional injuries	17,521
65 Years and Older	
■ Heart disease	606,913
■ Cancer	382,913
■ Stroke	140,366

Bullets above link to the conditions listed in the charts in figure 8.

Source: Centers for Disease Control and Prevention, National Center for Health Statistics. National Vital Statistics System. 1999.

Leading Health Indicators

The Leading Health Indicators reflect the major public health concerns in the United States and were chosen based on their ability to motivate action, the availability of data to measure their progress, and their relevance as broad public health issues.

The Leading Health Indicators illuminate individual behaviors, physical and social environmental factors, and important health system issues that greatly affect the health of individuals and communities. Underlying each of these indicators is the significant influence of income and education (see Income and Education, page 12).

The process of selecting the Leading Health Indicators mirrored the collaborative and extensive efforts undertaken to develop Healthy People 2010. The process was led by an interagency work group within the U.S. Department of Health and Human Services. Individuals and organizations provided comments at national and regional meetings or via mail and the Internet. A report by the Institute of Medicine, National Academy of Sciences, provided several scientific models on

Leading Health Indicators

- Physical activity
- Overweight and obesity
- Tobacco use
- Substance abuse
- Responsible sexual behavior
- Mental health
- Injury and violence
- Environmental quality
- Immunization
- Access to health care

which to support a set of indicators. Focus groups were used to ensure that the indicators are meaningful and motivating to the public.

For each of the Leading Health Indicators, specific objectives derived from Healthy People 2010 will be used to track progress. This small set of measures will provide a snapshot of the health of the Nation. Tracking and communicating progress on the Leading Health Indicators through national- and State-level report cards will spotlight achievements and challenges in the next decade. The Leading Health Indicators serve as a link to the 467 objectives in *Healthy People 2010* and can become the basic building blocks for community health initiatives.

A major challenge throughout the history of Healthy People has been to balance a comprehensive set of health objectives with a smaller set of health priorities.

The Leading Health Indicators are intended to help everyone more easily understand the importance of health promotion and disease prevention and to encourage wide participation in improving health in the next decade. Developing strategies and action plans to address one or more of these indicators can have a profound effect on increasing the quality of life and the years of healthy life and on eliminating health disparities—creating *healthy people in healthy communities*.

Physical Activity

Leading Health Indicator

Regular physical activity throughout life is important for maintaining a healthy body, enhancing psychological well-being, and preventing premature death.

In 1999, 65 percent of adolescents engaged in the recommended amount of physical activity. In 1997, only 15 percent of adults performed the recommended amount of physical activity, and 40 percent of adults engaged in no leisure-time physical activity.

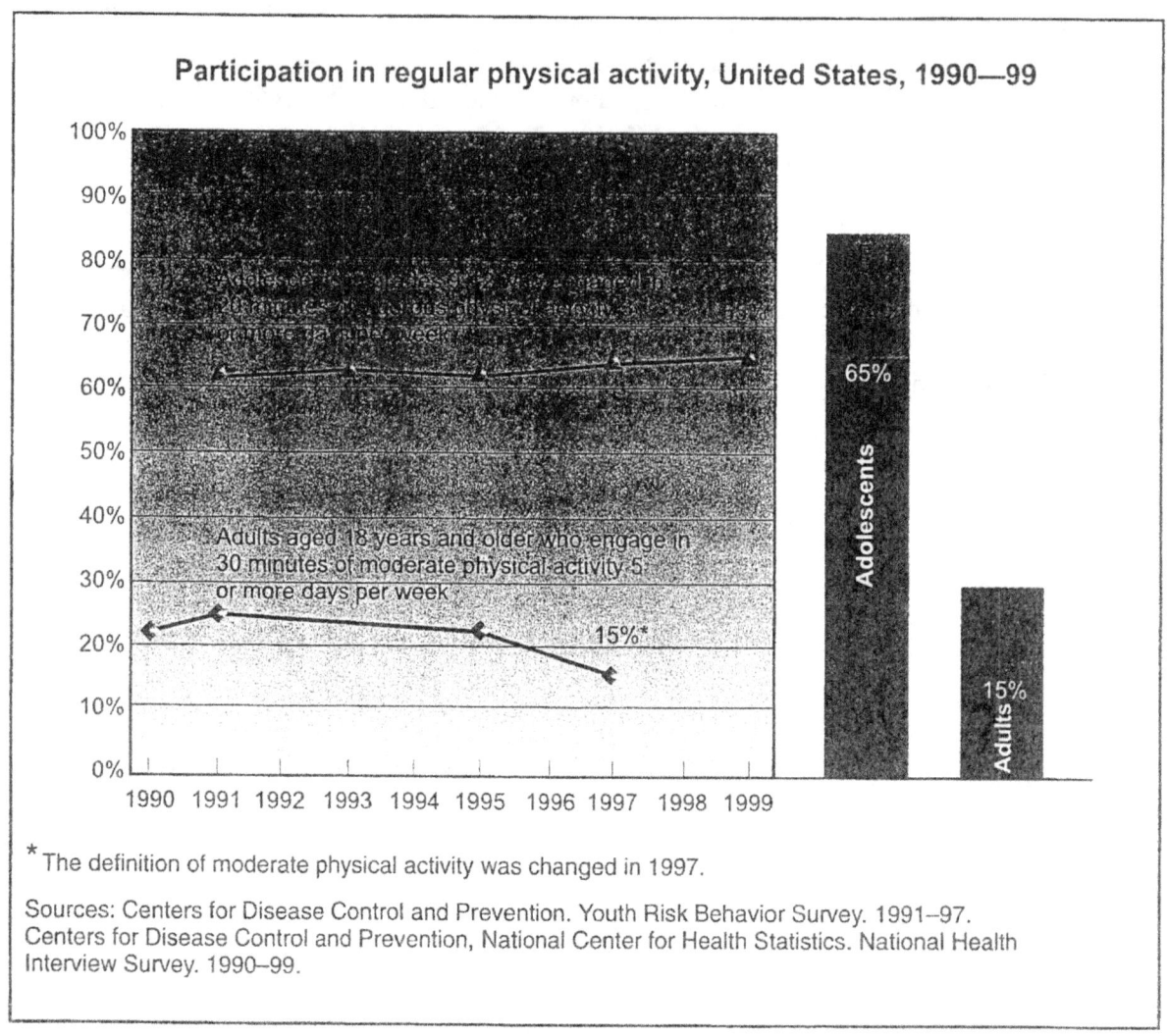

*The definition of moderate physical activity was changed in 1997.

Sources: Centers for Disease Control and Prevention. Youth Risk Behavior Survey. 1991–97. Centers for Disease Control and Prevention, National Center for Health Statistics. National Health Interview Survey. 1990–99.

The objectives selected to measure progress among adolescents and adults for this Leading Health Indicator are presented below. These are only indicators and do not represent all the physical activity and fitness objectives included in Healthy People 2010.

22-7. **Increase the proportion of adolescents who engage in vigorous physical activity that promotes cardiorespiratory fitness 3 or more days per week for 20 or more minutes per occasion.**

22-2. **Increase the proportion of adults who engage regularly, preferably daily, in moderate physical activity for at least 30 minutes per day.**

Leading Health Indicator

Health Impact of Physical Activity

Regular physical activity is associated with lower death rates for adults of any age, even when only moderate levels of physical activity are performed. Regular physical activity decreases the risk of death from heart disease, lowers the risk of developing diabetes, and is associated with a decreased risk of colon cancer. Regular physical activity helps prevent high blood pressure and helps reduce blood pressure in persons with elevated levels.

Regular physical activity also:

- Increases muscle and bone strength.
- Increases lean muscle and helps decrease body fat.
- Aids in weight control and is a key part of any weight loss effort.
- Enhances psychological well-being and may even reduce the risk of developing depression.
- Appears to reduce symptoms of depression and anxiety and to improve mood.

In addition, children and adolescents need weight-bearing exercise for normal skeletal development, and young adults need such exercise to achieve and maintain peak bone mass. Older adults can improve and maintain strength and agility with regular physical activity. This can reduce the risk of falling, helping older adults maintain an independent living status. Regular physical activity also increases the ability of people with certain chronic, disabling conditions to perform activities of daily living.

Populations With Low Rates of Physical Activity

- Women generally are less active than men at all ages.
- People with lower incomes and less education are typically not as physically active as those with higher incomes and education.
- African Americans and Hispanics are generally less physically active than whites.
- Adults in northeastern and southern States tend to be less active than adults in North-Central and Western States.
- People with disabilities are less physically active than people without disabilities.
- By age 75, one in three men and one in two women engage in *no* regular physical activity.

Other Issues

The major barriers most people face when trying to increase physical activity are lack of time, lack of access to convenient facilities, and lack of safe environments in which to be active.

Overweight and Obesity

Leading Health Indicator

Overweight and obesity are major contributors to many preventable causes of death. On average, higher body weights are associated with higher death rates. The number of overweight children, adolescents, and adults has risen over the past four decades. Total costs (medical cost and lost productivity) attributable to obesity alone amounted to an estimated $99 billion in 1995.

During 1988–94, 11 percent of children and adolescents aged 6 to 19 years were overweight or obese. During the same years, 23 percent of adults aged 20 years and older were considered obese.

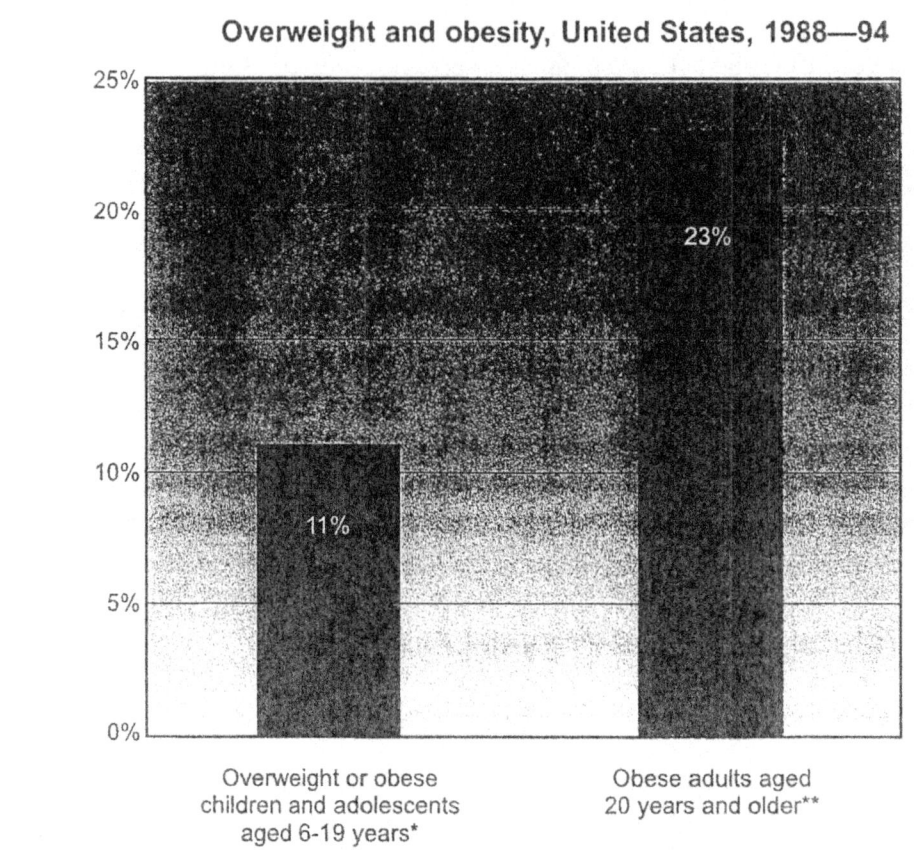

Overweight and obesity, United States, 1988—94

* In those aged 6 to 19 years, overweight or obesity is defined as at or above the sex- and age-specific 95th percentile of Body Mass Index (BMI) based on CDC Growth Charts: United States.
** In adults, obesity is defined as a BMI of 30 kg/m² or more; overweight is a BMI of 25 kg/m² or more.

Body mass index (BMI) is calculated as weight in kilograms (kg) divided by the square of height in meters (m²) (BMI = weight[kg]/height[m²]). To estimate BMI using pounds (lbs) and inches (in), divide weight in pounds by the square of height in inches. Then multiply the resulting number by 704.5 (BMI = weight[lbs]/height[in²] X 704.5).

Source: Centers for Disease Control and Prevention, National Center for Health Statistics. National Health and Nutrition Examination Survey. 1988–94.

The objectives selected to measure progress among children, adolescents, and adults for this Leading Health Indicator are presented below. These are only indicators and do not represent all the nutrition and overweight objectives included in Healthy People 2010.

19-3c. **Reduce the proportion of children and adolescents who are overweight or obese.**

19-2. **Reduce the proportion of adults who are obese.**

Leading Health Indicator

Health Impact of Overweight and Obesity

Overweight and obesity substantially raise the risk of illness from high blood pressure, high cholesterol, type 2 diabetes, heart disease and stroke, gallbladder disease, arthritis, sleep disturbances and problems breathing, and certain types of cancers. Obese individuals also may suffer from social stigmatization, discrimination, and lowered self-esteem.

Populations With High Rates of Overweight and Obesity

More than half of adults in the United States are estimated to be overweight or obese. The proportion of adolescents from poor households who are overweight or obese is twice that of adolescents from middle- and high-income households. Obesity is especially prevalent among women with lower incomes and is more common among African American and Mexican American women than among white women. Among African Americans, the proportion of women who are obese is 80 percent higher than the proportion of men who are obese. This gender difference also is seen among Mexican American women and men, but the percentage of white, non-Hispanic women and men who are obese is about the same.

Reducing Overweight and Obesity

Obesity is a result of a complex variety of social, behavioral, cultural, environmental, physiological, and genetic factors. Efforts to maintain a healthy weight should start early in childhood and continue throughout adulthood, as this is likely to be more successful than efforts to lose substantial amounts of weight and maintain weight loss once obesity is established.

A healthy diet and regular physical activity are both important for maintaining a healthy weight. Over time, even a small decrease in calories eaten and a small increase in physical activity can help prevent weight gain or facilitate weight loss. It is recommended that obese individuals who are trying to lose substantial amounts of weight seek the guidance of a health care provider.

Dietary and Physical Activity Recommendations

The *Dietary Guidelines for Americans* recommend that to build a healthy base, persons aged 2 years and older choose a healthful assortment of foods that includes vegetables; fruits; grains (especially whole grains); fat-free or low-fat milk products; and fish, lean meat, poultry, or beans. The guidelines further emphasize the importance of choosing foods that are low in saturated fat and added sugars most of the time and, whatever the food, eating a sensible portion size. It is recognized, however, that this guidance may be particularly challenging when eating out because the consumer may be offered large portion sizes with unknown amounts of saturated fat and added sugars.

The *Dietary Guidelines for Americans* recommend that all adults be more active throughout the day and get at least 30 minutes of moderate physical activity most, or preferably all, days of the week. Adults who are trying to maintain healthy weight after weight loss are advised to get even more physical activity. The guidelines also recommend that children get at least 60 minutes of physical activity daily and limit inactive forms of play such as television watching and computer games.

Tobacco Use

Leading Health Indicator

Cigarette smoking is the single most preventable cause of disease and death in the United States. Smoking results in more deaths each year in the United States than AIDS, alcohol, cocaine, heroin, homicide, suicide, motor vehicle crashes, and fires—combined.

Tobacco-related deaths number more than 430,000 per year among U.S. adults, representing more than 5 million years of potential life lost. Direct medical costs attributable to smoking total at least $50 billion per year.

In 1999, 35 percent of adolescents were current cigarette smokers. In 1998, 24 percent of adults were current cigarette smokers.

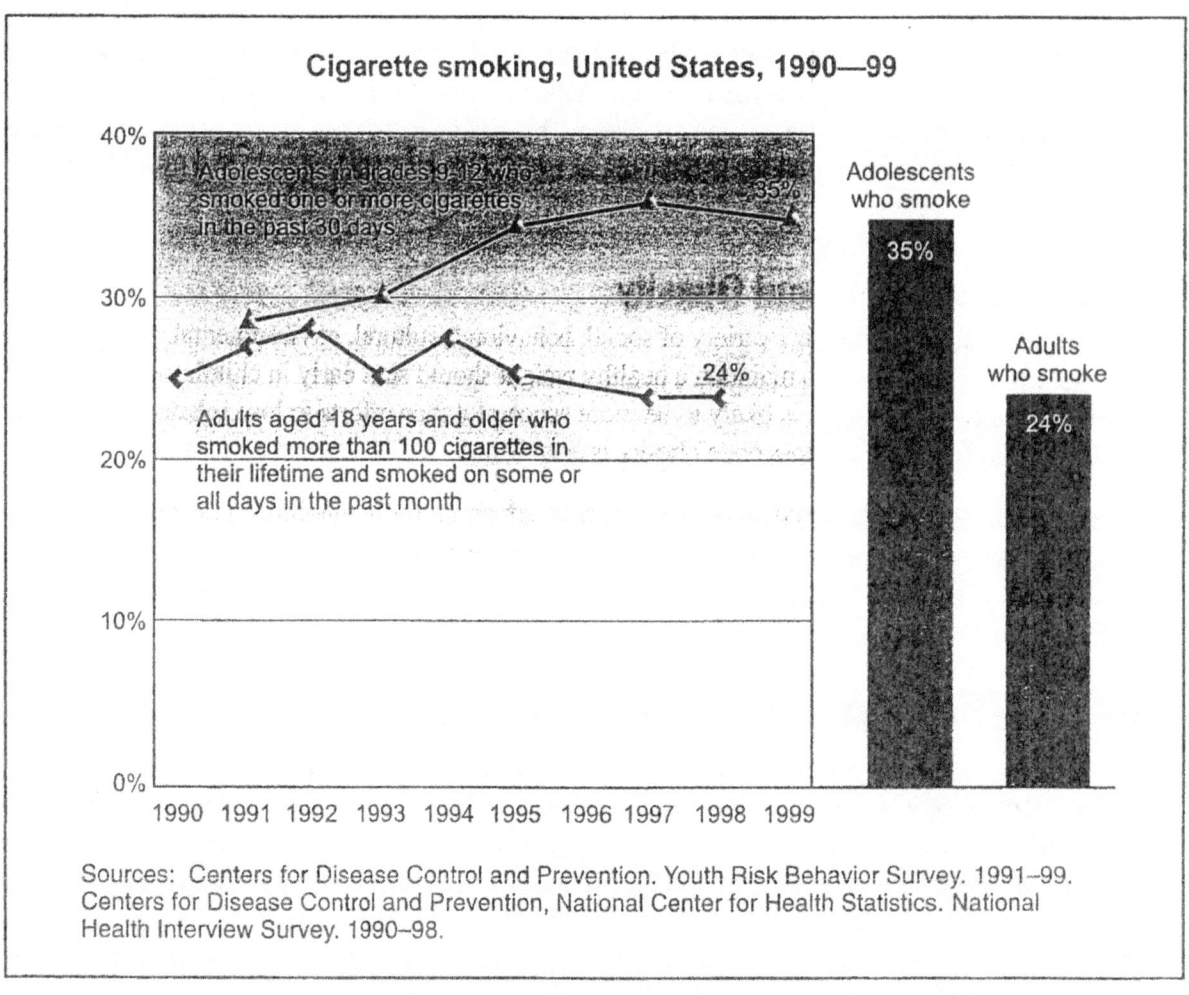

The objectives selected to measure progress among adolescents and adults for this Leading Health Indicator are presented below. These are only indicators and do not represent all the tobacco use objectives included in Healthy People 2010.

27-2b. Reduce cigarette smoking by adolescents.
27-1a. Reduce cigarette smoking by adults.

Health Impact of Cigarette Smoking

Smoking is a major risk factor for heart disease, stroke, lung cancer, and chronic lung diseases all leading causes of death. Smoking during pregnancy can result in miscarriages, premature delivery, and sudden infant death syndrome. Other health effects of smoking result from injuries and environmental damage caused by fires.

Environmental tobacco smoke (ETS) increases the risk of heart disease and significant lung conditions, especially asthma and bronchitis in children. ETS is responsible for an estimated 3,000 lung cancer deaths each year among adult nonsmokers.

Trends in Cigarette Smoking

Adolescents. Overall, the percentage of adolescents in grades 9 through 12 who smoked in the past month increased in the 1990s. Every day, an estimated 3,000 young persons start smoking. These trends are disturbing because the vast majority of adult smokers tried their first cigarette before age 18 years; more than half of adult smokers became daily smokers before this same age. Almost half of adolescents who continue smoking regularly will die eventually from a smoking-related illness.

Adults. Following years of steady decline, rates of smoking among adults appear to have leveled off in the 1990s.

Populations With High Rates of Smoking

Adolescents. Adolescent rates of cigarette smoking have increased in the 1990s among white, African American, and Hispanic high school students after years of declining rates during the 1970s and 1980s. In 1999, 39 percent of white high school students currently smoked cigarettes compared with 33 percent for Hispanics and 20 percent for African Americans. Among African Americans in 1999, only 19 percent of high school girls, compared with 22 percent of boys, currently smoked cigarettes.

Adults. Overall, American Indians and Alaska Natives, blue-collar workers, and military personnel have the highest rates of smoking in adults. Rates of smoking in Asian and Pacific Islander men are more than four times higher than for women of the same race. Men have only somewhat higher rates of smoking than women within the total U.S. population. Low-income adults are more likely to smoke than are high-income adults. The percentage of people aged 25 years and older with less than 12 years of education who are current smokers is nearly three times that for persons with 16 or more years of education.

Other Important Tobacco Issues

There is no safe tobacco alternative to cigarettes. Spit tobacco (chew) causes cancer of the mouth, inflammation of the gums, and tooth loss. Cigar smoking causes cancer of the mouth, throat, and lungs and can increase the risk of heart disease and chronic lung problems.

Substance Abuse

Leading Health Indicator

Alcohol and illicit drug use are associated with many of this country's most serious problems, including violence, injury, and HIV infection. The annual economic costs to the United States from alcohol abuse were estimated to be $167 billion in 1995, and the costs from drug abuse were estimated to be $110 billion.

In 1998, 79 percent of adolescents aged 12 to 17 years reported that they did *not* use alcohol or illicit drugs in the past month. In the same year, 6 percent of adults aged 18 years and older reported using illicit drugs in the past month; 17 percent reported binge drinking in the past month, which is defined as consuming five or more drinks on one occasion.

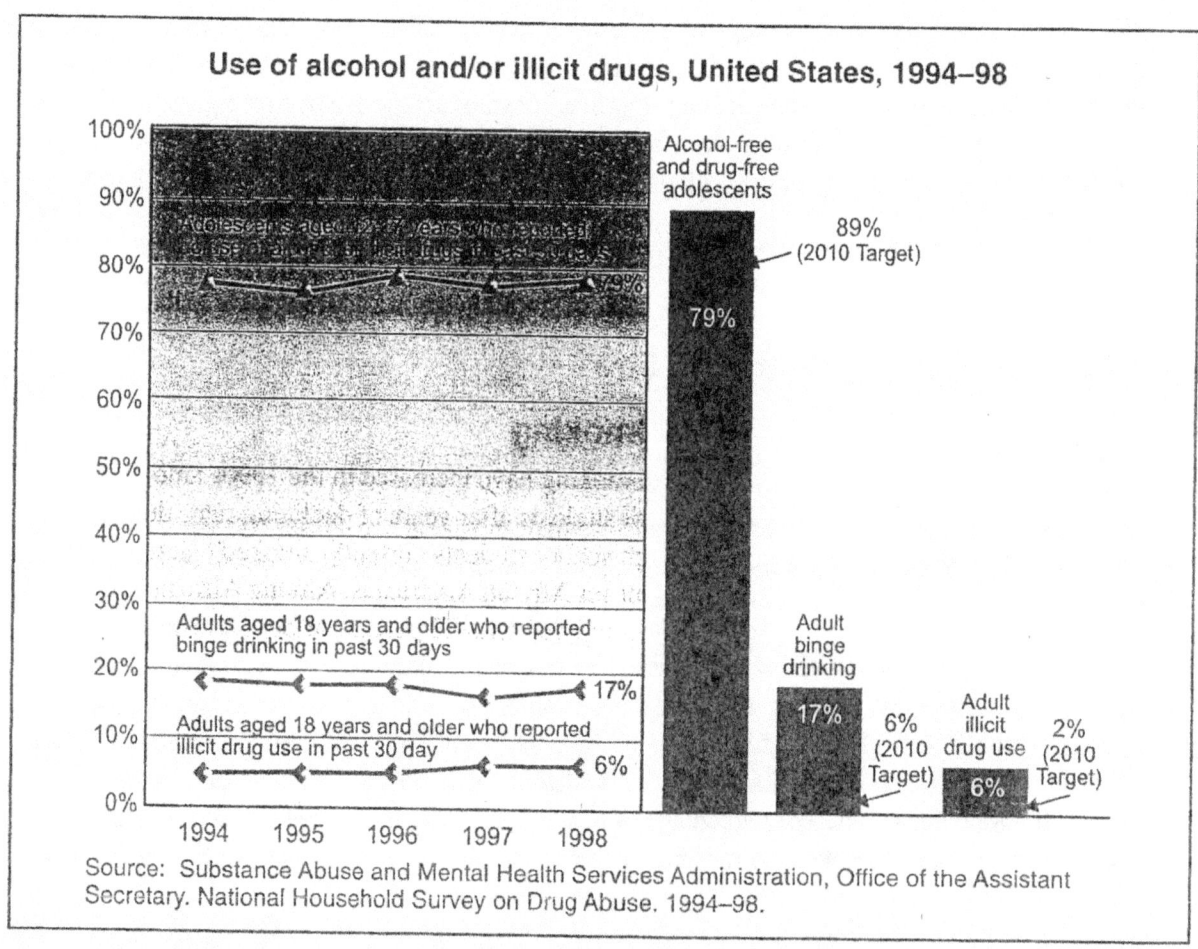

Source: Substance Abuse and Mental Health Services Administration, Office of the Assistant Secretary. National Household Survey on Drug Abuse. 1994–98.

The objectives selected to measure progress among adolescents and adults for this Leading Health Indicator are presented below. These are only indicators and do not represent all the substance abuse objectives in Healthy People 2010.

- 26-10a. **Increase the proportion of adolescents not using alcohol or any illicit drugs during the past 30 days.**
- 26-10c. **Reduce the proportion of adults using any illicit drug during the past 30 days.**
- 26-11c. **Reduce the proportion of adults engaging in binge drinking of alcoholic beverages during the past month.**

Leading Health Indicator

Health Impact of Substance Abuse

Alcohol and illicit drug use are associated with child and spousal abuse; sexually transmitted diseases, including HIV infection; teen pregnancy; school failure; motor vehicle crashes; escalation of health care costs; low worker productivity; and homelessness. Alcohol and illicit drug use also can result in substantial disruptions in family, work, and personal life.

Alcohol abuse alone is associated with motor vehicle crashes, homicides, suicides, and drowning—leading causes of death among youth. Long-term heavy drinking can lead to heart disease, cancer, alcohol-related liver disease, and pancreatitis. Alcohol use during pregnancy is known to cause fetal alcohol syndrome, a leading cause of preventable mental retardation.

Trends in Substance Abuse

Adolescents. Although the trend from 1994 to 1998 has shown some fluctuations, about 77 percent of adolescents aged 12 to 17 years report being both alcohol-free and drug-free in the past month.

Alcohol is the drug most frequently used by adolescents aged 12 to 17 years. In 1998, 19 percent of adolescents aged 12 to 17 years reported drinking alcohol in the past month. Alcohol use in the past month for this age group has remained at about 20 percent since 1992. Eight percent of this age group reported binge drinking, and 3 percent were heavy drinkers (five or more drinks on the same occasion on each of 5 or more days in the past 30 days).

Data from 1998 show that 10 percent of adolescents aged 12 to 17 years reported using illicit drugs in the past 30 days. This rate remains well below the all-time high of 16 percent in 1979. Current illicit drug use had nearly doubled for those aged 12 to 13 years between 1996 and 1997 but then decreased between 1997 and 1998. Youth are experimenting with a variety of illicit drugs, including marijuana, cocaine, crack, heroin, acid, inhalants, and methamphetamines, as well as misuse of prescription drugs and other "street" drugs. The younger a person becomes a habitual user of illicit drugs, the stronger the addiction becomes and the more difficult it is to stop use.

Adults. Binge drinking has remained at the same approximate level of 17 percent for all adults since 1988, with the highest current rate of 32 percent among adults aged 18 to 25 years. Illicit drug use has been near the present rate of 6 percent since 1980. Men continue to have higher rates of illicit drug use than women have, and rates of illicit drug use in urban areas are higher than in rural areas.

Responsible Sexual Behavior

Leading Health Indicator

Unintended pregnancies and sexually transmitted diseases (STDs), including infection with the human immunodeficiency virus that causes AIDS, can result from unprotected sexual behaviors. Abstinence is the only method of complete protection. Condoms, if used correctly and consistently, can help prevent both unintended pregnancy and STDs.

In 1999, 85 percent of adolescents abstained from sexual intercourse or used condoms if they were sexually active. In 1995, 23 percent of sexually active women reported that their partners used condoms.

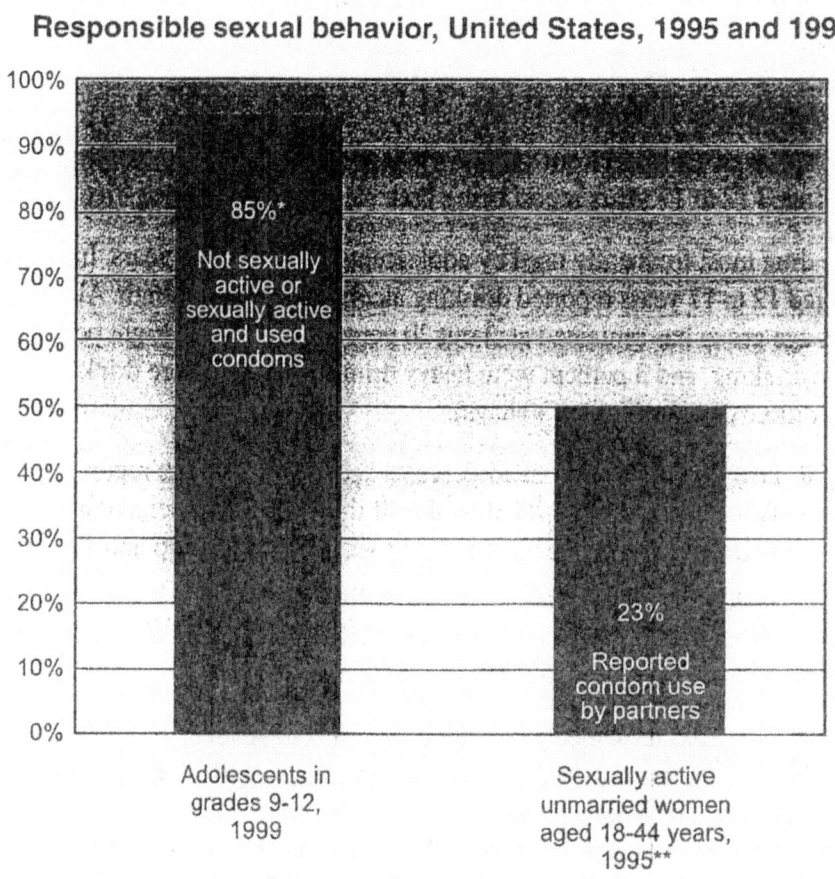

Responsible sexual behavior, United States, 1995 and 1999

- Adolescents in grades 9-12, 1999: 85%* Not sexually active or sexually active and used condoms
- Sexually active unmarried women aged 18-44 years, 1995**: 23% Reported condom use by partners

* This 85 percent includes 50 percent of students in grades 9-12 who were not ever sexually active, 14 percent who were not sexually active in the past 3 months, and 21 percent who were sexually active but used a condom at the last intercourse.

** Data on males aged 15 to 49 years will be collected in 2003.

Sources: Centers for Disease Control and Prevention. Youth Risk Behavior Survey. 1999. Centers for Disease Control and Prevention, National Center for Health Statistics. National Survey of Family Growth. 1995.

The objectives selected to measure progress among adolescents and adults for this Leading Health Indicator are presented below. These are only indicators and do not represent all the responsible sexual behavior objectives in Healthy People 2010.

25-11. Increase the proportion of adolescents who abstain from sexual intercourse or use condoms if currently sexually active.

13-6a. Increase the proportion of sexually active persons who use condoms.

Leading Health Indicator

Trends in Sexual Behavior

In the past 6 years there has been both an increase in abstinence among all youth and an increase in condom use among those young people who are sexually active. Research has shown clearly that the most effective school-based programs are comprehensive ones that include a focus on abstinence *and* condom use. Condom use in sexually active adults has remained steady at about 25 percent.

Unintended Pregnancies

Half of all pregnancies in the United States are unintended; that is, at the time of conception the pregnancy was not planned or not wanted. Unintended pregnancy rates in the United States have been declining. The rates remain highest among teenagers, women aged 40 years or older, and low-income African American women. Approximately 1 million teenage girls each year in the United States have unintended pregnancies. Nearly half of all unintended pregnancies end in abortion.

The cost to U.S. taxpayers for adolescent pregnancy is estimated at between $7 billion and $15 billion a year.

Sexually Transmitted Diseases

Sexually transmitted diseases are common in the United States, with an estimated 15 million new cases of STDs reported each year. Almost 4 million of the new cases of STDs each year occur in adolescents. Women generally suffer more serious STD complications than men, including pelvic inflammatory disease, ectopic pregnancy, infertility, chronic pelvic pain, and cervical cancer from the human papilloma virus. African Americans and Hispanics have higher rates of STDs than whites.

The total cost of the most common STDs and their complications is conservatively estimated at $17 billion annually.

HIV/AIDS

Nearly 700,000 cases of AIDS have been reported in the United States since the HIV/AIDS epidemic began in the 1980s. The latest estimates indicate that 800,000 to 900,000 people in the United States currently are infected with HIV. The lifetime cost of health care associated with HIV infection, in light of recent advances in HIV diagnostics and therapies, is $155,000 or more per person.

About one-half of all new HIV infections in the United States are among people under age 25 years, and the majority are infected through sexual behavior. HIV infection is the leading cause of death for African American men aged 25 to 44 years. Compelling worldwide evidence indicates that the presence of other STDs increases the likelihood of both transmitting and acquiring HIV infection.

Mental Health

Leading Health Indicator

Approximately 20 percent of the U.S. population is affected by mental illness during a given year; no one is immune. Of all mental illnesses, depression is the most common disorder. More than 19 million adults in the United States suffer from depression. Major depression is the leading cause of disability and is the cause of more than two-thirds of suicides each year.

In 1997, only 23 percent of adults diagnosed with depression received treatment.

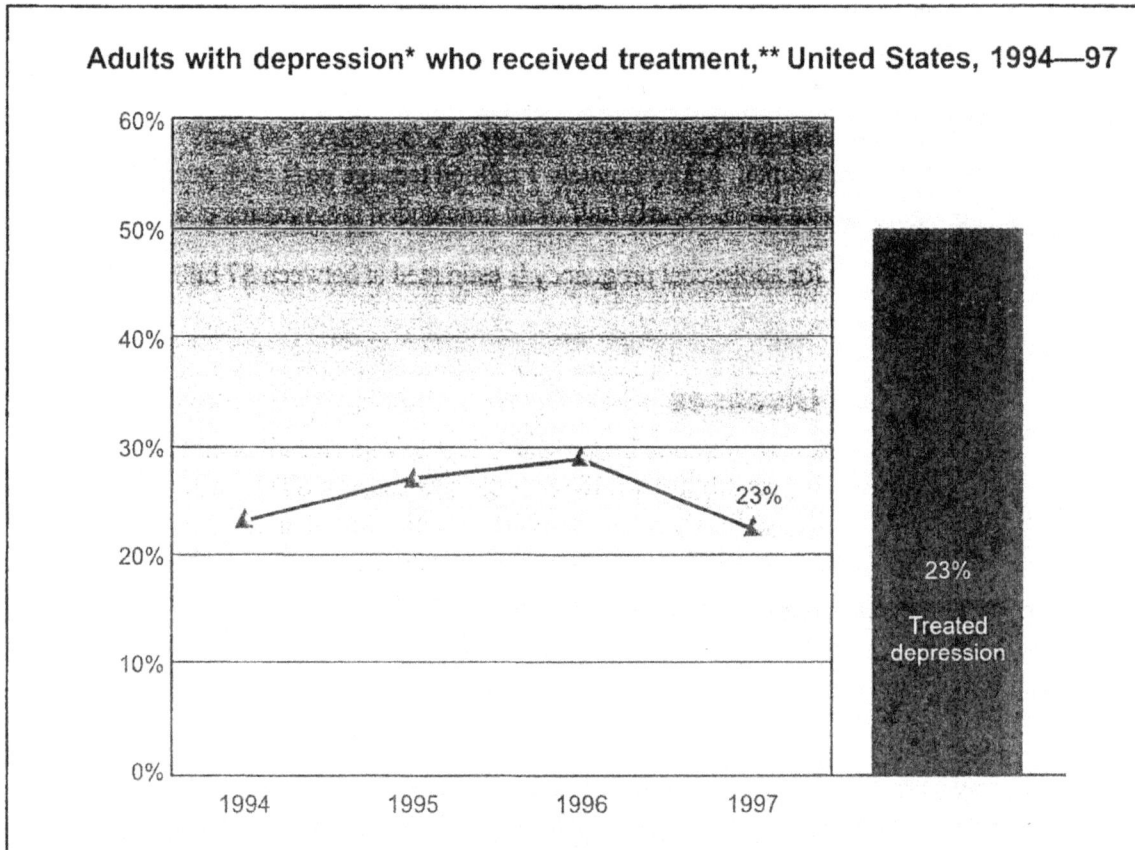

Adults with depression* who received treatment,** United States, 1994—97

* Depression is defined as major depressive episode in the past year.

** Treatment is defined as treatment in the past year for psychological problems or emotional difficulties at a mental health clinic or by a mental health professional on an outpatient basis or treatment for psychological or emotional difficulties at a hospital overnight or longer.

Source: Substance Abuse and Mental Health Services Administration, Office of Applied Studies. National Household Survey on Drug Abuse. 1994–97.

The objective selected to measure progress among adults for this Leading Health Indicator is presented below. This is only an indicator and does not represent all the mental health objectives in Healthy People 2010.

18-9b. Increase the proportion of adults with recognized depression who receive treatment.

Leading Health Indicator

Definition of Mental Health

Mental health is sometimes thought of as simply the absence of a mental illness but is actually much broader. Mental health is a state of successful mental functioning, resulting in productive activities, fulfilling relationships, and the ability to adapt to change and cope with adversity. Mental health is indispensable to personal well-being, family and interpersonal relationships, and one's contribution to society.

Impact of Depression

A person with a depressive disorder often is unable to fulfill the daily responsibilities of being a spouse, partner, or parent. The misunderstanding of mental illness and the associated stigmatization prevent many persons with depression from seeking professional help. Many people will be incapacitated for weeks or months because their depression goes untreated.

Depression is associated with other medical conditions, such as heart disease, cancer, and diabetes as well as anxiety and eating disorders. Depression also has been associated with alcohol and illicit drug abuse. An estimated 8 million persons aged 15 to 54 years had coexisting mental and substance abuse disorders within the past year.

The total estimated direct and indirect costs of mental illness in the United States in 1996 was $150 billion.

Treatment of Depression

Depression is treatable. Available medications and psychological treatments, alone or in combination, can help 80 percent of those with depression. With adequate treatment, future episodes of depression can be prevented or reduced in severity. Treatment for depression can enable people to return to satisfactory, functioning lives.

Populations With High Rates of Depression

Serious mental illness clearly affects mental health and can affect children, adolescents, adults, and older adults of all ethnic and racial groups, both genders, and people at all educational and income levels.

Adults and older adults have the highest rates of depression. Major depression affects approximately twice as many women as men. Women who are poor, on welfare, less educated, unemployed, and from certain racial or ethnic populations are more likely to experience depression. In addition, depression rates are higher among older adults with coexisting medical conditions. For example, 12 percent of older persons hospitalized for problems such as hip fracture or heart disease are diagnosed with depression. Rates of depression for older persons in nursing homes range from 15 to 25 percent.

Injury and Violence

Leading Health Indicator

More than 400 Americans die each day from injuries due primarily to motor vehicle crashes, firearms, poisonings, suffocation, falls, fires, and drowning. The risk of injury is so great that most persons sustain a significant injury at some time during their lives.

Motor vehicle crashes are the most common cause of serious injury. In 1998, there were 15.6 deaths from motor vehicle crashes per 100,000 persons.

Because no other crime is measured as accurately and precisely, homicide is a reliable indicator of all violent crime. In 1998, the murder rate in the United States fell to its lowest level in three decades—6.5 homicides per 100,000 persons.

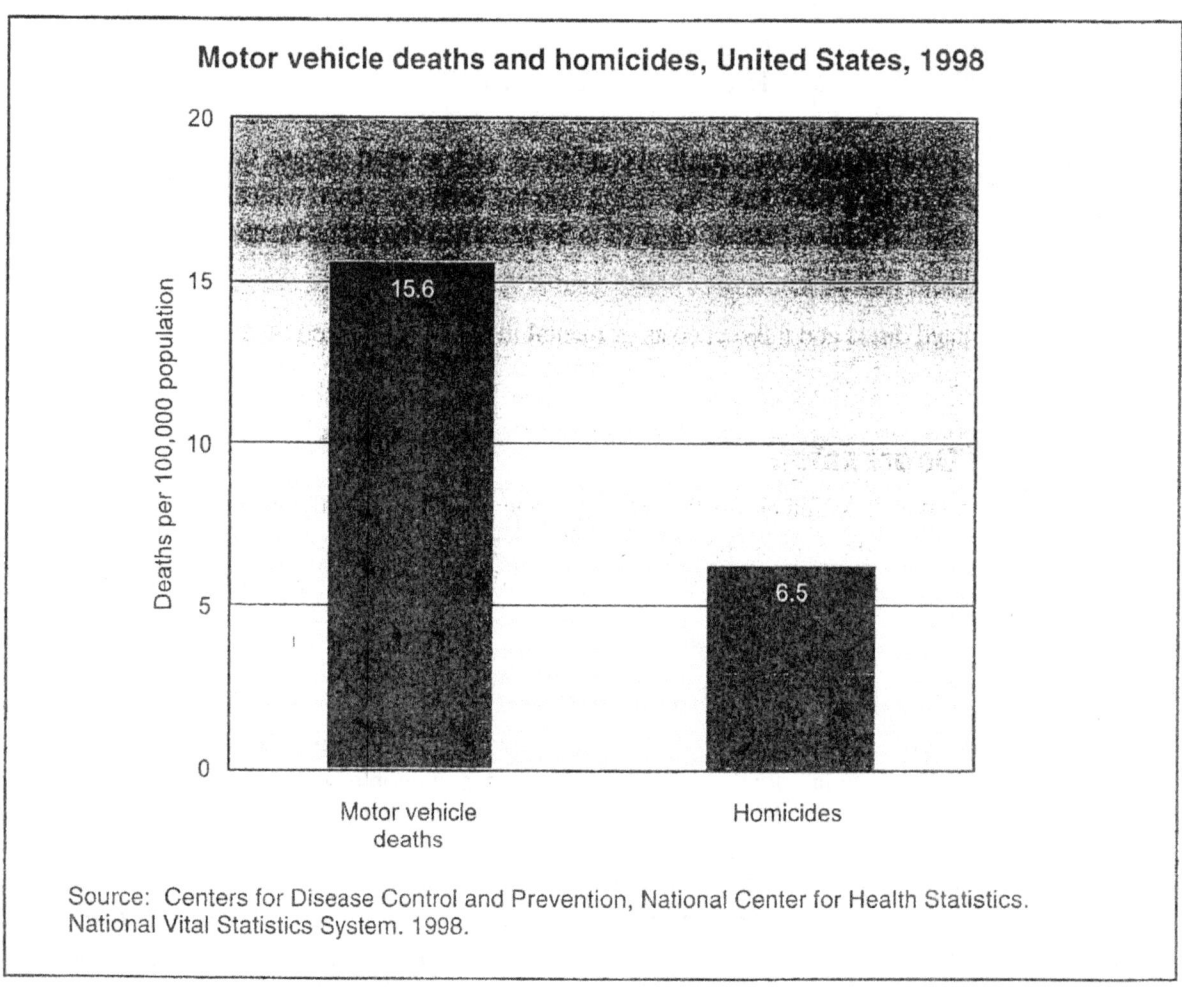

The objectives selected to measure progress for this Leading Health Indicator are presented below. These are only indicators and do not represent all the injury and violence prevention objectives in Healthy People 2010.

15-15a. Reduce deaths caused by motor vehicle crashes.
15-32.   Reduce homicides.

Leading Health Indicator

Impact of Injury and Violence

In 1995, the cost of injury and violence in the United States was estimated at more than $224 billion per year. These costs include direct medical care and rehabilitation as well as productivity losses to the Nation's workforce. The total societal cost of motor vehicle crashes alone exceeds $150 billion annually.

Motor Vehicle Crashes

Motor vehicle crashes often are predictable and preventable. Increased use of safety belts and reductions in driving while impaired are two of the most effective means to reduce the risk of death and serious injury of occupants in motor vehicle crashes.

Death rates associated with motor vehicle-traffic injuries are highest in the age group 15 to 24 years. In 1996, teenagers accounted for only 10 percent of the U.S. population but 15 percent of the deaths from motor vehicle crashes. Those aged 75 years and older had the second highest rate of motor vehicle-related deaths.

Nearly 40 percent of traffic fatalities in 1997 were alcohol related. Each year in the United States it is estimated that more than 120 million episodes of impaired driving occur among adults. In 1996, 21 percent of traffic fatalities of children aged 14 years and under involved alcohol; 60 percent of the time the driver of the car in which the child was a passenger was impaired.

The highest intoxication rates in fatal crashes in 1995 were recorded for drivers aged 21 to 24 years. Young drivers who have been arrested for driving while impaired are more than four times as likely to die in future alcohol-related crashes.

Homicides

In 1997, 32,436 individuals died from firearm injuries; of this number, 42 percent were victims of homicide. In 1997, homicide was the third leading cause of death for children aged 5 to 14 years, an increasing trend in childhood violent deaths. In 1996, more than 80 percent of infant homicides were considered to be fatal child abuse.

Many factors that contribute to injuries are also closely associated with violent and abusive behavior, such as low income, discrimination, lack of education, and lack of employment opportunities.

Males are most often the victims and the perpetrators of homicides. African Americans are more than five times as likely as whites to be murdered. There has been a decline in the homicide of intimates, including spouses, partners, boyfriends, and girlfriends, over the past decade, but this problem remains significant.

Environmental Quality

Leading Health Indicator

An estimated 25 percent of preventable illnesses worldwide can be attributed to poor environmental quality. In the United States, air pollution alone is estimated to be associated with 50,000 premature deaths and an estimated $40 billion to $50 billion in health-related costs annually. Two indicators of air quality are ozone (outdoor) and environmental tobacco smoke (indoor).

In 1997, approximately 43 percent of the U.S. population lived in areas designated as nonattainment areas for established health-based standards for ozone. During the years 1988 to 1994, 65 percent of nonsmokers were exposed to environmental tobacco smoke (ETS).

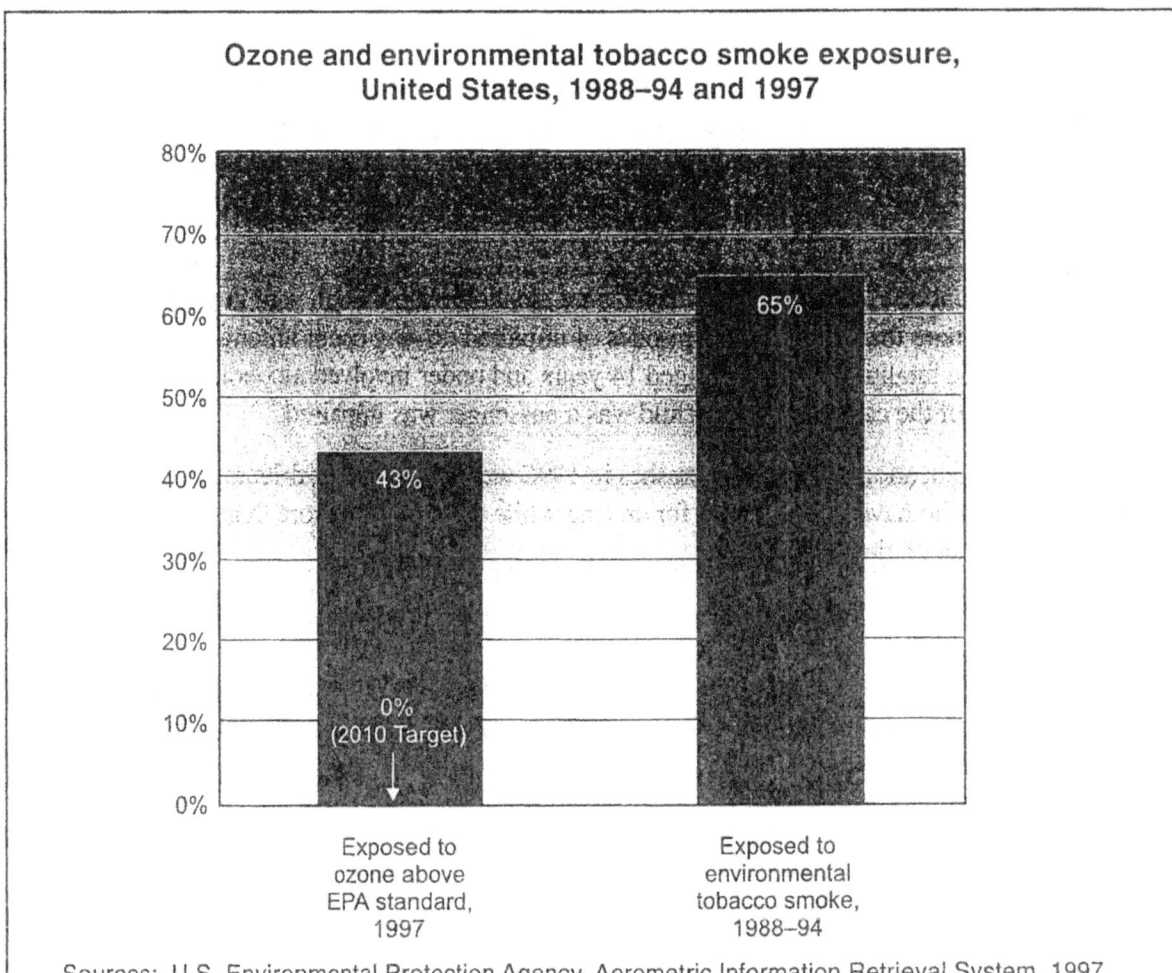

Ozone and environmental tobacco smoke exposure, United States, 1988–94 and 1997

Sources: U.S. Environmental Protection Agency. Aerometric Information Retrieval System. 1997. Centers for Disease Control and Prevention, National Center for Health Statistics. National Health and Nutrition Examination Survey. 1988–94.

The objectives selected to measure progress among children, adolescents, and adults for this Leading Health Indicator are presented below. These are only indicators and do not represent all the environmental quality objectives in Healthy People 2010.

8-1a. **Reduce the proportion of persons exposed to air that does not meet the U.S. Environmental Protection Agency's health-based standards for ozone.**

27-10. **Reduce the proportion of nonsmokers exposed to environmental tobacco smoke.**

Leading Health Indicator

Defining the Environment

Physical and social environments play major roles in the health of individuals and communities. The physical environment includes the air, water, and soil through which exposure to chemical, biological, and physical agents may occur. The social environment includes housing, transportation, urban development, land use, industry, and agriculture and results in exposures such as work-related stress, injury, and violence.

Global Concern

Environmental quality is a global concern. Ever-increasing numbers of people and products cross national borders and may transfer health risks such as infectious diseases and chemical hazards. For example, pesticides that are not registered or are restricted for use in the United States potentially could be imported in the fruits, vegetables, and seafood produced abroad.

Health Impact of Poor Air Quality

Poor air quality contributes to respiratory illness, cardiovascular disease, and cancer. For example, asthma can be triggered or worsened by exposure to ozone and ETS. The overall death rate from asthma increased 57 percent between 1980 and 1993, and for children it increased 67 percent.

Air Pollution. Dramatic improvements in air quality in the United States have occurred over the past three decades. Between 1970 and 1997, total emissions of the six principal air pollutants decreased 31 percent. Still, million of tons of toxic pollutants are released into the air each year from automobiles, industry, and other sources. In 1997, despite continued improvements in air quality, approximately 120 million people lived in areas with unhealthy air based on established standards for one or more commonly found air pollutants, including ozone. In 1996, a disproportionate number of Hispanics and Asian and Pacific Islanders lived in areas that failed to meet these standards compared with whites, African Americans, and American Indians or Alaska Natives.

Tobacco Smoke. Exposure to ETS, or secondhand smoke, among nonsmokers is widespread. Home and workplace environments are major sources of exposure. A total of 15 million children are estimated to have been exposed to secondhand smoke in their homes in 1996. ETS increases the risk of heart disease and respiratory infections in children and is responsible for an estimated 3,000 cancer deaths of adult nonsmokers.

Improvement in Environmental Quality

In the United States, ensuring clean water, safe food, and effective waste management has contributed greatly to a declining threat from many infectious diseases; however, there is still more that can be done. Work to improve the air quality and to understand better threats such as chronic, low-level exposures to hazardous substances also must continue.

Immunization

Leading Health Indicator

Vaccines are among the greatest public health achievements of the 20th century. Immunizations can prevent disability and death from infectious diseases for individuals and can help control the spread of infections within communities.

In 1998, 73 percent of children received all vaccines recommended for universal administration.

In 1998, influenza immunization rates were 64 percent in adults aged 65 years and older—almost double the 1989 immunization rate of 33 percent. In 1998, only 46 percent of persons aged 65 years and older had ever received a pneumococcal vaccine.

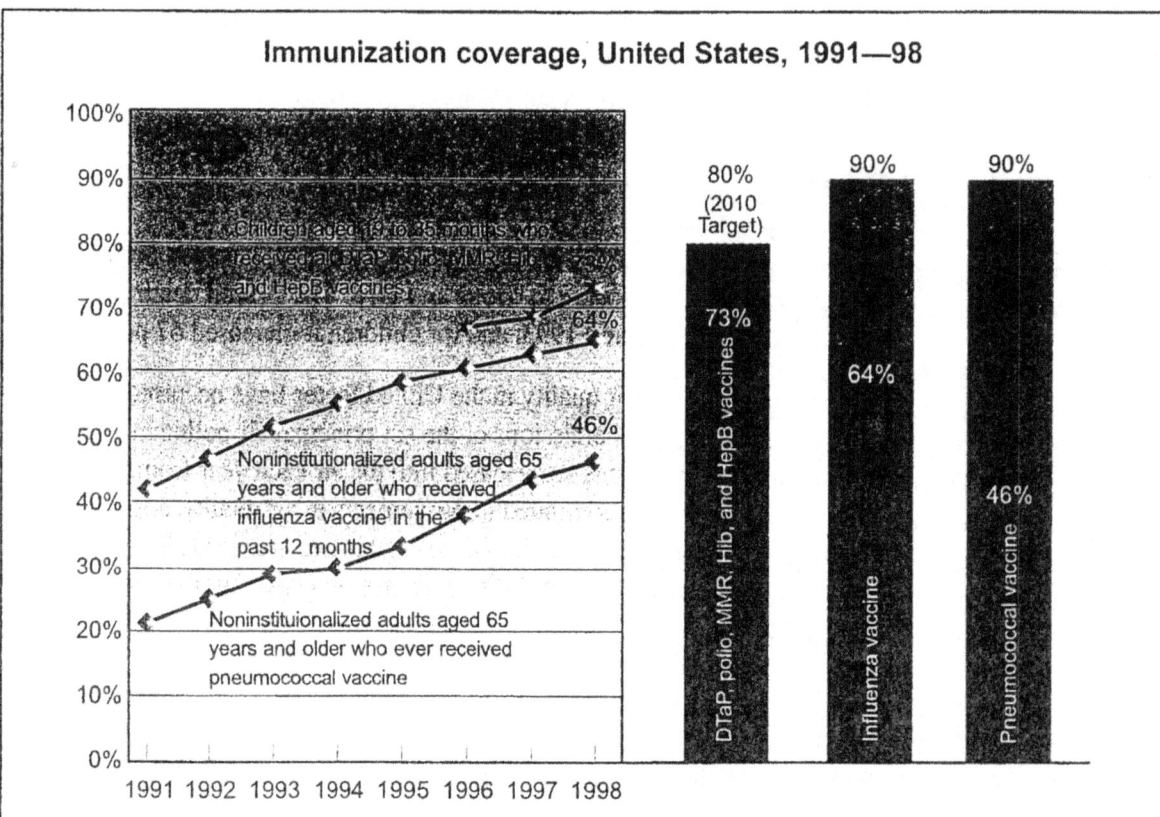

*Four or more doses of diphtheria/tetanus/acellular pertussis (DTaP) vaccine, three or more doses of polio vaccine, one or more dose of measles/mumps/rubella (MMR) vaccine, three or more doses of *Haemophilus influenzae* type b (Hib) vaccine, and three or more doses of hepatitis B (Hep B) vaccine.

Sources: Centers for Disease Control and Prevention, National Center for Health Statistics and National Immunization Program. National Immunization Survey. 1996–98. Centers for Disease Control and Prevention, National Center for Health Statistics. National Health Interview Survey. 1991–98.

The objectives selected to measure progress among children and adults for this Leading Health Indicator are presented below. These are only indicators and do not represent all the immunization and infectious diseases objectives in Healthy People 2010.

14-24a. **Increase the proportion of young children who receive all vaccines that have been recommended for universal administration for at least 5 years.**

14-29a, b. **Increase the proportion of noninstitutionalized adults who are vaccinated annually against influenza and ever vaccinated against pneumococcal disease.**

Leading Health Indicator

Impact of Immunization

Many once-common vaccine-preventable diseases now are controlled. Smallpox has been eradicated, poliomyelitis has been eliminated from the Western Hemisphere, and measles cases in the United States are at a record low.

Immunizations against influenza and pneumococcal disease can prevent serious illness and death. Pneumonia and influenza deaths together constitute the sixth leading cause of death in the United States. Influenza causes an average of 110,000 hospitalizations and 20,000 deaths annually; pneumococcal disease causes 10,000 to 14,000 deaths annually.

Recommended Immunizations

As of November 1, 1999, all children born in the United States (11,000 per day) should be receiving 12 to 16 doses of vaccine by age 2 years to be protected against 10 vaccine-preventable childhood diseases. This recommendation will change in the years ahead as new vaccines are developed, including combinations of current vaccines that may even reduce the number of necessary shots.

Recommended immunizations for adults aged 65 years and older include a yearly immunization against influenza (the "flu shot") and a one-time immunization against pneumococcal disease. Most of the deaths and serious illnesses caused by influenza and pneumococcal disease occur in older adults and others at increased risk for complications of these diseases because of other risk factors or medical conditions.

Trends in Immunization

National coverage levels in children now are greater than 90 percent for each immunization recommended during the first 2 years of life, except for hepatitis B and varicella vaccines. The hepatitis B immunization rate in children was 87 percent in 1998—the highest level ever reported. In 1998, 70 percent of children aged 19 to 35 months from the lowest income households received the combined series of recommended immunizations, compared with 77 percent of children from higher income households.

Both influenza and pneumococcal immunization rates are significantly lower for African American and Hispanic adults than for white adults.

Other Immunization Issues

Coverage levels for immunizations in adults are not as high as those achieved in children, yet the health effects may be just as great. Barriers to adult immunization include not knowing immunizations are needed, misconceptions about vaccines, and lack of recommendations from health care providers.

Access to Health Care

Leading Health Indicator

Strong predictors of access to quality health care include having health insurance, a higher income level, and a regular primary care provider or other source of ongoing health care. Use of clinical preventive services, such as early prenatal care, can serve as indicators of access to quality health care services.

In 1997, 83 percent of persons under age 65 years had health insurance. In 1998, 87 percent of persons of all ages had a usual source of health care. Also in that year, 83 percent of pregnant women received prenatal care in the first trimester of pregnancy.

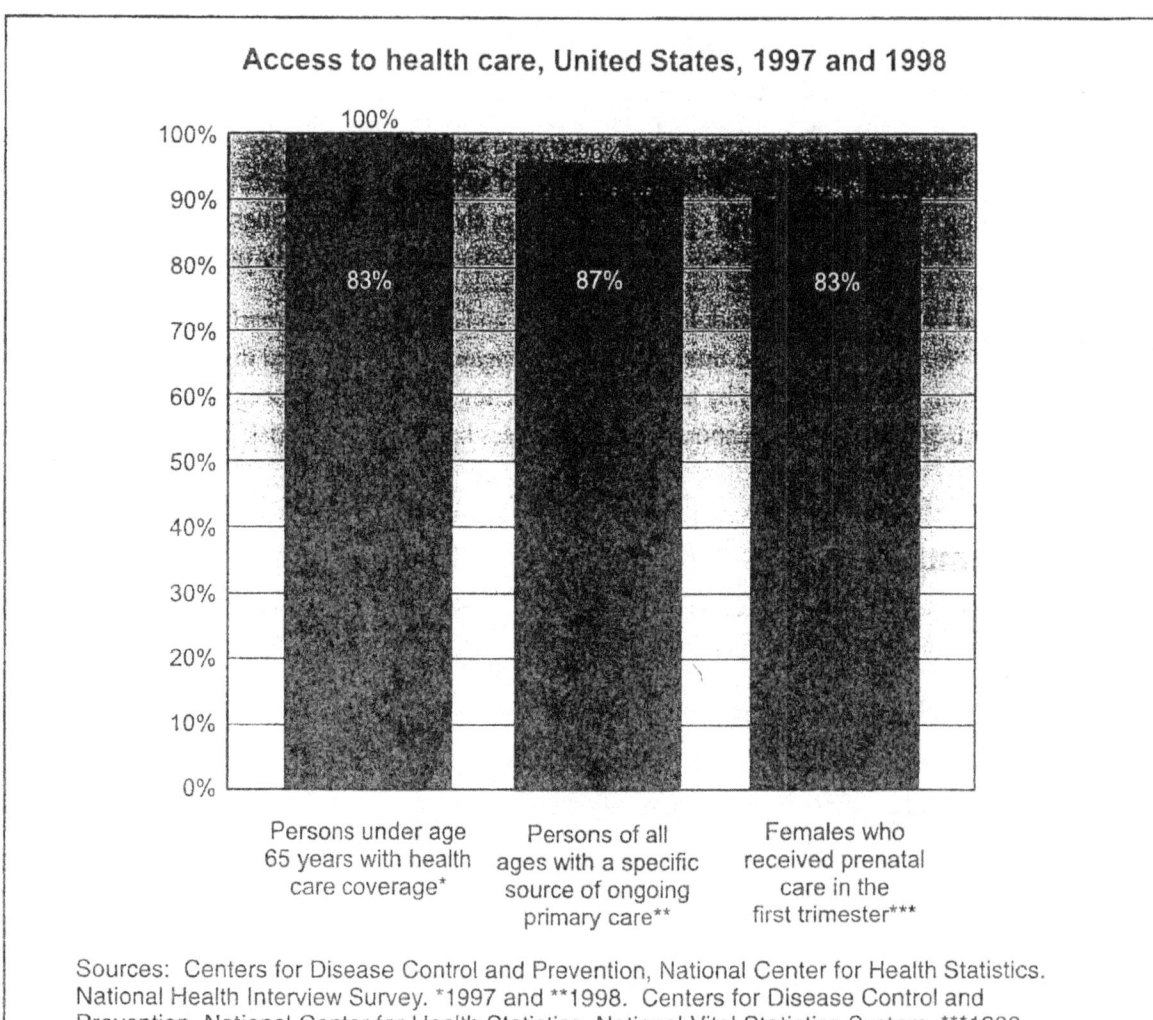

Access to health care, United States, 1997 and 1998

Sources: Centers for Disease Control and Prevention, National Center for Health Statistics. National Health Interview Survey. *1997 and **1998. Centers for Disease Control and Prevention, National Center for Health Statistics. National Vital Statistics System. ***1998.

The objectives selected to measure progress for this Leading Health Indicator are presented below. These are only indicators and do not represent all the access to quality health services objectives in Healthy People 2010.

1-1. Increase the proportion of persons with health insurance.
1-4a. Increase the proportion of persons who have a specific source of ongoing care.
16-6a. Increase the proportion of pregnant women who begin prenatal care in the first trimester of pregnancy.

Leading Health Indicator

Health Insurance

Health insurance provides access to health care. Persons with health insurance are more likely to have a primary care provider and to have received appropriate preventive care such as a recent Pap test, immunization, or early prenatal care. Adults with health insurance are twice as likely to receive a routine checkup as are adults without health insurance.

More than 44 million persons in the United States do not have health insurance, including 11 million uninsured children. Over the past decade, the proportion of persons under age 65 years with health insurance remained steady at about 85 percent. About one-third of adults under age 65 years below the poverty level were uninsured. For persons of Hispanic origin, approximately one in three was without health insurance coverage in 1997. Mexican Americans had one of the highest uninsured rates at 40 percent.

Ongoing Sources of Primary Care

More than 40 million Americans do not have a particular doctor's office, clinic, health center, or other place where they usually go to seek health care or health-related advice. Even among privately insured persons, a significant number lacked a usual source of care or reported difficulty in accessing needed care due to financial constraints or insurance problems.

People aged 18 to 24 years were the most likely to lack a usual source of ongoing primary care. Only 80 percent of individuals below the poverty level and 79 percent of Hispanics had a usual source of ongoing primary care.

Barriers to Access

Financial, structural, and personal barriers can limit access to health care. Financial barriers include not having health insurance, not having enough health insurance to cover needed services, or not having the financial capacity to cover services outside a health plan or insurance program. Structural barriers include the lack of primary care providers, medical specialists, or other health care professionals to meet special needs or the lack of health care facilities. Personal barriers include cultural or spiritual differences, language barriers, not knowing what to do or when to seek care, or concerns about confidentiality or discrimination.

Appendix: Short Titles for Healthy People 2010 Objectives

1. Access to Quality Health Services

Goal: Improve access to comprehensive, high-quality health care services.

Objective Number and Short Title

Clinical Preventive Care
- 1-1 Persons with health insurance
- 1-2 Health insurance coverage for clinical preventive services
- 1-3 Counseling about health behaviors

Primary Care
- 1-4 Source of ongoing care
- 1-5 Usual primary care provider
- 1-6 Difficulties or delays in obtaining needed health care
- 1-7 Core competencies in health provider training
- 1-8 Racial and ethnic representation in health professions
- 1-9 Hospitalization for ambulatory-care-sensitive conditions

Emergency Services
- 1-10 Delay or difficulty in getting emergency care
- 1-11 Rapid prehospital emergency care
- 1-12 Single toll-free number for poison control centers
- 1-13 Trauma care systems
- 1-14 Special needs of children

Long-Term Care and Rehabilitative Services
- 1-15 Long-term care services
- 1-16 Pressure ulcers among nursing home residents

2. Arthritis, Osteoporosis, and Chronic Back Conditions

Goal: Prevent illness and disability related to arthritis and other rheumatic conditions, osteoporosis, and chronic back conditions.

Objective Number and Short Title

Arthritis and Other Rheumatic Conditions
- 2-1 Mean number of days without severe pain
- 2-2 Activity limitations due to arthritis
- 2-3 Personal care limitations
- 2-4 Help in coping
- 2-5 Employment rate
- 2-6 Racial differences in total knee replacement
- 2-7 Seeing a health care provider
- 2-8 Arthritis education

Osteoporosis
- 2-9 Cases of osteoporosis
- 2-10 Hospitalization for vertebral fractures

Chronic Back Conditions
- 2-11 Activity limitations due to chronic back conditions

3. Cancer

Goal: Reduce the number of new cancer cases as well as the illness, disability, and death caused by cancer.

Objective Number and Short Title

- 3-1 Overall cancer deaths
- 3-2 Lung cancer deaths
- 3-3 Breast cancer deaths
- 3-4 Cervical cancer deaths
- 3-5 Colorectal cancer deaths
- 3-6 Oropharyngeal cancer deaths
- 3-7 Prostate cancer deaths
- 3-8 Melanoma deaths
- 3-9 Sun exposure and skin cancer
- 3-10 Provider counseling about cancer prevention
- 3-11 Pap tests
- 3-12 Colorectal cancer screening
- 3-13 Mammograms
- 3-14 Statewide cancer registries
- 3-15 Cancer survival

4. Chronic Kidney Disease

Goal: Reduce new cases of chronic kidney disease and its complications, disability, death, and economic costs.

Objective Number and Short Title

- 4-1 End-stage renal disease
- 4-2 Cardiovascular disease deaths in persons with chronic kidney failure
- 4-3 Counseling for chronic kidney failure care
- 4-4 Use of arteriovenous fistulas
- 4-5 Registration for kidney transplantation
- 4-6 Waiting time for kidney transplantation
- 4-7 Kidney failure due to diabetes
- 4-8 Medical therapy for persons with diabetes and proteinuria

5. Diabetes

Goal: Through prevention programs, reduce the disease and economic burden of diabetes, and improve the quality of life for all persons who have or are at risk for diabetes.

Objective Number and Short Title

- 5-1 Diabetes education
- 5-2 New cases of diabetes
- 5-3 Overall cases of diagnosed diabetes
- 5-4 Diagnosis of diabetes
- 5-5 Diabetes deaths
- 5-6 Diabetes-related deaths
- 5-7 Cardiovascular disease deaths in persons with diabetes
- 5-8 Gestational diabetes
- 5-9 Foot ulcers
- 5-10 Lower extremity amputations
- 5-11 Annual urinary microalbumin measurement
- 5-12 Annual glycosylated hemoglobin measurement
- 5-13 Annual dilated eye examinations
- 5-14 Annual foot examinations
- 5-15 Annual dental examinations
- 5-16 Aspirin therapy
- 5-17 Self-blood-glucose-monitoring

6. Disability and Secondary Conditions

Goal: Promote the health of people with disabilities, prevent secondary conditions, and eliminate disparities between people with and without disabilities in the U.S. population.

Objective Number and Short Title

- 6-1 Standard definition of people with disabilities in data sets
- 6-2 Feelings and depression among children with disabilities
- 6-3 Feelings and depression interfering with activities among adults with disabilities
- 6-4 Social participation among adults with disabilities
- 6-5 Sufficient emotional support among adults with disabilities
- 6-6 Satisfaction with life among adults with disabilities
- 6-7 Congregate care of children and adults with disabilities
- 6-8 Employment parity
- 6-9 Inclusion of children and youth with disabilities in regular education programs
- 6-10 Accessibility of health and wellness programs
- 6-11 Assistive devices and technology
- 6-12 Environmental barriers affecting participation in activities
- 6-13 Surveillance and health promotion programs

7. Educational and Community-Based Programs

Goal: Increase the quality, availability, and effectiveness of educational and community-based programs designed to prevent disease and improve health and quality of life.

Objective Number and Short Title

School Setting

- 7-1 High school completion
- 7-2 School health education
- 7-3 Health-risk behavior information for college and university students
- 7-4 School nurse-to-student ratio

Worksite Setting

- 7-5 Worksite health promotion programs
- 7-6 Participation in employer-sponsored health promotion activities

Health Care Setting

- 7-7 Patient and family education
- 7-8 Satisfaction with patient education
- 7-9 Health care organization sponsorship of community health promotion activities

Community Setting and Select Populations

- 7-10 Community health promotion programs
- 7-11 Culturally appropriate and linguistically competent community health promotion programs
- 7-12 Older adult participation in community health promotion activities

8. Environmental Health

Goal: Promote health for all through a healthy environment.

Objective Number and Short Title

Outdoor Air Quality

- 8-1 Harmful air pollutants
- 8-2 Alternative modes of transportation
- 8-3 Cleaner alternative fuels
- 8-4 Airborne toxins

Water Quality

- 8-5 Safe drinking water
- 8-6 Waterborne disease outbreaks
- 8-7 Water conservation
- 8-8 Surface water health risks
- 8-9 Beach closings
- 8-10 Fish contamination

Toxics and Waste

- 8-11 Elevated blood lead levels in children
- 8-12 Risks posed by hazardous sites
- 8-13 Pesticide exposures
- 8-14 Toxic pollutants
- 8-15 Recycled municipal solid waste

Healthy Homes and Healthy Communities

- 8-16 Indoor allergens
- 8-17 Office building air quality
- 8-18 Homes tested for radon
- 8-19 Radon-resistant new home construction
- 8-20 School policies to protect against environmental hazards
- 8-21 Disaster preparedness plans and protocols
- 8-22 Lead-based paint testing
- 8-23 Substandard housing

Infrastructure and Surveillance

- 8-24 Exposure to pesticides
- 8-25 Exposure to heavy metals and other toxic chemicals
- 8-26 Information systems used for environmental health
- 8-27 Monitoring environmentally related diseases
- 8-28 Local agencies using surveillance data for vector control

Global Environmental Health

- 8-29 Global burden of disease
- 8-30 Water quality in the U.S.-Mexico border region

9. Family Planning

Goal: Improve pregnancy planning and spacing and prevent unintended pregnancy.

Objective Number and Short Title

- 9-1 Intended pregnancy
- 9-2 Birth spacing
- 9-3 Contraceptive use
- 9-4 Contraceptive failure
- 9-5 Emergency contraception
- 9-6 Male involvement in pregnancy prevention
- 9-7 Adolescent pregnancy
- 9-8 Abstinence before age 15 years
- 9-9 Abstinence among adolescents aged 15 to 17 years
- 9-10 Pregnancy prevention and sexually transmitted disease (STD) protection
- 9-11 Pregnancy prevention education
- 9-12 Problems in becoming pregnant and maintaining a pregnancy
- 9-13 Insurance coverage for contraceptive supplies and services

10. Food Safety

Goal: Reduce foodborne illnesses.

Objective Number and Short Title

- 10-1 Foodborne infections
- 10-2 Outbreaks of foodborne infections
- 10-3 Antimicrobial resistance of *Salmonella* species
- 10-4 Food allergy deaths
- 10-5 Consumer food safety practices
- 10-6 Safe food preparation practices in retail establishments
- 10-7 Organophosphate pesticide exposure

11. Health Communication

Goal: Use communication strategically to improve health.

Objective Number and Short Title

- 11-1 Households with Internet access
- 11-2 Health literacy
- 11-3 Research and evaluation of communication programs
- 11-4 Quality of Internet health information sources
- 11-5 Centers for excellence
- 11-6 Satisfaction with health care providers' communication skills

12. Heart Disease and Stroke

Goal: Improve cardiovascular health and quality of life through the prevention, detection, and treatment of risk factors; early identification and treatment of heart attacks and strokes; and prevention of recurrent cardiovascular events.

Objective Number and Short Title

Heart Disease

- 12-1 Coronary heart disease (CHD) deaths
- 12-2 Knowledge of symptoms of heart attack and importance of calling 911
- 12-3 Artery-opening therapy
- 12-4 Bystander response to cardiac arrest
- 12-5 Out-of-hospital emergency care
- 12-6 Heart failure hospitalizations

Stroke

- 12-7 Stroke deaths
- 12-8 Knowledge of early warning symptoms of stroke

Blood Pressure

- 12-9 High blood pressure
- 12-10 High blood pressure control
- 12-11 Action to help control blood pressure
- 12-12 Blood pressure monitoring

Cholesterol

- 12-13 Mean total blood cholesterol levels
- 12-14 High blood cholesterol levels
- 12-15 Blood cholesterol screening
- 12-16 LDL-cholesterol level in CHD patients

13. HIV

Goal: Prevent HIV infection and its related illness and death.

Objective Number and Short Title

- 13-1 New AIDS cases
- 13-2 AIDS among men who have sex with men
- 13-3 AIDS among persons who inject drugs
- 13-4 AIDS among men who have sex with men and who inject drugs
- 13-5 New HIV cases
- 13-6 Condom use
- 13-7 Knowledge of serostatus
- 13-8 HIV counseling and education for persons in substance abuse treatment
- 13-9 HIV/AIDS, STD, and TB education in State prisons
- 13-10 HIV counseling and testing in State prisons
- 13-11 HIV testing in TB patients
- 13-12 Screening for STDs and immunization for hepatitis B
- 13-13 Treatment according to guidelines
- 13-14 HIV-infection deaths
- 13-15 Interval between HIV infection and AIDS diagnosis
- 13-16 Interval between AIDS diagnosis and death from AIDS
- 13-17 Perinatally acquired HIV infection

14. Immunization and Infectious Diseases

Goal: Prevent disease, disability, and death from infectious diseases, including vaccine-preventable diseases.

Objective Number and Short Title

Diseases Preventable Through Universal Vaccination

- 14-1 Vaccine-preventable diseases
- 14-2 Hepatitis B in infants and young children
- 14-3 Hepatitis B in adults and high-risk groups
- 14-4 Bacterial meningitis in young children
- 14-5 Invasive pneumococcal infections

Diseases Preventable Through Targeted Vaccination
- 14-6 Hepatitis A
- 14-7 Meningococcal disease
- 14-8 Lyme disease

Infectious Diseases and Emerging Antimicrobial Resistance
- 14-9 Hepatitis C
- 14-10 Identification of persons with chronic hepatitis C
- 14-11 Tuberculosis
- 14-12 Curative therapy for tuberculosis
- 14-13 Treatment for high-risk persons with latent tuberculosis infection
- 14-14 Timely laboratory confirmation of tuberculosis cases
- 14-15 Prevention services for international travelers
- 14-16 Invasive early onset group B streptococcal disease
- 14-17 Peptic ulcer hospitalizations
- 14-18 Antibiotics prescribed for ear infections
- 14-19 Antibiotics prescribed for common cold
- 14-20 Hospital-acquired infections
- 14-21 Antimicrobial use in intensive care units

Vaccination Coverage and Strategies
- 14-22 Universally recommended vaccination of children aged 19 to 35 months
- 14-23 Vaccination coverage for children in day care, kindergarten, and first grade
- 14-24 Fully immunized young children and adolescents
- 14-25 Providers who measure childhood vaccination coverage levels
- 14-26 Children participating in population-based immunization registries
- 14-27 Vaccination coverage among adolescents
- 14-28 Hepatitis B vaccination among high-risk groups
- 14-29 Influenza and pneumococcal vaccination of high-risk adults

Vaccine Safety
- 14-30 Adverse events from vaccinations
- 14-31 Active surveillance for vaccine safety

15. Injury and Violence Prevention

Goal: Reduce injuries, disabilities, and deaths due to unintentional injuries and violence.

Objective Number and Short Title

Injury Prevention
- 15-1 Nonfatal head injuries
- 15-2 Nonfatal spinal cord injuries
- 15-3 Firearm-related deaths
- 15-4 Proper firearm storage in homes
- 15-5 Nonfatal firearm-related injuries
- 15-6 Child fatality review
- 15-7 Nonfatal poisonings
- 15-8 Deaths from poisoning
- 15-9 Deaths from suffocation
- 15-10 Emergency department surveillance systems
- 15-11 Hospital discharge surveillance systems
- 15-12 Emergency department visits

Unintentional Injury Prevention
- 15-13 Deaths from unintentional injuries
- 15-14 Nonfatal unintentional injuries
- 15-15 Deaths from motor vehicle crashes
- 15-16 Pedestrian deaths
- 15-17 Nonfatal motor vehicle injuries
- 15-18 Nonfatal pedestrian injuries
- 15-19 Safety belts
- 15-20 Child restraints
- 15-21 Motorcycle helmet use
- 15-22 Graduated driver licensing
- 15-23 Bicycle helmet use
- 15-24 Bicycle helmet laws
- 15-25 Residential fire deaths
- 15-26 Functioning smoke alarms in residences
- 15-27 Deaths from falls
- 15-28 Hip fractures
- 15-29 Drownings
- 15-30 Dog bite injuries
- 15-31 Injury protection in school sports

Violence and Abuse Prevention
- 15-32 Homicides
- 15-33 Maltreatment and maltreatment fatalities of children
- 15-34 Physical assault by intimate partners
- 15-35 Rape or attempted rape
- 15-36 Sexual assault other than rape
- 15-37 Physical assaults
- 15-38 Physical fighting among adolescents
- 15-39 Weapon carrying by adolescents on school property

16. Maternal, Infant, and Child Health

Goal: Improve the health and well-being of women, infants, children, and families.

Objective Number and Short Title

Fetal, Infant, Child, and Adolescent Deaths
- 16-1 Fetal and infant deaths
- 16-2 Child deaths
- 16-3 Adolescent and young adult deaths

Maternal Deaths and Illnesses
- 16-4 Maternal deaths
- 16-5 Maternal illness and complications due to pregnancy

Prenatal Care
- 16-6 Prenatal care
- 16-7 Childbirth classes

Obstetrical Care
- 16-8 Very low birth weight infants born at level III hospitals
- 16-9 Cesarean births

Risk Factors
- 16-10 Low birth weight and very low birth weight
- 16-11 Preterm births
- 16-12 Weight gain during pregnancy
- 16-13 Infants put to sleep on their backs

Developmental Disabilities and Neural Tube Defects
- 16-14 Developmental disabilities
- 16-15 Spina bifida and other neural tube defects
- 16-16 Optimum folic acid levels

Prenatal Substance Exposure
- 16-17 Prenatal substance exposure
- 16-18 Fetal alcohol syndrome

Breastfeeding, Newborn Screening, and Service Systems
- 16-19 Breastfeeding
- 16-20 Newborn bloodspot screening
- 16-21 Sepsis among children with sickle cell disease
- 16-22 Medical homes for children with special health care needs
- 16-23 Service systems for children with special health care needs

17. Medical Product Safety

Goal: Ensure the safe and effective use of medical products.

Objective Number and Short Title

- 17-1 Monitoring of adverse medical events
- 17-2 Linked, automated information systems
- 17-3 Provider review of medications taken by patients
- 17-4 Receipt of useful information about prescriptions from pharmacies
- 17-5 Receipt of oral counseling about medications from prescribers and dispensers
- 17-6 Blood donations

18. Mental Health and Mental Illness

Goal: Improve mental health and ensure access to appropriate, quality mental health services.

Objective Number and Short Title

Mental Health Status Improvement
- 18-1 Suicide
- 18-2 Adolescent suicide attempts
- 18-3 Serious mental illness (SMI) among homeless adults
- 18-4 Employment of persons with SMI
- 18-5 Eating disorder relapses

Treatment Expansion
- 18-6 Primary care screening and assessment
- 18-7 Treatment for children with mental health problems
- 18-8 Juvenile justice facility screening
- 18-9 Treatment for adults with mental disorders
- 18-10 Treatment for co-occurring disorders
- 18-11 Adult jail diversion programs

State Activities
- 18-12 State tracking of consumer satisfaction
- 18-13 State plans addressing cultural competence
- 18-14 State plans addressing elderly persons

19. Nutrition and Overweight

Goal: Promote health and reduce chronic disease associated with diet and weight.

Objective Number and Short Title

Weight Status and Growth
- 19-1 Healthy weight in adults
- 19-2 Obesity in adults
- 19-3 Overweight or obesity in children and adolescents
- 19-4 Growth retardation in children

Food and Nutrient Consumption
- 19-5 Fruit intake
- 19-6 Vegetable intake
- 19-7 Grain product intake
- 19-8 Saturated fat intake
- 19-9 Total fat intake
- 19-10 Sodium intake
- 19-11 Calcium intake

Iron Deficiency and Anemia
- 19-12 Iron deficiency in young children and in females of childbearing age
- 19-13 Anemia in low-income pregnant females
- 19-14 Iron deficiency in pregnant females

Schools, Worksites, and Nutrition Counseling
- 19-15 Meals and snacks at school
- 19-16 Worksite promotion of nutrition education and weight management
- 19-17 Nutrition counseling for medical conditions

Food Security
- 19-18 Food security

20. Occupational Safety and Health

Goal: Promote the health and safety of people at work through prevention and early intervention.

Objective Number and Short Title
- 20-1 Work-related injury deaths
- 20-2 Work-related injuries
- 20-3 Overexertion or repetitive motion
- 20-4 Pneumoconiosis deaths
- 20-5 Work-related homicides
- 20-6 Work-related assaults
- 20-7 Elevated blood lead levels from work exposure
- 20-8 Occupational skin diseases or disorders
- 20-9 Worksite stress reduction programs
- 20-10 Needlestick injuries
- 20-11 Work-related, noise-induced hearing loss

21. Oral Health

Goal: Prevent and control oral and craniofacial diseases, conditions, and injuries and improve access to related services.

Objective Number and Short Title
- 21-1 Dental caries experience
- 21-2 Untreated dental decay
- 21-3 No permanent tooth loss
- 21-4 Complete tooth loss
- 21-5 Periodontal diseases
- 21-6 Early detection of oral and pharyngeal cancers
- 21-7 Annual examinations for oral and pharyngeal cancers
- 21-8 Dental sealants
- 21-9 Community water fluoridation
- 21-10 Use of oral health care system
- 21-11 Use of oral health care system by residents in long-term care facilities
- 21-12 Dental services for low-income children
- 21-13 School-based health centers with oral health component
- 21-14 Health centers with oral health service components
- 21-15 Referral for cleft lip or palate
- 21-16 Oral and craniofacial State-based surveillance system
- 21-17 Tribal, State, and local dental programs

22. Physical Fitness and Activity

Goal: Improve health, fitness, and quality of life through daily physical activity.

Objective Number and Short Title

Physical Activity in Adults
- 22-1 No leisure-time physical activity
- 22-2 Moderate physical activity
- 22-3 Vigorous physical activity

Muscular Strength/Endurance and Flexibility
- 22-4 Muscular strength and endurance
- 22-5 Flexibility

Physical Activity in Children and Adolescents
- 22-6 Moderate physical activity in adolescents
- 22-7 Vigorous physical activity in adolescents
- 22-8 Physical education requirement in schools
- 22-9 Daily physical education in schools
- 22-10 Physical activity in physical education class
- 22-11 Television viewing

Access
- 22-12 School physical activity facilities
- 22-13 Worksite physical activity and fitness
- 22-14 Community walking
- 22-15 Community bicycling

23. Public Health Infrastructure

Goal: Ensure that Federal, Tribal, State, and local health agencies have the infrastructure to provide essential public health services effectively.

Objective Number and Short Title

Data and Information Systems

- 23-1 Public health employee access to the Internet
- 23-2 Public access to information and surveillance data
- 23-3 Use of geocoding in health data systems
- 23-4 Data for all population groups
- 23-5 Data for Leading Health Indicators, Health Status Indicators, and Priority Data Needs at Tribal, State, and local levels
- 23-6 National tracking of Healthy People 2010 objectives
- 23-7 Timely release of data on objectives

Workforce

- 23-8 Competencies for public health workers
- 23-9 Training in essential public health services
- 23-10 Continuing education and training by public health agencies

Public Health Organizations

- 23-11 Performance standards for essential public health services
- 23-12 Health improvement plans
- 23-13 Access to public health laboratory services
- 23-14 Access to epidemiology services
- 23-15 Model statutes related to essential public health services

Resources

- 23-16 Data on public health expenditures

Prevention Research

- 23-17 Population-based prevention research

24. Respiratory Diseases

Goal: Promote respiratory health through better prevention, detection, treatment, and education efforts.

Objective Number and Short Title

Asthma

- 24-1 Deaths from asthma
- 24-2 Hospitalizations for asthma
- 24-3 Hospital emergency department visits for asthma
- 24-4 Activity limitations
- 24-5 School or work days lost
- 24-6 Patient education
- 24-7 Appropriate asthma care
- 24-8 Surveillance systems

Chronic Obstructive Pulmonary Disease (COPD)

- 24-9 Activity limitations due to chronic lung and breathing problems
- 24-10 Deaths from COPD

Obstructive Sleep Apnea (OSA)

- 24-11 Medical evaluation and followup
- 24-12 Vehicular crashes related to excessive sleepiness

25. Sexually Transmitted Diseases

Goal: Promote responsible sexual behaviors, strengthen community capacity, and increase access to quality services to prevent sexually transmitted diseases (STDs) and their complications.

Objective Number and Short Title

Bacterial STD Illness and Disability

- 25-1 Chlamydia
- 25-2 Gonorrhea
- 25-3 Primary and secondary syphilis

Viral STD Illness and Disability

- 25-4 Genital herpes
- 25-5 Human papillomavirus infection

STD Complications Affecting Females

- 25-6 Pelvic inflammatory disease (PID)
- 25-7 Fertility problems
- 25-8 Heterosexually transmitted HIV infection in women

STD Complications Affecting the Fetus and Newborn
25-9 Congenital syphilis
25-10 Neonatal STDs

Personal Behaviors
25-11 Responsible adolescent sexual behavior
25-12 Responsible sexual behavior messages on television

Community Protection Infrastructure
25-13 Hepatitis B vaccine services in STD clinics
25-14 Screening in youth detention facilities and jails
25-15 Contracts to treat nonplan partners of STD patients

Personal Health Services
25-16 Annual screening for genital chlamydia
25-17 Screening of pregnant women
25-18 Compliance with recognized STD treatment standards
25-19 Provider referral services for sex partners

26. Substance Abuse

Goal: Reduce substance abuse to protect the health, safety, and quality of life for all, especially children.

Objective Number and Short Title

Adverse Consequences of Substance Use and Abuse
26-1 Motor vehicle crash deaths and injuries
26-2 Cirrhosis deaths
26-3 Drug-induced deaths
26-4 Drug-related hospital emergency department visits
26-5 Alcohol-related hospital emergency department visits
26-6 Adolescents riding with a driver who has been drinking
26-7 Alcohol- and drug-related violence
26-8 Lost productivity

Substance Use and Abuse
26-9 Substance-free youth
26-10 Adolescent and adult use of illicit substances
26-11 Binge drinking
26-12 Average annual alcohol consumption
26-13 Low-risk drinking among adults
26-14 Steroid use among adolescents
26-15 Inhalant use among adolescents

Risk of Substance Use and Abuse
26-16 Peer disapproval of substance abuse
26-17 Perception of risk associated with substance abuse

Treatment for Substance Abuse
26-18 Treatment gap for illicit drugs
26-19 Treatment in correctional institutions
26-20 Treatment for injection drug use
26-21 Treatment gap for problem alcohol use

State and Local Efforts
26-22 Hospital emergency department referrals
26-23 Community partnerships and coalitions
26-24 Administrative license revocation laws
26-25 Blood alcohol concentration (BAC) levels for motor vehicle drivers

27. Tobacco Use

Goal: Reduce illness, disability, and death related to tobacco use and exposure to secondhand smoke.

Objective Number and Short Title

Tobacco Use in Population Groups
27-1 Adult tobacco use
27-2 Adolescent tobacco use
27-3 Initiation of tobacco use
27-4 Age at first tobacco use

Cessation and Treatment
27-5 Smoking cessation by adults
27-6 Smoking cessation during pregnancy
27-7 Smoking cessation by adolescents
27-8 Insurance coverage of cessation treatment

Exposure to Secondhand Smoke
27-9 Exposure to tobacco smoke at home among children
27-10 Exposure to environmental tobacco smoke
27-11 Smoke-free and tobacco-free schools
27-12 Worksite smoking policies
27-13 Smoke-free indoor air laws

Social and Environmental Changes
27-14 Enforcement of illegal tobacco sales to minors laws
27-15 Retail license suspension for sales to minors
27-16 Tobacco advertising and promotion targeting adolescents and young adults
27-17 Adolescent disapproval of smoking
27-18 Tobacco control programs
27-19 Preemptive tobacco control laws
27-20 Tobacco product regulation
27-21 Tobacco tax

28. Vision and Hearing

Goal: Improve the visual and hearing health of the Nation through prevention, early detection, treatment, and rehabilitation.

Objective Number and Short Title

Vision

- 28-1 Dilated eye examinations
- 28-2 Vision screening for children
- 28-3 Impairment due to refractive errors
- 28-4 Impairment in children and adolescents
- 28-5 Impairment due to diabetic retinopathy
- 28-6 Impairment due to glaucoma
- 28-7 Impairment due to cataract
- 28-8 Occupational eye injury
- 28-9 Protective eyewear
- 28-10 Vision rehabilitation services and devices

Hearing

- 28-11 Newborn hearing screening, evaluation, and intervention
- 28-12 Otitis media
- 28-13 Rehabilitation for hearing impairment
- 28-14 Hearing examination
- 28-15 Evaluation and treatment referrals
- 28-16 Hearing protection
- 28-17 Noise-induced hearing loss in children
- 28-18 Noise-induced hearing loss in adults

www.ingramcontent.com/pod-product-compliance
Lightning Source LLC
Chambersburg PA
CBHW081815300426
44116CB00014B/2370